William Augustus Berkey

The Money Question

The Legal Tender Paper Monetary System of the United States

William Augustus Berkey

The Money Question
The Legal Tender Paper Monetary System of the United States

ISBN/EAN: 9783337123963

Printed in Europe, USA, Canada, Australia, Japan

Cover: Foto ©Suzi / pixelio.de

More available books at **www.hansebooks.com**

THE LEGAL TENDER PAPER

MONETARY SYSTEM

OF THE

UNITED STATES.

An Analysis of the Specie Basis or Bank Currency System, and of the Legal Tender Paper Money System; together with an Historical Account of Money as it has been Instituted in the Principal Nations of Europe and in the United States.

By WILLIAM A. BERKEY.

GRAND RAPIDS, MICH.:
W. W. HART, STEAM BOOK AND JOB PRINTER.
1876.

Entered according to Act of Congress, in the year 1876, by
WILLIAM A. BERKEY,
In the Office of the Librarian of Congress, at Washington, D. C.

PREFACE.

IN appearing before the public in the character of a writer, upon what is commonly supposed to be a very abstruse subject, a word of explanation seems to be necessary. For over a quarter of a century I have been actively engaged in business, as a manufacturer, and have naturally been led to enquire into the laws which govern the production and distribution of wealth. It was a matter of perplexity to me why it was that a nation possessed of the wonderful natural resources and the enormous productive powers that are possessed by the American people, should not enjoy general and uninterrupted prosperity; and, knowing that wealth is chiefly the product of labor, that the industrial classes of society are unable to retain anything like a fair proportion of the wealth produced by their labor. The farmer, usually considered the most independent of mortals, is engaged in a never-ending struggle to secure a mere competency; the same is true of the mechanic, the laborer, etc.; and the merchant, the manufacturer and others engaged in the production and distribution of wealth, aided by capital, are oppressed with a consciousness that their capital may at any time take to itself wings and fly away, no matter how wisely or prudently they may conduct their affairs. On the other hand, wealth is seen flowing in a constant stream into the laps of those who do not employ their capital in any wealth producing pursuit, but use it, in the shape of money, as an instrument to control property and labor. This certainly is sufficient to justify the suspicion that the unequal distribution of the products of labor which is constantly going on in the land, greatly to the disadvantage of society, is due to the manner in which money is instituted; and the questions arise, in what respect is money improperly instituted, and what is the remedy?

If it had not been for the experience furnished during the Rebellion, the great body of the American people would doubtless have continued to struggle on, in entire ignorance of the fact that it is possible to establish a monetary system on any other principles than those inculcated by the advocates of the specie basis or bank currency system. Fortunately, however, it was then fully demonstrated that a system of money, such as was suggested by Jefferson and other eminent founders of the republic, could be instituted upon entirely different principles; a system that would distribute the products of labor in entire harmony with the laws of trade, and far more equitably than could possibly be done through the instrumentality of bank currency. The masses undoubtedly realize the truth of this, but are at loss to give a reason for the faith that is in them. This is not at all strange. The wealth, intelligence and ability of the nation, as well as the power of the press, are arrayed on the side of the banks, precisely as the same elements were arrayed on the side of the United States Bank in the memorable contest between that institution and the people, under the patriotic leadership of General Jackson. Even professors of political economy are dragooned into the same ignoble service, and compelled to distort the principles of the science, to which they profess to be devoted, for the purpose of deceiving the public. In pursuing my own investigations, I found, to my surprise, that, except Kellogg's admirable work, written some years before the war, there was no book extant of a popular character, from which anything like a clear understanding of the questions involved in the present crisis could be obtained; and that the public was entirely dependent upon the fugitive writings of the few earnest and able men, who have espoused the cause of the people, for information upon the subject. It was in view of these circumstances that this work was undertaken. I would have been glad, indeed, if some one, who was better prepared for the duty, had undertaken it; but as that did not seem probable, and, knowing the great want of such a work from my own experience, I determined that it should be written at all events, in order that the American people might have a fair opportunity to decide intelligently upon this all important question. No claim is made to originality, nor has there been any effort made in regard to style. My sole aim has been to present the facts and principles relating to the subject correctly, and in plain, simple language; and, as will be observed, I have not hesitated to quote extensively whenever it could be done to advantage. In preparing the work for the press I have also availed myself of competent assistance, in order that the subject matter might be presented to the public as forcibly as possible. Special care has been taken to give credit to those whose ideas or language have been adopted, but I am much indebted to the fugitive writings above referred to, and I desire in a general way to express my acknowledgments for the same, and especially to Hon. W. D. Kelley, General Wm. Brindle, Henry Carey Baird and E. M. Davis, of Philadelphia; Peter Cooper and Pliny Freeman, of New York City; John G. Drew, of New Jersey; and to the Cincinnati Enquirer, the Chicago Industrial Age and the Indianapolis Sun.

WILLIAM A. BERKEY.

GRAND RAPIDS, MICH.,
May 20th, 1876.

CONTENTS.

CHAPTER I.—THE WEALTH AND RESOURCES OF THE UNITED STATES.—WHY THE AMERICAN PEOPLE DO NOT ENJOY GENERAL PROSPERITY.   9

CHAPTER II.—MONEY AND ITS FUNCTIONS.   25
The Nature of Money.................................. 26
The Intrinsic Value of Money....................... 30
The Uses of Money.................................... 37
Systems of Money..................................... 48
The Power to Make Money a Governmental Function.. 53
How Paper Money issued by the Government Represents Value.. 70

CHAPTER III.—BANKS AND BANKING.   75

CHAPTER IV.—BANKS OF THE OLD WORLD.   80
The Bank of Venice................................... 80
The Bank of Genoa.................................... 87
The Bank of Amsterdam................................ 87
The Bank of Hamburg.................................. 88
The Bank of England.................................. 88
The Banks of Scotland................................ 97
The French System of Finance........................ 100

CHAPTER V.—PAPER MONEY AND BANKS OF THE UNITED STATES.   109
Early Colonial Currency............................. 109
Continental Money................................... 112
State Banks of Issue................................ 117
The First Bank of the United States................ 119
The Money Panic of 1809............................. 124
The Money Panic of 1814............................. 125
The Second Bank of the United States............... 126
The Money Panic of 1819............................. 127
The Money Panic of 1825............................. 133
The War with the United States Bank................ 133
The Money Panic of 1837–1839–1841.................. 150
The Money Panic of 1857............................. 153
The Suspension of 1861.............................. 154
State Banks of Issue Supplanted by National Banks... 158

CHAPTER VI.—HISTORY OF THE PAPER MONEY
ISSUED DURING THE REBELLION. 161
The First Loan Acts............................... 164
Treasury Note bearing interest and not a Legal Tender. 171
Full Legal Tender Treasury Note, not bearing interest. 172
Secretary Chase's First Annual Report.............. 173
The First Legal Tender Bill....................... 175
The Greenback.................................... 199
Temporary Deposits in the Sub-Treasury............. 203
Certificates of Indebtedness...................... 203
The Second Legal Tender Act...................... 204
The Second Annual Report of Secretary Chase....... 204
The Third Legal Tender Act—$900,000,000 Loan Act. 206
The National Bank Bill........................... 209
Public Debt Statement, 1863....................... 210
Amount and kind of Paper Circulation, June 30, 1864.. 215
Bonds Exempted from Taxation..................... 216
Greenbacks Limited to $400,000,000............... 216
Fessenden Appointed Secretary of the Treasury...... 216
McCulloch Appointed Secretary of the Treasury...... 217
Debt and Circulation of the United States, 1865...... 219
McCulloch's Contraction Policy.................... 219
Amount Contracted, July, 1868..................... 222
Act of Congress Suspending Contraction of Greenbacks 223
An Act to Strengthen the Public Credit............. 224
Refunding the Public Debt......................... 230
Public Debt Statement, November, 1875............. 231

CHAPTER VII.—THE NATIONAL BANKING SYSTEM. 244
Secretary Chase Recommends a National Banking Law. 244
National Bank Bill Reported in the Senate........... 245
The National Banking Law......................... 246
Of the Organization of National Banks.............. 247
The Profits of National Banks..................... 250
The Panic of 1873................................ 251
The Cost of Bank Currency........................ 263
Failures in the Country since 1863................ 264
Extravagance—Over Production..................... 266
An Act to Resume Specie Payments and Make Banking Free to Bondholders......................... 270
The Little Tariff Bill—an Act to Enable the National Banks to Monopolize the Currency................ 271

CHAPTER VIII.—RESUMPTION OF SPECIE PAYMENTS.. 273
How Interest on Government Bonds is Paid.......... 274
The Specie Resumption Act....................... 279
The Amount of Gold in the Country............... 281
Resumption Impossible........................... 282
The Consequences of Forced Resumption........... 289
The Experience of Great Britain in 1819—1823....... 290
The Consequences of Forced Resumption in the United
  States... 300

CHAPTER IX.— A MONETARY SYSTEM FOUNDED
  UPON SOUND PRINCIPLES.   305
The Real Issue in the Impending Crisis............. 311
An Analysis of the Specie Basis or Bank Currency System of Money.................................... 312
The Cost of the Credit System.................... 324
Commercial Crashes and Money Panics............. 326
An Analysis of the Legal Tender Paper Money System. 330
What is a Dollar?............................... 333
Money of Account............................... 334
The Legal Tender Question....................... 341
How Much Money a Nation Should Have........... 344
How Interest Should be Regulated................. 349
The 3.65 Bond Plan............................. 352
How the Public Note is Put in Circulation.......... 355
The National Debt.............................. 356
Conclusion..................................... 359

APPENDIX.

Horace Greeley's Famous Editorial on the 3.65 Bond
  Plan.. 363
The Legal Tender Bill as it passed the House of Representatives, Feb. 6, 1862..................... 367
The Legal Tender Act of February 25, 1862.......... 370
Speech of the Hon. Thaddeus Stevens in the House of
  Representatives, December 19, 1862.............. 373
Table Showing the Monthly Range of the Gold Premium since 1862................................ 381
The French Assignats............................ 382

CORRECTIONS.

The table given on page 231 exhibiting the amount and character of the public debt, bearing interest, on the 30th day of November, 1875, is incomplete. By an oversight the currency bonds issued to the Pacific Railroads were omitted. The amount of the currency bonds outstanding at that date was $64,623,512, which, added to the amount given on page 231, would make the total public debt, bearing interest, November 30, 1875, $1,758,874,812.

On page 88 for "out," the last word on the page, read "about."

On page 17, in the seventh line from the bottom of the page, substitute "April" for "March."

THE MONEY QUESTION.

CHAPTER I.

THE WEALTH AND RESOURCES OF THE UNITED STATES.—
WHY THE AMERICAN PEOPLE DO NOT ENJOY
GENERAL PROSPERITY.

THE prosperity of a people depends chiefly on the use which they are enabled to make of their natural resources. It frequently happens that nations possessing great natural advantages fail, through want of properly directed industry or defective laws, to attain even a reasonable degree of prosperity; and, on the other hand, that nations possessing but limited resources succeed, under wise laws and by means of well directed energy, in achieving great wealth. History abounds in instances illustrating the truth of this statement. At the present time Ireland and Holland may be cited as cases in point. Ireland possesses a fertile soil, salubrious climate, fine harbors, noble rivers, and a population naturally brave, quick and capable of great labor; but her people, by reason of unequal laws and bad government, are chained to poverty and ignorance. Holland, a land reclaimed from the ocean and held only by sleepless vigilance, was originally destitute of even ordinary advantages; but under enlightened laws, industry and art have accomplished the most marvelous results. "Below the level of the sea, and the surface of adjacent rivers and canals, have been created by human art, fat pastures teeming with flocks and herds, rich artificial garden land, nourishing the industrious and thriving population of innumerable cities, towns and villages. The very coast is an artificial fortification against the ocean, the ancient and natural monarch of the country. Here he is defied by leagues of artificial sea banks—there by miles of granite masonry. Rivers and canals are made to run many feet above the level of the country. Armies of indefatigable wind mills are perpetually pumping and draining. Amsterdam and Rotterdam, populous, opulent and splendid cities, rest on piles driven into the mud." Thus, by well directed industry, under wise laws, have the people of Holland been enabled to achieve a wonderful victory over the forces of nature, and to clothe themselves with general prosperity.

The people of the United States are peculiarly rich in all the bounties of nature. They possess a land whose area exceeds 4,000,000 of square miles. Within its boundaries are embraced every variety of soil and climate; inexhaustible mines of iron, coal, copper, lead, zinc, gold and silver; immense forests; grand lakes and mighty rivers. A better idea of its great extent may be formed by comparing some of the States of the Union with the kingdoms of Europe. California, for example, is equal in size to England, Scotland, Ireland, Wales, Belgium, Holland and Portugal; and Texas is equal to France, Holland, Belgium and Denmark. The mineral resources of the country are almost beyond computation. For example, it is estimated that coal enough has already been discovered to supply a population of 1,000,000,000 for 60,000 years. Other minerals, comparatively speaking, are equally abundant. The gold producing region of the country covers an area of over 1,000,000 of square miles. Prior to the discovery of gold in California in 1849, the gold yield of the world did not exceed $20,000,000 a year.

Now the United States alone produce annually over $75,000,000 worth of bullion.

The agricultural resources of the country are equally boundless. In almost every section the soil yields bountifully, while in some regions, as in the great States of the West, its fertility is unsurpassed. The agricultural productions of that region alone have reached an almost fabulous amount.

The great natural advantages possessed by the country have enabled its manufacturing interests to make great progress, in spite of the ever changing and illy devised tariff laws, which, for the greater part of the time, have disfigured the statute books of the nation. While agriculture and manufactures flourish side by side, in all parts of the country, greatly to the advantage of both, it happens that the peculiar facilities and advantages enjoyed by different sections of the country have caused their industries to vary greatly in character. Thus, the people of the Eastern States are devoted chiefly to manufactures and commerce; the people of the Middle States, although engaged largely in commerce, manufactures and agriculture, are also occupied extensively in dealing in iron, coal, lumber, salt, petroleum, etc.; the people of the Western and South Western States, while possessed of large mineral and other interests, as yet find their chief profits in the vast agricultural resources which they enjoy; the people of the Southern States are engaged principally in the production of the valuable staples common to that section, such as cotton, rice, sugar, tobacco, etc.; and the people of the Pacific States, besides their immense agricultural and commercial interests, find a wide field for employment in developing the rich mines of gold, silver, etc., which have rendered that region famous throughout the world.

To glance briefly at a few details, the assessed value of the farms and stock in the United States in 1870 was nearly $11,000,000,000, and this sum did not cover one-half their actual value. The following statement, gathered from the Census Report of 1870, gives a partial view of the agricultural operations of the country during the preceding year:

Farm products, including additions to stock.$2,500,000,000
Farm wages, including value of board...... 310,000,000
Wheat..................... 288,000,000 bushels.
Rye....................... 17,000,000 "
Indian Corn............... 761,000,000 "
Oats...................... 282,000,000 "
Barley.................... 30,000,000 "
Buckwheat................. 10,000,000 "
Flax Seed................. 1,700,000 "
Clover Seed............... 600,000 "
Grass "................ 600,000 "
Potatoes.................. 144,000,000 "
" Sweet............... 21,000,000 "
Peas and Beans............ 5,500,000 "
Cotton....................1,200,000,000 pounds.
Flax...................... 27,000,000 "
Hemp...................... 25,000,000 "
Hops...................... 25,000,000 "
Rice...................... 74,000,000 "
Wool...................... 100,000,000 "
Tobacco................... 263,000,000 "
Butter.................... 500,000,000 "
Cheese.................... 23,000,000 "
Hay....................... 27,000,000 tons.

And the following statement presents a general view of the manufacturing interests of the country in 1870:

Number of manufacturing establishments... 252,148
Number of operatives..................... 2,053,997
Capital invested.........................$2,118,000,000
Annual salaries paid..................... 776,000,000
Raw material used........................ 2,488,000,000
Products................................. 4,232,000,000

In considering the resources and advantages of the country, it is proper to notice the labor saving machinery, largely the result of American ingenuity, which now performs such an important part in all the departments of labor. In Great Britain the power of the machinery of that country is estimated as equal to that of 600,000,000 of men. In this country it probably does not reach that amount, but it is sufficiently large to add enormously to the productions of the country. In many sections one thousand acres of land can now be cultivated with no more cost than was formerly required to cultivate one hundred.

The great and varied industries of the country are rendered vastly more useful and profitable by reason of the channels of communication, natural and artificial, which extend in every possible direction. In addition to the many lakes and rivers, which traverse the country, it is covered with a network of railroads from ocean to ocean, affording ample means of transportation to gather and distribute the products of the nation.

From this outline of the wealth and resources of the United States, it is apparent that the American people are possessed of vast advantages, such as are hardly possessed by any other nation on the globe. It is estimated that the United States are capable of sustaining a population of upwards of 350,000,000, while the population of the country now scarcely exceeds 40,000,000. If enabled by wise laws and well directed industry to make a proper use of their advantages, the people of the United States ought to enjoy general and uninterrupted prosperity. And, as the government of the United States is republican in form—based upon the theory that all power emanates from the people, the responsibility of any failure on their part to attain wealth and prosperity must rest with the people themselves.

DO THE AMERICAN PEOPLE ENJOY GENERAL PROSPERITY?

Notwithstanding their boasted industry, intelligence and enterprise, and the vast resources which they possess, the people of the United States, as a nation, have failed, utterly and disgracefully, to attain anything like a reasonable degree of general prosperity. We shall not resort to any elaborately prepared statistics to establish the truth of the assertion, but will simply call attention to a few important facts, the consideration of which, we believe, cannot fail to produce conviction.

TEN TIMES within the past sixty years has the country been visited by commercial crashes and money panics, accompanied or followed by general stagnation of business, ruin and bankruptcy. From 1814 to 1861 the country suffered NINE TIMES in this way, and *only once*, from 1841 to 1857, did it escape a financial crash for a longer period than *ten years*. At the present time the country is suffering from the crash of 1873, or rather from the same causes that produced that crash. These commercial crashes have invariably paralyzed all forms of productive industry, bankrupted business men, stripped the debtor class of their property, and occasioned want and distress amongst nearly all classes of people. When we look back over the past half century, we find that, as a matter of fact, the people at large have never had an opportunity, even between these seasons of financial disturbance, to enjoy more than a glimpse of prosperity. They have been kept busy, either struggling to avoid impending ruin, in view of a commercial crash, or laboring to rebuild their shattered fortunes, after the panic had subsided. And now, the CENTENNIAL YEAR, 1876, soon to be celebrated with great pomp on the banks of the Schuylkill, under the auspices of a great city writhing under the heel of a corrupt Ring, finds the people, in the midst of plenty, distressed, exhausted and poor. And how does this happen? Has nature frowned upon the husbandman and refused to respond to his toil? Has the earth declined to yield up her precious stores? Has the hand of the artisan or mechanic lost its cunning, or the arm of the laborer its strength? Not at all. The graneries of the West are bursting with the products of the soil; the valuable staples of the South are as ready as ever to respond to the touch of labor; the mineral wealth of the earth lies exposed on every hand; the wheels of the workshop and the factory are faithful as ever; and the mechanic and laborer are not only able and willing, but anxious to work. The cause of the whole trouble lies concealed in the simple word—MONEY.

In civilized nations at the present day a circulating medium of exchange, called money, is as essential to the production and distribution of wealth in all its forms as railroads and wagons are to its transportation. In 1873 an epidemic among the horses, for a few weeks, seriously interfered with trade and travel. Were all the railroads and canals of the country to suspend operations for a single season, it is not difficult to surmise the amount of disaster and distress that would ensue. And the public might as well try to conduct the affairs of life without railroads and wagons, or the farmer try to cultivate the soil without implements, as for a nation to attempt to develop its producing forces, or carry on successfully the operations of trade, without an adequate amount of money in the channels of circulation.

The business affairs of the country during and after the late war increased largely. The wealth of the nation, in spite of the ravages of war, increased from \$16,000,000,000 in 1860 to \$30,000,000,000 in 1870. All the money and evidences of indebtedness of the government, which could be used as a circulating medium of exchange, were actively employed. The people, for the first time in their history, had an abundance of money in circulation and were enabled to develop the resources of the country and add to its wealth in a corresponding degree. The increased production in every department of labor rendered the burdens of taxation light, and, at the same time, increased the revenues of the government to an enormous extent. The government, in consequence of its largely increased revenue, was enabled, at the close of the war, to begin the reduction of the public debt at a rapid rate. The people, notwithstanding the burden of taxation which they were compelled to bear, were, individually, *out of debt*. But matters began to change. The channels of trade became stagnant or sluggish, business began to languish, factories and workshops were obliged to suspend or reduce labor and wages, real estate fell in value, and enforced idleness began to grow common; and, as in times prior to the war, the climax was capped by a financial panic. The cause of this astonishing change in the condition of the country—from activity and prosperity to inactivity and distress—will be found in the following statement, taken from the books of the Treasury Department by Hon. Moses W. Field, which exhibits the contraction of the circulating medium of the country that took place from September 1, 1865, to December 1, 1873:

Amount of money, currency, and circulating medium, September 1, 1865, (exclusive of coin:)

United States Notes	$433,160,569
Fractional Currency	26,344,742
National Bank Notes	185,000,000
Compound Interest Legal-tender Notes	217,024,160
Temporary Loan Certificates, (10-d-d,)	107,148,713
Certificates of Indebtedness	85,093,000
Treasury five per cent. legal tenders	32,536,991
Treasury Notes, past due, legal-tenders, and not presented	1,503,020
State Bank Notes	78,867,575
Three year Treasury Notes	830,000,000
Total Sept. 1, 1865	$1,996,678,770

Circulating medium, exclusive of coin, December 1, 1873.
United States Notes...................... $367,001,685
Fractional Currency...................... 48,000,000
Certificates of Indebtedness (bearing Interest) 678,000
National Bank Currency.................. 350,000,000

Total December 1, 1873............... $765,679,685
Contraction from Sept. 1, 1865, to Dec. 1,
  1873, (causing a money panic).........$1,230,999,085

From the foregoing statement it appears that the circulating medium of the country (or evidences of indebtedness of the government used as such) was contracted over $1,200,000,000 in eight years. The greater part of this amount consisted of the Three year Treasury Notes ($830,000,000.) These notes were called in and bonds substituted in their stead prior to 1868. The crash of 1873 followed as an inevitable consequence. It won't do to say that it was the result of the war, or of extravagance, or of over production, or of anything of the kind. Crashes and money panics just like it occurred before the war, on an average, *every five years*, and this crash did not occur until *eight years after* the war. The periodical money panics, which occurred before the war, were the natural results of the specie basis system of money; and the panic of 1873 was caused by enforcing the policy of contraction, which was planned at the same time that the National Banking system was projected, in order that the specie basis system might be re-established. The act of Congress of March 12, 1866, authorizing a contraction of the currency, was adopted on the recommendation of Hugh McCulloch, Secretary of the Treasury. It gave him unlimited control over the finances of the country, and he did not fail to use the power placed in his hands, to the fullest extent, in aiding the money power, with which he was in league, to rob the country and the people. When McCulloch's infamous betrayal of the high trust reposed in him becomes fully understood, his name will be used as a by-word and reproach throughout the nation.

Apart from commercial crashes, or money panics, it is evident that there is something radically wrong in the monetary system of the country—that there is some constantly operating cause, which tends "to fertilize the rich man's field by the sweat of the poor man's brow." The masses toil, day after day and year after year, seeking to secure a competency and scarcely succeed in obtaining a subsistence. The better classes may succeed in building up homes, but they are never secure in their possession, until they have amassed sufficient property to at least enable them to outlive a season of financial depression. The profits of labor flow in a steady stream into the hands of non-producers, who are engaged in manipulating money. It is not difficult to discover the reason. Money is essential to the development of the producing forces of the country, and to the distribution of its products. It is far more necessary that money should be abundant and cheap, than that there should be abundant and cheap means of transportation. The contrary, however, has been the general rule since the American people have constituted a nation. They unfortunately inherited the British system of banks of issue, which clothes the moneyed classes with unlimited control over the circulating medium of a country. Money should be the servant and not the master of wealth, and then it will flow in the channels of trade, in obedience to the natural laws of supply and demand; but the people have permitted the power to furnish the circulating medium of the country to be filched from the nation and given over to individuals and corporations to be used as a monopoly. At present **money** has ceased to fill the channels of trade, and, refusing to perform its offices, has taken refuge in the banks in the commercial centers. Statesmen, like Senator Christiancy, may tell the people "to go to work in any and every form of productive industries," and command it to return, and imagine that they are uttering a great deal of wisdom, but where are the productive industries? If Senator Christiancy had been in Moses's place, the Jews, possibly, would have been at no loss how to "make bricks without straw;" but as such wisdom is not available in this country, it is to be regretted that he did not turn up in Egypt a few thousand years ago, instead of in the United States Senate at the present time.

It is of course mere matter of speculation as to what would be the condition of the country now if gold and silver had been its circulating medium in fact as well as theory, or if a legal tender paper money had been adopted at an early period, as urged by Franklin, Jefferson, Calhoun and others. With nothing but gold and silver the progress of the country would undoubtedly have been slow, but the people generally would doubtless be better off than they are now. With a legal tender paper money, in the light of late experience, it is more than probable that the United States would to-day be the richest, most powerful and most prosperous nation on the globe. Neither system of money, however, was adopted. The government allowed the circulating medium to be taken out of its hands and erected into a gigantic monopoly in the hands of individuals and corporations. The gold and silver of the country were locked up in bank vaults, as the pretended basis of bank notes, and the people were compelled to pay an exorbitant price for a false, fluctuating and unsafe currency, subject to the entire control of those who issued it.

Banks of issue have been a fruitful source of disaster, both in Great Britain and in the United States. By encouraging discounts and inflating their circulation they greatly stimulate business of all kinds. As the process goes on, credit becomes inflated to an unlimited extent, until a turning point, beyond which inflation cannot go without bursting, is reached. Whilst the process of inflating the currency and credit of the country is going on, great activity prevails in all departments of industry, and everybody seems to be on the high road to wealth and prosperity. But it becomes necessary or desirable for the banks to put themselves in funds, and they begin to convert their discounted bills into money as rapidly as possible. They cease discounting and call in their loans. "If by such means they do not actually obtain specie, they redeem their notes, which might otherwise be presented for redemption in coin. Prices begin to fall. Merchants, deprived of their accustomed facility for borrowing, and with obligations coming round every day, upon which they are liable as principals or endorsers, are anxious to sell, while none of them want to buy. The pressure begins in the great marts of foreign trade, and extends from them to the dealers in the interior. The latter are crowded for payment by their distressed creditors, and crowd their debtors in turn. Property of all kinds depreciates and becomes difficult to sell, when every body wants to sell, and is anxious to restrict his purchases to the lowest practicable amount. Sales, nevertheless, are made upon credit, for the purpose of obtaining contracts to deliver money at a future day, which can be sold to usurers, who riot in their harvest. Collections are enforced by suits at law, and effected at the expense of a heavy toll to attorneys and Sheriffs' officers, out of the proceeds of forced sales. Persons whose property is adequate, even at the depreciated rates, to the payment of their debts, become bankrupt from the failure of their debtors to pay promptly. When the doors of a banking house are closed in the afternoon, and a merchant's obligation is protested, his credit is gone, and he ceases the effort to maintain it by ruinous sacrifices. The failure of one increases the embarrassment of his creditors, and repeated failures spread general distrust. As one after another goes down, however, there is one less engaged in the scramble for money, and the survivors experience the same sort of relief as men in a crowd do when some of them faint and are carried out."* These financial crises invariably involve a general suspension of specie payments. The suspension is charged up to the people, who are told that they have been "producing too much," or "living too extravagantly;" and the banks are enabled to retain their reserve of gold and silver, to repeat the operation as soon as the Sheriff's services are no longer required, and "confidence has been restored."

The power which such a system confers upon those, to whom the right to furnish the circulating medium of the country has been delegated, is immense. The price which the people are compelled to pay for their circulating medium of exchange is of itself sufficient to rob labor and industry of their profits. The wealth of the country increases, as statistics show, a little over three per cent. a year, and with money in circulation that costs from 6 to 25 per cent., it is not difficult to see how it is that the wealth of the country has a constant tendency to accumulate in the hands of the few. The profits of industry are eaten up by interest on the circulating medium of exchange—if not entirely, a commercial crash will take what is left. How seldom do people, when handling money, think of the great difference which

*Political Economy by E. Peshine Smith.

exists between a United States legal tender note (greenback) and a National bank bill. The greenback represents the property of the people, on which it is a lien, and in the performance of its mission of usefulness, as it flies from hand to hand, feeding the hungry, clothing the naked, ministering to the sick or distressed, or furthering the operations of industry and trade, no keen eyed usurer marks its flight; it is not burdened with interest. But it is otherwise with the National bank bill. Whether serving the purposes of money in the channels of trade, or stowed away in the recesses of a bank vault, it is perpetually drawing interest. That interest, although paid by individuals, is a tax upon the community at large. No one can hope to escape his share of the tax by "keeping out of bank." General laws in the economical world are as universal and constant in their effect as the law of gravitation is in the natural world.

The specie basis system of money has existed in Great Britain for nearly two hundred years, and the result of its workings there can be seen at a glance. The bulk of the wealth and property of the kingdom is held by a small and constantly decreasing class, whilst the masses are steeped in poverty and ignorance. During the wars with France, from 1797 to 1823, the people of Great Britain had an irredeemable paper currency. For twenty-five years, notwithstanding the drain of a great war, they enjoyed unparalleled prosperity, by reason of the abundance of money in circulation. But the money power demanded a return to specie payments, and in 1819 an act of Parliament was passed decreeing a return to specie payments in 1823. England possessed abundance of gold, had no foreign debt, the balance of trade was in her favor, and the difference between gold and paper money was only three per cent. Notwithstanding all these favorable circumstances, the enforced return to specie payments prostrated the industries of the kingdom, ruined the farming, manufacturing and business interests, and plunged the entire nation into bankruptcy. The masses of Great Britain, whose labor and valor had just enabled the British government to prosecute to a successful termination one of the most gigantic wars of modern times, were hurled by an act of Parliament, at the instance of the money power of the kingdom, in the most heartless manner and without the slightest grounds of excuse, from a state of prosperity into the depths of ruin and poverty.

At the demands of the same power the people of the United States are now being subjected to like treatment. With but little gold, scarcely $100,000,000, in the country, with the balance of trade against the nation, with a large public debt mostly held abroad, and with a difference between gold and paper money of over twelve per cent., enforced resumption of specie payments has been decreed to take place in 1879. In the light of English experience under vastly more favorable circumstances, the people of the United States can look forward to nothing else but continued and increasing prostration of all forms of industry, and, when the fatal hour for resumption arrives, a general crash, burying the entire nation in its ruins.

The people of the United States are a forbearing and long suffering people, but it is scarcely possible that they would continue to submit in silence to the exactions of the money power, if they were fully apprised of the nature and extent of the robbery to which they have been, and are still, subjected, by reason of a false and corrupt monetary system. The public debt of the United States in 1865 was $2,682,593,026; on September 1, 1875, it was $2,127,393,836, showing a reduction of $555,199,190. Besides this $555,199,190, the people have paid in the past TEN YEARS, for interest on the public debt, navy, war, civil service, pensions and Indians, $3,324,560,785, or in all the enormous sum of **$3,879,759,-975**, which is one-half more than the original amount of the national debt, or a sum greater than the national debt of Great Britain. This vast sum has been paid principally by the producing classes, for the bondholder and money power generally bear no part of the expenses of government. It is high time that the burdens of taxation should be more equally distributed. This can be done only by the imposition of a graduated income tax, than which nothing can be more just.

President Grant suggested in his last annual message that the Centennial year would be a fit time to inaugurate reforms. We agree with him. Let the people take a lesson from experience and reform their monetary system. As it is the year for the general elections, something might also be done in the way of purifying the administration of public affairs. The Centennial year can thus be rendered doubly memorable in the annals of the country.

The celebrated Junius said: "The ruin or prosperity of a State depends so much on the administration of the government, that to be acquainted with the merit of a ministry we need only observe the condition of the people. If we see them obedient to the laws, prosperous in their industry, united at home and respected abroad, we may reasonably presume that their affairs are conducted by men of experience, ability and virtue. If on the contrary we see a universal spirit of distrust and dissatisfaction, a rapid decay of trade, dissensions in all parts of the empire, and a total loss of respect in the eyes of foreign powers, we may pronounce, without hesitation, that the government of that country is WEAK, DISTRACTED AND CORRUPT."

CHAPTER II.

MONEY AND ITS FUNCTIONS.

In a state of civilization money performs an important part in the production, distribution and accumulation of wealth; it is necessary, therefore, that it should be based on sound principles. A great deal of nonsense has been written about money and its "hidden power," partly through ignorance and partly through design. So widely have political economists differed in regard to its nature and functions that it is not surprising that people have been willing to ascribe to it some mysterious power, or that they should have almost despaired of being able to comprehend the principles on which it is founded and by which its movements are governed. And this delusion has been encouraged in every way possible by the moneyed and governing classes, who are thus enabled to found systems of money on the false theory that money is the master and not the servant of labor and property.

But the age is characterized by a spirit of progress, and old systems are rapidly yielding to new ones. The signs of the times indicate that the hoary tyranny of the money power, which has exercised despotic sway for ages over the masses of mankind, will, sooner or later, be compelled to succumb to the influences of an enlightened public sentiment. A distinguished English writer,[*] in commenting on the imperfect and rudimentary condition of the science of political economy, says: "The steam engine, steam navigation, railways, mechanical inventions, the electric telegraph,

[*] Sir John Barnard Byles.

modern chemistry, have not appeared for nothing. A science of political economy will yet dawn that shall perform as well as promise—a science that will rain the riches of nature into the laps of the starving poor. Men do not yet dream of the prosperity which is in store for all orders of the people." A large and increasing number of leading thinkers, statesmen and philanthropists of the day are calling public attention to the unequal and unjust distribution of the products of industry that is constantly going on through the agency of a false and corrupt monetary system, and their views have already made a profound impression on the public mind. The ignorant masses of Great Britain may be deluded into believing, as is taught by the dismal school of English political economists, "that it is natural, and if natural, proper—though we may not see the reason— that poverty and want and disease and misery should be next door neighbors of wealth and unbounded prosperity;" but the intelligent farmers, mechanics and laborers of the United States are not so easily convinced that the surplus wealth, which their labor produces annually, should naturally be owned at the end of the year by the financiering and non-producing classes of the country. When people find themselves being robbed, they are apt to try to discover the offender and the means by which it is accomplished. A very moderate amount of investigation, we think, will satisfy any candid mind that the theory, that the money power is the robber, which deprives labor of its just reward, and that a corrupt monetary system is the instrumentality, by means of which the robbery is perpetrated, is based on sound reasons.

THE NATURE OF MONEY.

Money, in its ordinary signification, is an agency of trade. Civilization has developed a great variety of wants and industries, and labor has come to be divided into innumerable forms, requiring a constant exchange of commodities. Individuals are dependent on their fellow men for every thing, except the particular product of their own labor. One class furnishes food, another the material for clothing, another builds houses, etc., etc., and each class is susceptible of innumerable subdivisions. When we come to individuals, each one has to give his labor, or the product of his labor, or the product of the labor of others, for that which he needs or desires. This exchange is effected through the agency of money. It is necessary, therefore, that money should possess a legal representative value. It must possess representative value to be the equivalent of the commodity or labor for which it is exchanged, and its representative value must be established by law, otherwise its acceptance by a creditor would be optional. As the value and power of money depend on law, its institution and regulation are duties which devolve upon the legislature or governing power of a nation.

The adoption of money or a medium of exchange was undoubtedly one of the first steps in civilization. In a simple state of society, as in newly settled countries now, the exchange of commodities took place by means of barter, but the necessity of a medium of exchange becoming apparent, different representatives of value were adopted, according to the wants, tastes and possessions of the communities or nations concerned. Thus the Spartans adopted iron, the ancient Romans bars of copper and cattle, the North American Indian beads, and the East Indian and African shells. At an early age gold and silver came to be regarded as the most suitable materials for the purposes of money for many reasons, among others on account of their possessing large value in a small and compact form. Coins or tokens made of these metals next appeared, but originally possessed no other power than that which they derived from the intrinsic value of the materials of which they were made, which was determined by weight, as is the case now, when used in commerce between different nations. Governments next assumed the right to make and regulate the value of money, in consequence of the necessity of establishing a common representative of value to be used in the payment of debts and taxes. As civilization progressed and wealth increased, requiring a more rapid and extensive exchange of commodities, it became necessary that the medium of exchange should be increased in the same proportion. It was impossible to obtain gold and silver in sufficient quantities to answer the purposes of money, and it would seemingly have been but the part of wisdom to have adopted new systems of money, but history gives but one or two instances where anything of the kind was attempted. The scarcity of money led to the use of credit, which now plays such an important part in the commerce of the world. Bills of exchange were invented, it is believed, by the Jews of Lombardy in the 7th century. In the 13th, 14th and 15th centuries the greater part of the commerce of Europe was accomplished at periodical markets or fairs. Merchants and traders, or their brokers, would meet at these fairs with their accounts or *bilans* (balance) made out, and by transferring debts and credits from one to another, effect a settlement with the use of no more money than was required to settle balances. In many parts of Europe these fairs are still held, although they have lost most of their former importance. Various other devices to increase the circulating medium of exchange have been resorted to by different nations, such as reducing the amount of bullion in their coins from time to time, until now they contain but a fraction of the value which their names originally called for. In the days of William, the Conqueror, the "pound" actually was a pound weight of silver, and a shilling was a twentieth part of a pound, but at the present time a pound of silver is coined into sixty-six shillings. The legal money of England has been regulated or altered in this way by the English government one hundred and eighty-four times.

The specie basis system of Great Britain, which was adopted nearly two hundred years ago, owes its origin to the same cause—the necessity of increasing the medium of exchange. The effect of the system is to centralize wealth. In Great Britain it has enabled the aristocratic and moneyed classes to acquire enormous wealth, and has reduced the industrial classes to a condition of abject poverty. In the United States it has had the same tendency.

The only people of former times, who seemed to fully understand the nature of money, were the Venetians. In the 12th century they adopted a system of money, based on the wealth and credit of the people, which lasted over 600 years. Inscriptions on the books of a bank, established by the State, which were divisible to any desired amount and transferable on the books of the bank from one to another, formed the chief medium of exchange during the period named. These inscriptions of credit were not redeemable in coin, but, notwithstanding that, they commanded a high premium over gold and silver. The Venetians were enabled, principally through their enlightened system of money, to attain great prosperity, which they enjoyed for centuries, and commercial crashes and money panics were unknown amongst them. (See Chap. IV.)

The French people manage their financial affairs with more wisdom than any other nation of the present day. When specie is scarce an irredeemable legal tender paper money is used in its stead. Great pains are taken by the French government to keep every section amply supplied with a circulating medium of exchange, in order to develop the producing forces of the country—a policy that has been crowned with marked success.

The American people have had some experience in regard to the advantages of a legal tender paper money system since 1861, but the notes of the government (greenbacks) were issued in such a mutilated form, and the workings of the system have been so materially interfered with by the money power, by means of corrupt legislation, that as yet they have had no fair opportunity to judge of its real merits.

From an early period, then, money came to derive its power, as an agent to represent, measure and exchange value, from public authority. Individuals and nations seek to exchange and accumulate property and commodities, and money is desirable only on account of the power, with which it is clothed by public authority, to command property or labor. It is not useful of itself, for it cannot be used as food, or clothing, or shelter. It must be parted with before any service or value can be obtained from it. In an accumulated form, as capital, it can bring no income until it is put to use—parted with. It is, therefore, the immaterial principle or power to represent value that is the essence of money, and this it can only derive from law. "Money is then," in the language of Kellogg, "a legal existence, being constituted a national representative of property; consequently it is a public lien on all property for sale in the nation, a public medium for the exchange of products, and a tender in payment of debts."

THE INTRINSIC VALUE OF MONEY.

As money is a legal public medium of exchange, possessing representative value, it is not necessary that the material of which it is made should possess intrinsic or commercial value. To use again the language of the author last quoted, "The value of money perpetually depends upon its power to represent value and not upon its material, because money never reaches a point at which it can be used as an article of actual value." The value of the material can add nothing to its power as money; it can only render its value more certain, as when money is issued by a weak and irresponsible government, or by a nation possessing few or no products for which it can be exchanged. When issued by a stable and responsible government, whose people possess ample property and valuable products, its value corresponds to the value of the products of the country for which it can be exchanged. If money made of paper will procure the same property or commodities, as if made of a material possessing intrinsic value, like gold or silver, it possesses the same power in one instance as in the other. If A. has a ten dollar gold piece and B. has a ten dollar legal tender note, and the gold piece and paper money will each purchase the same article of value, in parting with them A. does not part with anything more than B., although A's money possesses an intrinsic value and B's does not. And as long as the gold piece is used as money, it is not possible for any one to derive any more use or value from it, than that which belongs to it in its representative capacity by virtue of law. Dr. Walker, a political economist of the bullionist school, in speaking of money as an instrument of exchange, says: "Anything which by general consent, or in obedience to law, all receive in exchange will answer the purpose (of money.) So far as this function is concerned, it is of no consequence whether the article has value or not; safety and convenience are the only considerations of importance. Money in this respect is simply a counter, token or universal equivalent."

The power of money, then, whether made of a material possessing value or not, depends on its ability to represent value. How a piece of paper, possessing little or no intrinsic value, can acquire the power to represent value, will be explained further on. In the meantime it will appear from a slight examination that it is a disadvantage to money to possess an intrinsic value, and that gold and silver, however suitable they may be to adjust balances between nations, are not the proper substances out of which to make the circulating medium of a nation. If money possesses an intrinsic, as well as a representative value, it is then a commodity, as well as money, and is subject to two different and often antagonistic sets of laws. As money it seeks to perform the functions of money and to fill the channels of trade, while as a commodity it is compelled to obey the "uncontrollable laws of supply and demand." In commerce gold and silver are commodities and are taken in exchange for products, when they are preferable, in a business point of view, to other products or commodities, or in the settlement of balances, after an exchange of products has been made. They are thus liable to be taken at any time from the channels of circulation by the demands of commerce, and this can be done most readily when they are stored in bank vaults as the basis of bank notes. In this way the amount of the circulating medium in a country is rendered dependent on the wants and whims of other nations, and is, consequently, uncertain in amount and fluctuating in value. It may be safely asserted that there was scarcely ever a time in the history of the United States, when the specie basis system was in existence, that the Emperor of China could not have occasioned a commercial crash and money panic, by simply decreeing that the idols and images worshipped by his subjects should be made of gold.

Gold and silver money are objectionable on account of the inconvenience and risk which attend their use, and for many other reasons, but the chief objection to gold is its scarcity, which also renders it expensive. There is not sufficient gold money in circulation to answer the wants of any one of the leading commercial nations of the world, and for all to seek to use it as an exclusive medium of exchange is simply an absurdity. It is true the difficulty is remedied in part in some countries by issuing paper notes based on gold, but these notes are not legal representatives of value, but merely representatives of the credit of those who issue them, and constitute, as experience has proved, an unsafe and unreliable medium of exchange, as will hereafter more fully appear. As compared with the vast amount of money required to pay interest on debts, national, state, municipal and corporate, and the expenses of governments, and to carry on the transactions of hundreds of millions of people, the amount of gold in use as money is as a grain of sand to a mountain.

And when properly considered the intrinsic value of gold and silver is comparatively trifling. These metals owe their chief value to their use as money. If that use were discontinued to any considerable extent, their value would depreciate in a corresponding degree. Only recently Germany demonetized silver, and it depreciated so rapidly in value that it became a matter of importance to the German government to dispose of its supply at the earliest moment possible. In 1764 the British Board of Trade objected to the use of legal tender paper money in the colonies, doubtless because it rendered the people of the colonies independent of the money power of Great Britain, on the ground that "every medium of exchange should have an intrinsic value, which paper money has not." To this Dr. Franklin replied:

"However fit a particular thing may be for a particular purpose, whenever that thing is not to be had, or not to be had in sufficient quantity, it becomes necessary to use something else, the fittest that can be got in lieu of it. * * Bank bills and bankers' notes are daily used here [in England] as a medium of trade, and in large dealings perhaps the greater part is transacted by their means, and yet they have no intrinsic value, but rest on the credit of those that issued them, as paper bills in the colonies do on the credit of the respective settlements there. These (bank bills) being payable in cash upon sight by the drawers is, indeed, a circumstance that cannot attend the colony bills, for the reason, just above mentioned, their cash (bullion) being drawn from them by the British trade; but the legal tender being substituted in its place, is rather a greater advantage to the possessor, since he need not be at the trouble of going to a particular bank or banker to demand the money."

"At this very time even the silver money in England is obliged to the legal tender for a part of its value; that part which is the difference between its real weight and denomination. Great part of the shillings and six-pences now current are, by wearing, become five, ten, twenty, and some of the six-pences even fifty, per cent. too light. For this difference between the real and nominal you have no intrinsic value; you have not so much as paper; you have nothing. It is the legal tender, with the knowledge that it can easily be repassed *for the same value*, that makes *three pennyworth* of silver pass for *six-pence*."

"Gold and silver are not intrinsically of equal value with iron, a metal in itself capable of many more benefits to mankind. Their value rests chiefly in the estimation they happen to be in among the generality of nations, and the credit given to the opinion that the estimation will continue.

Otherwise a pound of gold would not be a real equivalent for even a bushel of wheat." [Franklin's Works: Duane's edition, 1809; volume 4.]

Gold or silver, or both, however, are used for the purposes of money by nearly all nations, and hence it is that these metals have come to be used in the commerce of the world, not as money, but as commodities, under the name of bullion, possessing an established and universally recognized value. Gold at the present time is a commonly accepted equivalent for all other commodities. It will be borne in mind, however, that this general recognition of the value of gold depends chiefly upon the fact that gold is a legal tender, when coined into money, in all nations where it is used. No law exists compelling citizens of different nations to receive from each other gold in payment of debts, but people will always take that in payment of debts which they can in turn apply to the same purpose. It is incorrect, therefore, to speak of gold as the "money of the world." No such money has ever been established, nor can be until all nations adopt a uniform unit of value as well as of money. Different units of weight, length, value, etc., have grown up in different nations, in the same manner as different languages, manners and customs have grown up, and it would be almost as easy to establish a universal language as to induce the various nations of the world to adopt a common system of money. A person who takes $100 in gold, coined in the United States, to England, is obliged to sell his coin, just as he would sell a bale of cotton, in order to obtain money which will pass current in that country; and if he crosses over to France he is obliged to sell English coin in the same way. And it may happen, and frequently has happened, that a person may be unable to obtain money for gold or silver. During the financial crisis in England, in 1847, it was impossible to borrow a £5 note on thousands of dollars worth of silver, because silver was not a legal tender for an amount over forty shillings, and was, therefore, practically useless for the purposes of money; and in Calcutta, where silver money is the legal tender of the country, during the stringency of 1864, it was impossible to borrow money on gold. It is well authenticated that, during that crisis, persons, with as much as $100,000 worth of gold in their possession, were obliged to allow their notes to go protest, because they could not borrow $10 in silver money on a bushel of gold.

Another clap-trap name given to gold and silver, now in common use, is "honest money." Money is honest or not honest according to the uses it performs and the manner in which it performs them. Gold or silver may perform the uses of money in an honest manner—it is then "honest money;" but it has been, and still is, the misfortune of these naturally honest metals to be made the basis of all the rascally systems of money ever founded.

And it may be well, too, to notice briefly another pet name which is much relied upon by the bullionists to deceive and influence a large and intelligent class of people. In the memorable fight between the people, under the fearless and patriotic leadership of President Jackson, and the money power, represented by the United States Bank, the term "hard money" became deservedly popular. Gold and silver coin were then the people's money—the "honest money" of the country, as the greenback is now; and the gist of the controversy was then, precisely as it is in the pending struggle now, whether the people should retain the control of the circulating medium of the nation in their own hands, where it is placed by the Constitution of the United States, or should permit individuals and corporations to usurp the functions of the general government, and, in its stead, make and regulate the medium of exchange of the country. (See Chapter V.)

If gold and silver were demonetized by the principal nations of the earth, they would owe their value as commodities to the use that could be made of them for other purposes, as for ornaments or in the arts; and as they could then be had for such purposes in abundance, their value would doubtless diminish to but a fraction of what it is now.

THE USES OF MONEY.

The uses of money correspond to its powers or properties, viz: to represent value, to measure value, to accumulate value and to exchange value.* Actual or real value belongs to property or products, which are necessary or desirable, and money is the legal medium by which it is represented, measured and exchanged. In an accumulated form, as capital, it represents accumulated property or labor, and is capable of accumulating value in the same manner that the property or labor which it represents could be used for that purpose. It measures value because it is the legal standard of value established by law, just as weights and measures to determine the weight, length and bulk of articles are established; and if based on sound principles, it would prove as unvarying, as a standard of value, as are the standards of measurement of weight and quantity. The value of property and products would then rise and fall in obedience to the laws of supply and demand, but the standard of value, money, would remain the same as previously determined by the law which instituted it, provided the law emanated from a responsible source. This may be illustrated in a measure by the greenback now in use, though not with the same degree of force and certainty that it could be done, if the

*See Kellogg, page 46.

greenback had not been mutilated and depreciated by law. The value of property and commodities is now measured by the greenback, because the value of the greenback corresponds to the idea of value carried in the minds of the people of the United States. The unit of value in the United States is the dollar, and this unit of value is fixed in the mind, just as the units of measurement expressed by a pound, a bushel, a yard or a degree, are fixed there, that is by use and custom. Partial legal tender paper money (the greenback) is now the money or medium of exchange of the country, and corresponds to the idea of value fixed in the minds of the people. People *think* in greenbacks when estimating value. If told that the price of a horse is $100, the amount or value is instantly referred to the greenback standard of measurement. The price of particular commodities, as well as the price of gold, may change daily without affecting the prices of other commodities, as measured by the greenback standard, which could not be the case if it were the greenback that fluctuated. Hence it may be inferred, among other things, that editors of newspapers, who quote greenbacks as worth so many cents on the dollar as compared with gold, are either grossly ignorant of the nature of money, or have become entangled in the toils of the money power.

But it is of the uses of money in a less technical sense that we wish to speak. Money has come to be a vital element in production, in the operations of trade and in the business details of life. In a simple state of society, as in new countries even now, individuals and families are for the most part self-supporting. The farm supplies food and the material for clothing, and the spinning wheel and loom are found in every household. But where the advantages of civilization and a medium of exchange have once become common, a very different condition of affairs exists. The merchant, the tailor, the carpenter, the shoemaker, the blacksmith, the doctor, etc., etc., have made their appearance, and individuals and families are no longer self-supporting, but wholly dependent upon each other. Money is then a necessity. Food, clothing, rent, fuel, light, taxes, insurance, railroad fares, etc., etc., require cash, and a general scarcity of money will occasion want and suffering, even in the midst of plenty. How dependent individuals are upon each other in a state of civilization, is thust set forth by Kellogg:

"The necessity for the *exchange of commodities* is generally acknowledged. Few, however, even among thinking men, are aware how indispensable these exchanges are to the subsistence and comfort of the human family. Men are social beings, and mutually dependent. To appreciate this important truth, we must consider the inability of each man to provide for the numerous wants of his nature; and the ignorance and discomfort to which each would be exposed, were he not benefited by the labor of others. If every man could build his own house, furnish his own food and clothing, and make all the instruments and utensils that he needs to use: if the materials for all these things were placed upon every acre of land, and every man, woman and child, were endowed with sufficient skill and strength to produce them, there might be no need of an exchange of commodities.

But all men are, in many, in most things, dependent on the labor of their fellow men. For example, take the farmer, who is acknowledged to be the least dependent of men, and see for how many things even he is indebted to the labor of others. He must have implements for the cultivation of his farm, a plow, harrow, shovel, hoe, sickle, cradle, scythes, a fan, or fanning mill, and a cart or wagon. The farmer is dependent on the miner for the iron ore; on the collier to dig the coal; on the furnace worker to smelt the iron; on the forger and the smith to make him his iron and steel instruments. He is dependent on the wagon maker for his wagon; on the machinist for his fanning mill; on the carpenter for his house; on the nail maker for nails; on the glass manufacturer for glass; on the stone cutter and the mason for mason work; on the brick maker for bricks; on the cooper for barrels, tubs and pails; on the saw maker for a saw, and on the rolling mill to roll out the iron or steel for it; on the tin-plate worker for kitchen utensils; on the moulder and caster of iron for iron pots; on the miner of copper, and on the copper and brass founder for brass and copper kettles; on the pump maker for a pump, etc., etc. He is dependent on the needle maker, the pin maker, the button maker, the silk grower, the tanner, the shoemaker, the hatter, the saddle and harness maker, the cabinet maker, and the type maker, type setter and printer. Not one of these artisans, in attending to his particular employment, produces his food and clothing; and all would be destitute of them, unless supplied with them by the labor of others. The farmer raises all of his food, except salt, tea, coffee, sugar, molasses, spices and the like; these, and the ships to transport them, must be furnished by others. These wants call into employment ship carpenters, sailors, compass makers, surveyors, chart makers, etc. The farmer must raise wool, cotton, hemp or flax, or else be dependent on others for clothing. If the farmer, who is the least dependent of men, receives from others so many supplies, how is it with the hatter and shoemaker? The former makes an article to cover the head, the latter one to cover the feet; and all the additional supplies of both must be furnished by the labor of others. Artisans, too, depend upon each other for the different parts of their work; the cotton manufacturer must be assisted by others to carry forward his manufacture. Many articles, such as watch springs, are useless unless they are combined with other parts. It is, then, of paramount importance that no obstacles be thrown in the way of a ready exchange of commodities.

A certain quantity of one kind of produce is worth as much as a certain quantity of another kind; and all civilized nations have adopted some *medium* by means of which all kinds of produce may be more easily exchanged than by direct barter. We hear it sometimes asserted that there is no need of a medium of exchange. But the articles of trade could not be divided and distributed to supply the numerous wants of a people without a representative of value through which the distribution could be made. For example, a man brings to market five hundred bushels of wheat. The purchaser tenders corn in payment; and they agree that seven hundred and fifty bushels of corn are worth as much as five hundred bushels of wheat. The seller can use but a small portion of the corn, and finds a purchaser, with whom he exchanges the surplus for hams. He disposes of the hams for hats and shoes. If he endeavor to divide the hats and shoes, and exchange them for the articles that he needs, he may spend two years before he can return to his farm to raise a second crop of wheat. Yet he is fairly dealt with. All those with whom he exchanges, give him, as nearly as possible, an equivalent of actual value for the actual value that they receive; and all the articles are such as all need. In fact, all trade is simply a barter of one useful thing for another. A person who produces more of an article than he needs for his own use, exchanges his surplus for the surplus articles of others. If the farmer had sold the wheat for *money*, the money would have been a tender for any other article that he wished to purchase."

In the large operations of trade, as with foreign countries

and between different sections of the country, vast sums of money are constantly required. The foreign trade of the United States in ordinary times amounts to nearly $1,000,000,000 a year, and the trade between the different sections of the country amounts to probably five times that sum. It is true that, in the trade with foreign nations and between different parts of the nation, the transfer and re-transfer of money from one to the other is rendered unnecessary by the use of checks, drafts and bills of exchange, except to settle balances; but in the production, transportation, repeated handling and distribution of the commodities, represented by the vast sums referred to, the amount of money required is enormous. For example, in the movement of the crops of the Western States alone more cash is required each year than can be had for the purpose; and in the days of the specie basis system the Western banks, as is well known, were in the habit at such times of issuing their notes without any regard to legal limitations. President Grant in his message of December, 1873, after the panic and before he had become debauched by the money power, called the attention of Congress to the fact in the following language:

"It is patent to the most casual observer that much more currency or money is required to transact the legitimate trade of the country during the fall and winter months, when the vast crops are being removed, than during the balance of the year. With our present system, the amount in the country remains the same throughout the entire year, resulting in an accumulation of all the surplus capital of the country in a few centers, when not employed in moving crops, tempted there by the offer of interest on call loans. Interest being paid, this surplus capital must earn the interest paid with a profit. Being subject to 'call,' it can not be loaned, only in part at best, to the merchant or manufacturer, for a fixed term. Hence, no matter how much currency there might be in the country, it would be absorbed, prices keeping pace with the volume, and panics, stringency and disasters would ever be recurring with the autumn. Elasticity in our monetary system, therefore, is the object to be attained first, and next to that, as far as possible, a prevention of the use of other people's money in stocks and other species of speculation."

Money is also an important element of production. When the channels of circulation are supplied with money, the industries of the country are quick and active, and the entire nation becomes engaged in adding to its wealth. It has been well said that "A nation, whether it consumes its own products, or with them purchases from abroad, can have no more value than it produces. The supreme policy of every nation, therefore, is to develop the producing forces of its own country. What are they? The workingmen, the land, the mines, the machinery, the water power, etc."* The producing forces of a country can be developed only slowly and laboriously without the aid of money. The productive soil, the iron, the coal, the timber, the water power, the machinery, the labor, etc., may all be at hand, but until touched by the vitalizing current of money, as it circulates in the channels of trade, they can give forth but a feeble spark of the life and power which they possess.

At an early day in the history of the colonies the inhabitants were subjected to great drawbacks for the want of a legal medium of exchange. Dr. Franklin, in 1764, stated to the British Board of Trade that: "In 1723 Pennsylvania was totally stripped of its gold and silver. * * * The difficulties for want of cash were accordingly very great, the chief part of the trade being carried on by the extremely

*Sir John Barnard Byles.

inconvenient method of barter, when, in 1723, paper money was first made there which gave new life to business, promoted greatly the settlement of new lands, whereby the province has so greatly increased in inhabitants that the export from thence thither [to England] is now more than ten fold what it then was."

In 1755 Virginia was badly in need of money or a medium of exchange. A paper money bottomed on a specific tax was issued, which afforded abundant relief, and, as we learn from Jefferson, never depreciated a farthing in value. But a more marked instance of the value of money as an element of production is furnished by the experience of Pennsylvania during the present century. In 1841 the people of Pennsylvania were on the verge of bankruptcy. The State was unable to pay interest on the public debt, or even pay the wages of laborers for work done on the public works. Corporations were bankrupt, and merchants were in nearly as bad a situation. There was no money, and consequently trade and production were completely paralyzed. The State of Pennsylvania in this crisis issued $3,100,000 of what were called relief notes, bearing simply a promise that they would be received by the Treasury of the State in payment of all taxes and other obligations due to the State. "These notes were taken greedily by the people. Banks inserted in the front of their books an agreement that the depositor should receive on check the same kind of money he deposited, and then took these notes. They discounted paper with them. The wheels of industry were set in motion by these notes, which promised nothing but that they would be received in payment of State taxes. The State paid her domestic creditors, and these hastened to pay theirs or to supply their wants by purchase. Crops, for which there had been no market, moved; the loom and the spindle were again heard; labor, lifted from despair, found work and wages, and with the great resources of Pennsylvania under full and free development, she was soon exporting more than she imported. Gold and silver flowed in upon her; and the broken banks resumed specie payments. We then did," says the Hon. William D. Kelley, of Pennsylvania, from whom we quote, "what France does; we were wise enough then to know that it is labor, not coin, that maintains the public credit and gives prosperity to the people."

But the people of the United States have had ample proof, during the past few years, of the great advantages to be derived from an abundance of money. The activity in all forms of productive industry during and immediately after the war, which constituted an inexhaustible fountain of strength to the Federal Government, and which, in spite of the ravages of war, enabled the country to double its wealth in ten years, from 1860 to 1870, was attributable entirely to the vast amount of money, or evidences of indebtedness of the government used as such, that then filled the channels of circulation. The condition of the country then, when money was plenty, and now, under the policy of contraction, which has withdrawn the circulating medium of exchange from the channels of trade, is thus eloquently portrayed by the distinguished statesman quoted above (Kelley), in a recent address to the citizens of Philadelphia:

"You have seen a strong man, full of life, rise in the morning as a lion shakes the dew from his mane and go forward to the battle of life, full of vigor, full of hope, full of energy, full of enterprise. His brawny nether limbs bear his stout body ably; his muscular arm and his cunning hand go glibly and gladly to their duties, performing their functions. But an accident happens, an artery is cut; the blood does not ooze, but flows from him. The surgeon comes just in time to save his life. He staunches the wound and binds it up. But the man is another being, he lies there pallid and shrunken. His sturdy limbs will not even bear his wasted body. His muscles are flaccid, and his fingers have lost their skill. His energy is gone, and he dreams not of enterprise. This is our condition to-day as a people. In 1865 and 1866 every man in America who had the skill and the will to labor could earn wages to support his family and lay something by. All industries were quick and active. Production ran on. The American people waked up each new morning to feel that there were great duties before them; that there were mines to be opened, forges and furnaces to be erected to work the iron, the copper, the silver and the gold. New houses were built. Skill, energy, science and genius were taxed to quicken and cheapen productive processes. Our wealth grew as it, or that of any other people, had never grown. We were moving onward, when one Hugh McCulloch tapped a great artery and let nearly all the blood flow from the body politic. Diseased, paralyzed, shrinking from day to day, what American has the energy to engage in developing a new mine? Pennsylvanians, who of you are ready to construct a new forge or a new furnace? Where are factories building to-day? Your laborers—moody, sullen, in want—are begging the poor privilege of earning a day's food by an honest day's labor. Their homes are being stripped of everything they cherish. Go through the suburbs of your city, halt before the houses where of a Sunday afternoon you would, a few years ago, have found the family gathered about the melodeon or the cheap piano, singing the praises of Him who had given them their lines in these pleasant places. Ah! the house is silent now; the father is out of employment, the sons are in idleness, the daughters have no work; the melodeon or piano is gone.

Aye, worse than that, the most cherished mementoes, though of little value measured in dollars and cents—the cheap jewelry—the trinket that the young lover toiled in over hours that he might buy and see it grace the person of his sweetheart, the amulet he hung upon the neck of his bride —the silver cup that marked the birth or christening of their first born—cherished by all, but they have gone to the pawnbroker or jeweler to bring them food. Courage gone, hope gone, despair crushing him to the earth, and destroying all the pride that made the American mechanic the boast and honor of his country, how many a man to-day, longing for honest work but powerless to obtain it, creeps and crawls from town to town, foot-sore, ragged, dusty, to beg from strangers rather than from those who know him and will remember it—to be denounced as a 'tramp' and commended to the custody of the police!"

As the end and object of money are to exchange commodities and promote production, it should be increased in amount in proportion to the increase of population and trade. Bullionists assert the contrary, but they can furnish no sound reason or proof upon which to base their theory. They invariably rest their argument on the fact that nations have increased in wealth and population without adding to their monetary circulation, and most always cite Great Britain as a case in point. Properly considered the experience of Great Britain does not sustain their theory. How does Great Britain manage to conduct its large and increasing business without a corresponding increase of money? The answer is by means of *inflated bank credit*. On account of the want of a sufficient medium of exchange, the British people are compelled to use and pay for the credit of banks to an enormous extent. This is a heavy tax upon the industrial classes of that kingdom, and explains why the wealth of the people is constantly flowing into the hands of the few. We find the following statement used by Dr. Walker, a political economist of the bullionist school, to show how nicely the people of Great Britain can get along with but a limited amount of money. We submit that it shows much more forcibly to what a desperate use of inflated credit that nation has been driven by a false monetary system. He says: "As an illustration in point, Sir John Lubbock gave, in a paper read before the Statistical Society, in June, 1865, an analysis of £19,000,000 paid into his banking house *in a few days*, as follows:

Checks and bills..............£18,395,000, or 97 per cent.
Bank of England notes........   408,000 ⎫
Country notes...............   79,000 ⎬ 3 per cent.
Coin........................   118,000 ⎭

From which statement it appears that only three per cent. were paid in the form of money, i. e., notes and coin together, of which a little more than *one-half of one per cent. was in coin.*" The bullionists pretend to be very much afraid of the evil consequences of inflation; but when the mask is torn off, it is apparent that they are only concerned about retaining the power to inflate in their own hands.

SYSTEMS OF MONEY.

Every nation has its own peculiar system of finance, the difference consisting more in details than in principles. The financial system of the United States is now composed of the Independent Treasury Bureau for the receipt, custody and disbursement of the revenues; of the Treasury proper, which maintains an issue of about $370,000,000 of Treasury notes (greenbacks), constituting the legal tender medium of the country, and about $45,000,000 of fractional currency; of the National Banks, over 2,200 in number, with a circulation of over $360,000,000; and a number of State Banks, established under State authority.

The medium of exchange of the United States, it will be observed, is composed of Treasury notes (greenbacks) and bank notes. It is important to notice the difference between the Treasury note and the bank note, because they belong to two entirely different and distinct systems of money; and a clear perception of the difference is essential to a proper understanding of the money question and of the political issues, growing out of it, which now agitate the country.

A bank note is a bill of credit, promising payment in lawful money on demand, issued by and resting on the credit of a private corporation established by law. Being payable or redeemable in money on demand, it represents money and circulates as such, and performs nearly all of its functions. Private corporations, therefore, upon whom the privilege or power to issue bank notes is conferred, are practically invested with the authority and power to make and put in circulation a medium of exchange. If the bank note is secured by a deposit of stock or bonds to insure its payment and maintain its value, as is the case with the National Bank note, which is secured by a deposit of United States bonds in the Treasury of the Federal Government, it will form a perfectly safe, uniform and convenient medium of exchange. But a bank note possesses two peculiar features, which do not belong to money, (of any kind, whether made of gold, silver, or paper) and which render it a costly medium of exchange. One peculiarity of a bank note is that it enters into circulation encumbered with interest, and constantly accumulates value, whether it is in use or not. Its very existence, therefore, is a tax upon production and trade. The other peculiarity, which grows out of the one just mentioned, is that a bank note is not free to obey the natural laws of trade, but is subject to the will and control of the corporation which puts it in circulation. This can be made perfectly clear by supposing two notes, a greenback and a National Bank note, to be put into circulation at the same time and observing the course taken by each. A greenback dollar is paid out by the United States government to A. for its equivalent in labor or value. A. pays it to B. for a dollar's worth of commodities. B. lends it to C. for thirty days at 6 per cent interest. C. pays it to D. for a debt. D. retains it in his possession for three months and then puts it in circulation again. It passes from hand to hand, until finally it reaches Z., who pays it to a collector of internal revenue, when it is returned to the Federal Treasury, to be used over and over again in the same manner. While performing its use as a medium of exchange, it bore no interest. When held by D. for three months in a state of idleness, it accumulated no value for any one. It is true B. lent it to C. for thirty days at 6 per cent. interest, but that was an individual transaction and extended no further than the parties concerned. As soon as C. put it in circulation again, it went on its way, as free and unencumbered as when it left the Treasury of the United States. But it is very different with a bank note. The bank, which issues it, lends it to A. for sixty days at say 6 per cent. interest, and A. puts it in circulation. At the expiration of sixty days, A., unable to return the identical note which he borrowed, pays the bank with a greenback or another bank note. This note in turn is immediately lent to B., and the process goes on indefinitely. The original bank note thus constantly realizes interest and accumulates value for the bank, whether it circulates in the channels of trade, or reposes in the vaults of the bank as a deposit, or lies rotting at the bottom of the ocean. This interest comes out of the profits of production, and is a tax upon the community at large. The tax thus imposed upon the public for a medium of exchange is a greater burden than industry can bear, and every few years labor is driven to the wall and production, except of the necessities of life, ceases. To promote production, or in other words, to "develop the producing forces of a country," it is, as we have seen, more essential to have a cheap medium of exchange, than it is to have cheap transportation; but a bank note is the most expensive medium of exchange that could possibly be devised, because it is accumulating value all the time, whether it is performing the uses of money or not. The bank note is subject to the will and control of the corporation which issues it, because when the bank ceases to discount paper, as it usually does whenever there is a money stringency, and calls in its circulation, it is obliged to leave the channels of trade, no matter how much its services are needed as a medium of exchange, and return to the bank. But this is not all. The tax which banks are thus authorized to impose on the medium of exchange issued by them, enables them to control not only their own notes, but the money of the country, whether coin or legal tender paper money, as will be more fully explained in another chapter, and thus it happens, as at the present time, that the circulating medium of the nation every few years becomes concentrated in the money centers of the country.

A bank note medium of exchange, whether redeemable in coin, as in England, or in greenbacks, as in the United States at the present time, it will, therefore, be observed, constitutes a peculiar and distinct system of money, and one, it may be added, that has proved an infinite source of disaster and weakness in both England and America.

It was for these reasons, in days gone by, that Jefferson insisted that "Bank paper must be suppressed and the circulation restored to the nation to whom it belongs;" that John Adams denounced bank paper as a vile freak of those who were shapen in Toryism and British idolatry; that Jackson waged war on banks of issue; that Calhoun labored to establish a legal tender paper money, to be issued by the Federal Government; and it is for the same reasons that a host of the foremost statesmen, political economists and philanthropists of the country are to-day urging the people of the United States to assert their rights and prevent the money power from destroying the greenback, in order that they may substitute the National Bank note in its stead, and thus secure the entire control of the medium of exchange of the nation.

A Treasury note issued by the Federal Government represents the property and productions of the country to the amount or value inscribed on its face. It rests on the credit of the government in the same manner that a bank note rests on the credit of a corporation, and represents the property and productions of the country (including gold and silver) for which it is exchangeable, just as a bank note represents the coin or Treasury note in which it is payable or redeemable. The foundation of the Treasury note is the same as that of a United States bond, which secures the payment and maintains the value of the bank note, and it, therefore, possesses the highest and best security that a medium of exchange can possibly have.* A bank note is a promise to pay money, but a Treasury note, being a legal representative of value (property and products), is money. It is not, therefore, a *promise to pay*—it would be more accurate to describe it as a *promise to receive*. It is true that the present legal tender money of the United States (the greenback) professes to be a promise to pay, which is a

*See note at the end of this chapter.

misfortune, because it misleads people, even professors of political economy,* but the promise is an empty phrase, wholly foreign to the nature of the Treasury note and the principles upon which it is based. It was spread on the face of the greenback at the instance of the money power, which was unwilling to recognize any other kind of money than that based on bullion, and for the purpose of depreciating its value as a medium of exchange.

It is apparent, therefore, that legal tender paper money or Treasury notes and bank notes belong to two separate and distinct systems of money, based on entirely different principles. In the one case the medium of exchange is furnished by the government and subject only to the natural laws which govern trade. In the other, it is furnished by private corporations, who tax the public heavily for its use, and is subject, not to the laws of trade, but to the control of the corporations issuing it. In Great Britain, where the system originated, the legal tender money of the country, in which bank notes are payable, is gold and silver, as was the case in the United States prior to the war, and hence the system is commonly known, and is generally referred to in these pages, as the specie basis system. When the medium of exchange is limited to gold and silver, or paper money based on gold and silver, the public is compelled, on account of the scarcity of these metals, to use bank credit, which explains why the money power is now striving to force the American people to submit to a return to specie payments, no matter at what sacrifice.

THE POWER TO MAKE MONEY A GOVERNMENTAL FUNCTION.

The power to make and regulate money has long been recognized as a governmental function, or, in the language of Tooke, "In every civilized country supplying and regu-

*See Professor Newcomb's silly comments on this point in Appendix.

lating the circulating medium is a function of sovereign prerogative." The reason of this is obvious. Money to be a public medium of exchange must possess legal representative value, and this can be derived only from the sovereign or law making power of a nation. The bullionists do not concede this, but profess to believe that the government is vested simply with the power to coin gold and silver, because "the State can do the work best, * * as no attestation (of the weight and purity of coin) furnished by private persons can compete in authority with the stamp imposed by the government mint."* This view of the matter grows out of the peculiar ideas in regard to the nature of money held by those who advocate the specie basis system. Bonamy Price, Professor of political economy in the University of Oxford, England, says: "Coin, metallic coin, alone is true money and nothing else is, unless it be a commodity, as an ox, a cow, or a piece of salt,"—precisely the same theory of money, it will be observed, as that held by the ancient Romans, who used bars of copper and cattle, and by the American Indian of the present day.

The Constitution of the United States confers upon Congress the following, among other, powers, viz: "To lay and collect taxes, duties, imposts and excises, to pay the debts and provide for the common defense and general welfare of the United States; * * to borrow money on the credit of the United States; * * to coin money, regulate the value thereof and of foreign coins; * * and to make all laws which shall be necessary and proper to carry into effect the foregoing powers, etc." It also prohibits the States from coining money, emitting bills of credit, or making anything but gold or silver coin a tender in payment of debts. The exclusive power to make and regulate the

*Currency and Banking, by Bonamy Price, page 17.

medium of exchange, therefore, devolves upon the Federal Government At the time the Federal Constitution was framed the money question was one that had to be handled with great delicacy. The money power, then as always in fact, was on the alert, and care had to be taken not to incur its hostility, lest it might prevent the ratification of the Constitution by the several States. When it was proposed to insert a clause in the Constitution empowering the Federal Government "to emit bills of credit," it was boldly stated on the floor of the Convention that "the moneyed interest would oppose the plan of government if paper emissions (bills of credit) be not prohibited," and the clause was rejected by a vote of nine States against to two for. As "bills of credit" are promises to pay in lawful money and belong to the specie basis system of money, it is fortunate that no such provision was inserted in the Constitution. In this respect its framers, perhaps, "builded better than they knew." As the Federal Government is clothed with no power "to emit bills of credit," and States are expressly prohibited from doing so, it is a very pertinent question as to how either the Federal or a State government can delegate that power to a private corporation. Individuals can issue promises to pay, because they are in the nature of a common contract, but when it comes to corporations issuing promises to pay (bills of credit), under special authority of law, which are clothed with the attributes of money, it is a very different matter. The well known legal maxim that what one "does through another he does himself," would seem to fit the case pretty closely. But the people can not afford to waste time with constitutional quibbles. They can compel their Representatives in Congress to extinguish banks of issue and "restore the circulation to the nation to whom it belongs,"* and if it is necessary to amend

*Thomas Jefferson.

the Constitution in order to accomplish that purpose, they can also do that.

But there seems to be no difficulty so far as the Constitution is concerned. That the framers of the Constitution, when they refused to empower the Federal Government "to emit bills of credit," did not intend to prohibit paper money or in any way curtail the legitimate functions of government with respect to making and regulating the medium of exchange of the country, is apparent from cotemporaneous history, as well as the subsequent course of the government. Mr. Madison, who was a member of the Convention which framed the Constitution, in speaking of his vote against empowering the Federal Government "to emit bills of credit," says:

"The vote in the affirmative by Virginia was occasioned by the acquiescence of Mr. Madison, who became satisfied that striking out the words ['to emit bills of credit'] would not disable the government from the use of public notes, as far as they could be safe and proper; and would only cut off the pretext for a paper currency, and particularly for making the bills [of credit currency] a tender either for public or private debts." [See "Madison Papers."]

Mr. Jefferson repeatedly urged that banks of issue should be suppresed and that public notes issued by the Federal Government should be substituted for bank notes as a medium of exchange. In a letter dated June 24, 1813, to his son-in-law Eppis, who was a member of the committee of ways and means of the national House of Representatives, urging this point, he said:

"In the war of 1755, our State availed itself of this fund, by issuing a paper currency, bottomed on a specific tax for its redemption, and to insure the credit, bearing an interest of five per cent. Within a very short time, not a bill of this emission was found in circulation. It was locked up in the chests of executors, guardians, widows, farmers," etc.

"We then issued bills bottomed on a redeeming tax, but bearing no interest. These were received, and never depreciated a single farthing."

"In the revolutionary war, the old Congress, and the States, issued bills, without interest and without tax. They occupied the channels of circulation very freely, until those channels were overflowed by an excess beyond the calls of circulation. But although we have so improvidently suffered the field of circulating medium to be filched from us by private individuals, yet I think we may recover it, in part, and even in the whole, if the States will co-operate with us."

"If Treasury bills are emitted, on a tax appropriated for their redemption in fifteen years, and (to insure preference in the first moments of competition) bearing an interest of six per cent., there is no one who would not take them in preference to bank paper now afloat, on a principle of patriotism, as well as interest, and they would be withdrawn from circulation into private hoards to a considerable amount. Their credit once established, others might be emitted, bottomed also on a tax, but not bearing interest; and if ever their credit faltered, open public loans, on which these bills alone should be received as specie. These operating as a sinking fund, would reduce the quantity in circulation, so as to maintain them in an equilibrium with specie. It is not easy to estimate the obstacles which, in the beginning, we should encounter in ousting the banks from the possession of circulation."

Mr. Jefferson's plan, it will be observed, is identical in principle with the much derided 3.65 inter-convertible bond plan, so ably advocated by Pliny Freeman, Judge Kelley,

Horace Greeley* and a host of able and earnest friends of the American masses.

The issue of Treasury notes under the Constitution accordingly began at an early day, though not without meeting with fierce opposition from the money power, and their legality has been sanctioned from the first by all departments of the government. The first issue of Treasury notes was made in pursuance of an act of Congress of June 30, 1812. Further issues were authorized by the acts of Congress of February 25, 1813; March 4, and December 26, 1814; October 12, 1837; January 31, and August 31, 1842; July 22, 1846; and January 28, 1857.

The validity and constitutionality of these acts were tested and affirmed in the Supreme Court of the United States, in the case of Thorndike against the United States. Judge Story, in delivering the opinion of the court, said:

"By the statutes of the United States, under which the Treasury notes have been issued, it is enacted that such notes shall be receivable in payment to the United States for duties, taxes, and sales of public lands, to the full amount of the principle and interest accruing, due on such notes. It follows, of course, that they are a legal tender in payment of debts of this nature, due to the United States; and, by the very terms of the acts, public officers are bound to receive them."

When the act of Congress of October 12, 1837, authorizing an issue of Treasury notes, was pending, Mr. Calhoun advocated the measure in strong terms. The following extracts from a speech delivered by him September 19th, prior to the passage of the bill, confirm the distinction which we have made between public notes and bills of credit, and explain what was meant when we stated that it would be

*Horace Greeley's famous editorial on the 3.65 Bond plan will be found in the Appendix.

more accurate to describe a greenback as a promise to receive than a promise to pay.* He said:

"It is, then, my impression, that in the present condition of the world, a paper currency, in some form, * * is almost indispensable in financial and commercial operations of civilized and extensive communities. In many respects it has a vast superiority over a metallic currency, especially in great and extended transactions, by its greater cheapness, lightness, and the facility of determining the amount." * *

"It may throw some light on this subject to state, that North Carolina, just after the revolution, issued a large amount of paper, which was made receivable in dues to her; it was also made a legal tender, but which, of course, was not obligatory after the adoption of the Federal Constitution. A large amount, say between four and five hundred thousand dollars, remained in circulation after that period, and continued to circulate, for more than twenty years, at par with gold and silver during the whole time, with no other advantage than being received in the revenue of the State, which was much less than one hundred thousand dollars per annum."

"No one can doubt but that the government credit is better than that of any bank; more reliable—more safe. Why, then, should it mix it up with the less perfect credit of those institutions? Why not use its own credit to the amount of its own transactions? Why should it not be safe in its own hands, while it shall be considered safe in the hands of eight hundred private institutions, scattered all over the country. and which have no other object but their own private profit; to increase which they extend their business to the most dangerous extremes. And why should the community be compelled to give six per cent. discount

*See page 52.

for the government credit, blended with that of the bank, when the superior credit of the government could be furnished separate, without discount, to the mutual advantage of the government and the community?" * * *

"Believing that there might be a sound and safe paper currency, founded on the credit of the government exclusively, I was desirous that those who are responsible, and have the power, should have availed themselves of the opportunity." * *

"We are told the form I suggested is but a repetition of the 'old Continental money; a ghost that is ever conjured up by all who wish to give the banks an exclusive monopoly of government credit. The assertion is not true; there is not the least analogy between them. The one was a promise to pay, when there was no revenue; and the other a promise to receive in the dues of government when there is abundant revenue."

"We are told that there is no instance of a government paper that did not depreciate. In reply, I affirm, that there is none, assuming the form I propose, that ever did depreciate. Whenever a paper, receivable in dues of government, had anything like a fair trial, it has succeeded. Instance the case of North Carolina, referred to in my opening remarks. The drafts of the Treasury, at this moment, with all their incumbrance, are nearly at par with gold and silver. * * * The case of Russia might also be mentioned. In 1827 she had a fixed paper circulation in the form of bank notes, but which were inconvertible, of upward of one hundred and twenty millions of dollars, estimated in the metallic rouble, and which had for years remained without fluctuation, having nothing to sustain it, but that it was received in the dues of the government, and that too with a revenue of only about ninety millions of dollars annually. I speak on the authority of a respectable traveller. Other instances, no doubt, might be added, but it needs no such support."

"It has another striking advantage over bank circulation, in its superior cheapness, as well as greater stability and safety. Bank paper is cheap to those who make it; but dear, very dear, to those who use it, fully as much as gold and silver. It is the little cost of its manufacture, and the dear rates at which it is furnished to the community, which gives the great profit to those who have a monopoly of the article. Some idea may be formed of the extent of the profit, by the splendid palaces which we see under the name of banking houses, and the vast fortunes which have been accumulated in this branch of business; all of which must ultimately be derived from the productive powers of the community, and of course adds so much to the cost of production. On the other hand, the credit of government, while it would greatly facilitate its financial operations, would cost nothing, or next to nothing, both to it and to the people, and of course would add nothing to the cost of production; which would give to every branch of industry, agriculture, commerce and manufactures, as far as circulation might extend, great advantages, both at home and abroad."

Subsequently, March, 1838, Mr. Calhoun, in his speech on the Independent Treasury bill, said:

"I now undertake to affirm positively, and without the least fear that I can be answered—what heretofore I have but suggested—that a paper issued by government, with the simple promise to receive it in all dues, leaving its creditors to take it, or gold and silver, at its option, would, to the extent to which it would circulate, form a perfect paper circulation, which could not be abused by the government; that would be as steady and uniform in value as the metals themselves. I shall not go into the discussion now, but on a suitable occasion I shall be able to make good every word I have uttered. I will be able to do more—to prove that it is within the constitutional power of Congress to use such a paper, in the management of its finances, according to the most rigid rule of construing the Constitution; and that those at least who think that Congress can authorize the notes of private corporations to be received in the public dues are estopped from denying its right to receive its own paper."

The United States Treasury notes, issued prior to the war of 1861, had never been made a tender in payment of private debts, nor had they been issued in a suitable form to use as a circulating medium of exchange. But when the Rebellion broke out in 1861, the necessity for an increased amount of money became imperative, and it became necessary to issue public notes better adapted to the wants of the times. The banks of New York, Boston, and Philadelphia, soon after the war began, agreed to lend the Federal Government $150,000,000. After the loan had been negotiated, the Secretary of the Treasury, unexpectedly to the banks, required it to be paid in specie instead of bank notes, and the result was that the banks throughout the country were obliged to suspend specie payments.

The government stood in need of soldiers, ships, gunboats, cannon, guns, ammunition, commissary stores, quartermaster stores, transportation, etc. The people at large were obliged to supply the wants of the government, and fortunately possessed both the ability and willingness to do so, but it was impracticable to accomplish the ends desired except through the instrumentality of a medium of exchange—money. Congress, by virtue of the sovereign prerogative inherent in the people, and as their representative duly authorized by the Constitution, enacted a law authorizing and directing the Treasury Department of the Federal Government to issue public notes which should be a legal tender for debts, both public and private. As they were issued by the people in their collective capacity, and represented the property and products of the nation, it was eminently just and proper that they should declare that what they did in their collective capacity should be binding upon them individually. In fact, in no other way could the people all have been put upon the same platform with respect to the wants of the government, in the exigency which then existed, than by declaring their public notes a legal tender in payment of debts. These notes, as we have said, represented the property and products of the nation, and by virtue of their legal tender property they naturally and necessarily conformed to the unit and standard of value of the country. They therefore possessed the power to measure and exchange, as well as to represent value, and consequently possessed all the attributes of money—in a word were money, in every sense of the term; and the American people found themselves, unexpectedly, it is true, in the enjoyment (to use the language of President Grant) "of the best currency that was ever devised."

When public notes were issued, the people in a collective capacity in effect said to those who were able to supply the wants of the government: "Give the government all the guns, ships, food, transportation, etc., that is required, and the rest of the people will make good to you whatever amount you may contribute over and above your share out of any other property or products which they may possess that you need or desire." As it was a matter of compulsion on the part of the people to supply the wants of the government, it was an act of supreme folly in them to encumber their circulating medium with interest directly or indirectly, as was done, which can only be compared to a man paying somebody else interest for the privilege of using his own money. It simply made it the prey of speculators and money dealers, greatly to the disadvantage of the nation. That it was unnecessary appears from the fact that greenbacks to the amount of hundreds of millions of dollars circulated in the channels of trade and performed all the uses of money, as effectively as gold or silver could have done, for more than a year before the United States bonds, bearing six per cent. interest in gold, with which they were interchangeable, were issued, and continued to do so after their interchangeability was taken away by act of Congress. Mr. Spaulding, chairman of the sub-committee of Ways and Means of the House of Representatives, in a speech on January 12, 1863, said: "The Secretary has paid out nearly $250,000,000 legal tender notes, being all that he was authorized to issue; and notwithstanding he has had authority for the last ten months to sell $500,000,000 of five-twenty six per cent. bonds at the market price, he has only disposed of about $25,000,000, and has still authority to sell $475,000,000 at the market price, and take his pay for them in legal tender notes. One of the reasons why more of these bonds have not been disposed of is, that there has been no redundancy of currency, and it has been difficult for the Secretary of the Treasury to get legal tender notes on a sale of the bonds and seven-three-tenths notes that he has already negotiated." In other words, the people needed greenbacks far worse than anything else, and could not spare them to invest in five-twenty bonds, which have since been paid both principal and interest in gold. At this time gold ranged from 134 to 160.

Had Congress not yielded to the demands of the money power, but passed the legal tender act as originally framed and offered in the House of Representatives, that is to say, had made the greenback a full legal tender (receivable for duties on imports as well as other public dues), and not made the interest on the bonds, with which it was intended to be interchangeable, payable in gold; and resorted to a judicious system of taxation, using the bonds only to sustain the greenback in case its credit ever faltered, by receiving it alone as specie for bonds, there is every reason to believe, from the experience of the country at that time and since, that the war could have been carried through successfully without incurring but a fraction of the debt now owed by the Federal Government, and that the debt, whatever it might be, would be held mostly at home instead of abroad. But no sooner had the legal tender act made its appearance in Congress than the money power was up in arms against its passage. Delegations of bankers from New York, Boston and Philadelphia hurried to Washington; and formally organizing, by selecting one of their number chairman, they summoned the Finance Committee of the Senate, the Committee of Ways and Means of the House, and the Secretary of the Treasury into their presence. In the end the money power, although it did not succeed in preventing the passage of a legal tender act, secured a complete triumph. The *interest* of the bonds was made payable in gold in order to create a demand for gold, and then duties on imports were made payable in gold in order to get the gold to pay the interest on bonds. A premium on gold was thus established, and the public notes of the government were dishonored by the government itself; and, as we have seen, the premium on gold was run up to 160 *before ever the gold interest bearing bonds of the government were issued.* A National Banking law was also enacted to enable the money power to regain control of the monetary affairs of the nation. This was the beginning of the most stupendous robbery, boldly and openly planned and remorselessly executed, to be found in the annals of any nation, of either ancient or modern times, the details of which will be accurately set forth in a coming chapter (Chapter VI.), and the end is not yet.

The legal tender acts passed during the war not only received the sanction of every department of the government, but met with the universal approbation of the wealth producing classes of the nation. Their validity and constitutionality, which were of course contested by the money power, have been affirmed by the Supreme Court of the United States, and by the Supreme Court of fifteen States, and only in one instance has a State Court failed to endorse their constitutionality. The Constitution of the United States does not in express terms confer upon Congress the authority to make anything a tender in payment of debts, the word tender being no where mentioned in that instrument, except in the clause prohibiting States from making anything but gold and silver a tender, but the right to do so is so clearly an incident of the general powers of Congress over the currency of the country, that it has never hesitated to enact such laws upon the subject as the interests of the nation required. The right to declare by law what shall be a tender in payment of debts has thus been exercised by Congress in twenty-four statutes passed during the administrations of Washington, Jefferson, Madison, Monroe, Jackson, Tyler, Polk, Fillmore, Pierce, Lincoln and Johnson.

But driven out of the Supreme Court, the money power is now busy striving to inculcate the doctrine that Congress could only make public notes a tender in payment of private debts in time of war. A distinguished lawyer,* who has made himself conspicuous of late in his efforts to mislead the public upon this subject, says: "That the only currency

*Hon. Reverdy Johnson.

known to the Constitution is gold and silver, or paper convertible into it on demand," and gives it as his opinion that the Supreme Court did not intend to go so far, in the legal tender cases decided at the December term, 1870, as to decide that such an act would be constitutional if passed in time of peace. As the framers of the Constitution, as has already been explained, refused to authorize Congress "to emit bills of credit," (paper convertible into gold or silver on demand) it is evident that this distinguished advocate of banks of issue, in asserting that such a currency is "known to the Constitution," has allowed his zeal to outrun his judgment, and he is no less in error in regard to the opinion of the Supreme Court. Mr. Justice Bradley, one of the Judges of the Supreme Court, who read an opinion in the cases referred to, says:

"Another ground of the power to issue Treasury notes or bills is the necessity of providing a proper currency for the country, and especially of providing for the failure or disappearance of the ordinary currency in times of financial pressure and threatened collapse of commercial credit. Currency is a national necessity. The operations of the government, as well as private transactions, are wholly dependent upon it. The State governments are prohibited from making money or issuing bills. Uniformity of money was one of the objects of the Constitution. The coinage of money and regulation of its value is conferred upon the General Government exclusively. That government has also the power to issue bills. It follows as a matter of necessity, as a consequence of these various provisions, that it is specially the duty of the General Government to provide a national currency. The States cannot do it, except by the charter of local banks, and that remedy, if strictly legitimate and constitutional, is inadequate, fluctuating, uncertain and insecure, and operates with all the partiality to local interests, which it was the very object of the Constitution to avoid. But regarded as a duty of the General Government, it is strictly in accordance with the spirit of the Constitution, as well as in line with national necessities." (12 Wallace's Reports, 562.)

The necessities of peace may be as great, though of a different character, as those of war, as the American people are experiencing at the present time. For several years the nation has been suffering a daily loss of millions of dollars, by reason of its inability to develop the producing forces of the country, as they might be developed under wiser laws. Nor need any one indulge the hope that "times will change," because there can be no change, except from bad to worse, until the cause which has produced the present prostration of all forms of productive industry is removed. The repeal of the act decreeing specie resumption January 1, 1879, which rests as an incubus upon the industries of the country, might afford temporary relief, and would certainly avert the general bankruptcy, which is inevitable if its provisions are carried out, but to place the affairs of the nation on a sure foundation something more is required, viz., the extinction of banks or issue and the adoption of a monetary system based on sound principles. Specie circulation would then come naturally as soon as the nation produced a sufficient surplus of products to cause its return. This was witnessed in France after the late war with Germany. Stimulated by an abundance of irredeemable legal tender paper money, the French people bent every energy towards producing wealth, and in less than three years astonished the world by paying off the German indemnity of $1,000,000,000; and specie now circulates there side by side at par with irredeemable paper money. The immense sum paid by France to Germany was not paid in actual gold, but in bills of exchange, etc., which represented the proceeds of French industry. It is a common error in the United States to suppose that interest on the public debt is paid in gold, and that therefore it is necessary to require duties on imports to be paid in gold. It is a mere fiction. The interest of American securities held abroad are paid in products, and products do not sell for a farthing more or less in foreign markets, on account of being measured and exchanged in the United States by greenbacks instead of gold. The premium, however, on gold, which exists by reason of the law requiring duties on imports to be paid in gold, is a disadvantage to all classes, except the bondholder and money dealer, which should be remedied. If the greenback were made a full legal tender, and sustained by an interest-bearing bond with which it was interchangeable, there is every reason to believe that the premium on gold would almost totally disappear. In 1861, by the acts of July 17 and August 5, the Treasury Department was authorized to issue $50,000,000 in what were commonly known then as demand notes. An additional issue of $10,000,000 was authorized Feb. 10, 1862. These notes were receivable for all public dues, duties on imports included, and were subsequently made a legal tender for private debts, and the result was that they commanded the same premium over the ordinary greenback that gold did, and went up with gold, step by step, to the enormous premium of 285. Could any better evidence than this be required to prove that a greenback made a full legal tender would circulate at par, or nearly so, with gold? These "demand notes" were of course very obnoxious to the bullionists, because they gave the lie to all their theories about paper money, and accordingly they were got out of the way at the earliest moment possible—all except about $75,000, which are probably lost and, if such is the case, constitute a gain of that amount to the people at large.

HOW PAPER MONEY ISSUED BY THE GOVERNMENT REPRESENTS VALUE.

The nature of money has been so constantly and generally misrepresented that, as we have already suggested, it is not surprising that people find it difficult to understand how a piece of paper issued by the government represents value. This can be fully understood by considering briefly the attitude of the individual with respect to his duties and obligations to the government. In an organized state of society the controlling power, or sovereignty, is exercised for the common good through the agency of a government. As the sovereignty in the United States resides in the people at large, the duties of the individual may be said to be self-imposed. The powers with which the government, whether Federal, State, or local, is vested, imply a corresponding duty on the part of the individual. It is the duty of the Federal Government to provide for the common defense and general welfare. In time of peace it imposes taxes to defray the expenses of government and discharge its obligations; and in time of war it can demand the personal services of the individual. Thus the entire wealth of the nation is held subject to the needs of the State. Private property is taken daily, no matter how much it may be endeared to the individual by association, for public uses, as in the case of roads, streets, etc., and the tax warrant takes precedence over all other liens, without respect to priority.

The expenses of the government are paid out of the earnings of the people at large. When the government needs money it has to look to the people for it; taxes are laid and the people are obliged to respond. But if there is no money in the country, people are unable, not only to carry on private transactions, but to supply the necessities of the government. They may possess property and products in abundance, but they can not be made available for the uses of the government, except through the instrumentality of a medium of exchange, and it is necessary, therefore, that a medium of exchange be devised. The government might borrow gold or silver, or the credit of corporations in the shape of bank notes, by paying interest; but why should the people be compelled to pay interest for the use of a commodity like gold, when they have abundance of other commodities at the service of the government, which only require a medium of exchange to be made available, or for the credit of corporations, when their own credit is much better than that of any corporation? Through the agency of the Federal Government, upon whom, under the Constitution, that duty devolves exclusively, the people in a collective capacity can issue their own notes, which cover the entire property and wealth of the nation, including gold, silver— everything, in a word, that can be reached by a tax warrant. These notes represent property to the amount inscribed on their face, which the government was entitled to demand in the way of taxes at the time the notes were issued. It was in this sense that Calhoun declared that they were in reality "promises to receive," and bore no analogy to notes promising payment in money. As between citizen and government they are the same as money, and, if the individual in turn is not obliged to receive them as the representative of property to the amount inscribed on their face, it is tantamount to the people repudiating individually what they have done collectively. It is, therefore, but a matter of simple justice and equity that Congress should declare the public notes of the government a legal tender. It is also a matter of great advantage to the people, for when a public note is made a legal tender it acquires all the functions and serves all the purposes of money. The public note is not, then, one thing to the government and another to the people, but its value becomes fixed and certain, as determined by law. A dollar legal tender note of the government then represents a dollar's worth of property—neither more nor less. It consequently corresponds to the unit of value fixed in the minds of the people by usage and education, and is a measure of value. It has, therefore, representative value and the power to measure and exchange property; in other words, all the attributes or functions of money. As it represents a dollar's worth of property, it cannot vary as a standard or measure of value, except as the unit of value may vary in the minds of the people. This is not the case with money possessing intrinsic value, because its power as money then depends chiefly upon the value of the material of which it is made, and as that will fluctuate according to the laws of supply and demand, it cannot be used as a fixed measure of value. Thus gold fluctuates in value, and is itself, whether in coin or bullion, a thing to be measured. That a measure of value must possess *intrinsic* value is a dogma of the schools, which men of science, out of a desire to be consistent perhaps, adhere to—notwithstanding the fact that they are furnished with abundant proof to the contrary in almost every transaction of daily life—with as much pertinacity, as the men of science and the churchmen of the 17th century adhered to the opinion that it was the sun that revolved around the earth and not the earth around the sun.

When the Federal Government pays out a dollar legal tender note for value received, it will be asked how, when and where is the holder to obtain the property or value which it represents? The Federal Government could say, this note represents property, which the government is now entitled to receive, and a tax warrant can produce the property any moment, if it takes the last dollar's worth in the country; but the government is constantly receiving property, or its equivalent, in the shape of revenue, and there is no necessity to make a special levy of taxes to pay this particular dollar; nor is there any necessity to fix a time for its redemption in property. Being a legal tender, every individual in the nation will take it at the value inscribed on its face, and in the natural course of events it will redeem itself, in one sense, by returning to the Federal Treasury in the form of taxes or revenue. It was for this reason that, in the case of North Carolina, mentioned by Mr. Calhoun, several hundred thousand dollars of legal tender paper money, issued by the government of that State, circulated for years at par with gold and silver, with no other advantage than being received in the revenue of the State, which was less than one hundred thousand dollars per annum.

The wealth of the United States is estimated at over $40,000,000,000. The annual expenditures of the Federal Government amount to about $300,000,000, requiring a corresponding revenue. The amount of public notes, based on sound principles, which the Federal Government, backed by $40,000,000,000 of property, with a revenue of $300,000,000 a year, could safely issue, is a matter of opinion, arrived at in much the same way that the credit of an individual is measured. The amount of money required by a nation is just what can be used safely and profitably in carrying on its affairs, public and private. It will vary in different years and at different seasons of the same year, through the operation of causes existing in various parts of the world. Hence the necessity of sustaining the legal tender note of the government with a bond, with which it may be interchangeable in times of redundancy; and it might be possible, if the government were out of debt, to accomplish the same end by increasing or diminishing the rates of taxation as occasion required.

Note.—On page 52 we stated that "the foundation of the Treasury note (greenback) is the same as that of a United States bond, which secures the payment and sustains the value of the bank note, and it, therefore, possesses the highest and best security that a medium of exchange can possibly have." Professor Bonamy Price, although he seems to think that notes issued by a government are not as good as bank notes, because "there are no means for compelling a government to pay money, if it choses to say that it has none," (Currency and Banking, page 45) nevertheless, is of the opinion that no guarantee for the solvency of the notes of a bank is so natural and safe as a deposit of government securities. He says: "Bank notes circulate largely among the poor and uneducated, and when the bank breaks, the loss is severe and distressing. These facts supply ample warrant to the State to require of issuing bankers, not only that they should pay their debts to the utmost extent of their fortunes, as any other person, but further that they shall lodge such security as shall always provide for the payment of the debt acknowledged on the note. A guarantee for the solvency of the notes may be obtained in various ways, but none seems so natural and so simple as a deposit of government securities with some officer of the State. It combines two advantages—safety, and a natural and fitting profit for the banker from the interest accruing on the bonds or stock. The old Exchequer bill of the English government was an excellent specimen of this kind of security. It could always be paid in for taxes, bore a daily interest, and was thoroughly trusted, and with reason, by the whole community." (Currency and Banking, page 53.) It is a bad cause that obliges a professor of political economy to blow hot and cold in this manner.

CHAPTER III.

BANKS AND BANKING.

BANKING had its origin at an early period in the history of commerce, and a banker originally was simply a dealer in money. In the New Testament mention is made of a bank in which money could be placed at interest, and only recently the tablets of an ancient banker, with their inscriptions uneffaced, were brought to light by the explorations now being made amongst the ruins of Italy. In England, until as late as the beginning of the 18th century, the business of banking was carried on by goldsmiths. Banking, however, as it is now conducted, is an institution of modern growth. The check, certificate and bill of exchange have come to perform an important part in the work of exchange. It is not the intention to enter into a consideration of the principles and details of banking further than is necessary to a proper understanding of the question of money, with which it is intimately connected. Money, as has been explained, is an agency of trade, and, in an accumulated form as capital, an instrument of production. The first thought of the possessor of money is safety and the next profit. Money cannot accumulate value of itself, and consequently has to be put to use in order to bring its owner a return. When hoarded it is not only useless to the owner, but society is deprived of the advantage of an important agency of exchange and of production. It is, therefore, a matter of importance to society, as well as to the individual, that money should be afforded every opportunity to occupy the channels of trade and perform the uses for which it is designed. The interests of society, as we have seen, are best promoted by a division of labor. One class is devoted to agriculture, another to manufactures, trade, education, etc., etc., and each class is again subdivided into innumerable forms of industry. In this way it happens that a class has grown up which is specially engaged in the collection, custody and investment of money, and in dealing in debts and credits based on money. The banker offers reasonable safety and repayment on demand, or moderate interest, and in turn lends the money for the purposes of trade. The offices of a bank are to receive money on deposit subject to order, to collect money, to invest money, to lend money, and to buy and sell securities and exchange. The check and bill of exchange are invaluable aids to business and commerce, and for many purposes are preferable to money. The great facilities which a bank affords for the transaction of business, as well as its ability to promote the circulation of money and foster enterprise, render it an agency of trade, second in importance and usefulness only to money itself. Like all other human institutions, banking is of course liable to abuses, but when legitimately and properly conducted there is no other institution so closely connected with the well being of every individual, or one which is capable of rendering so much service to society. It is, therefore, important that banking, like money, should be based upon sound principles. Banking legitimately conducted is purely a matter of private enterprise, as much so as dealing in grain or lumber, and the relation, which the banker sustains to the community, differs in no respect from that of an individual, following any other pursuit or profession. Banking should, therefore, be free, and subject only to general laws, such as the laws under which partnerships are conducted. The generally recognized and acknowledged importance of banks, however, have led individuals to seek and governments to bestow upon them powers and privileges, such as are bestowed upon the vocation of no other class of society. We refer more particularly to the power, with which banks are clothed by law, of issuing promissory notes, nominally payable on demand, to circulate as money. There is no reason why bankers should be invested with this authority any more than any other class of society. The temporary relief which, by reason of this privilege, they are enabled to afford to individuals, and from which the community derives a benefit, has blinded society to the far greater evils which flow from the custom. A distinguished writer* upon the subject of money and finance, in speaking of this feature of banking, says: "The bad practice which originated with the Bank of England was an agreement to pay gold on demand for its inscriptions of credit. This was to undertake to do an impossibility. The general debts of a bank are redeemed by its general resources, and these consist mostly of loans and discounts which mature in the future. A more flagrant violation of sound banking was never conceived. It has repeatedly involved the banks of the United States in fatal embarrassments, and brought ruin upon thousands of merchants who were otherwise able to pay their debts and retain a handsome surplus." It is not alone the excessive and unfair profits which this system (banks of issue) enables those engaged in it to reap from the public, but the periodical derangement of business and trade, so fruitful of disaster, which it leads to, that renders it so obnoxious. Jefferson, who never failed to warn his countrymen against the evils of the system, in a letter upon the subject in 1813, said: "But it will be asked, 'Are we to have no banks? Are merchants and others to be deprived

*J. S. Gibbons, in Johnson's Universal Cyclopædia.

of the resource of short accommodations found so convenient?' I answer, let us have banks; but let them be such as are alone to be found in any country on earth, except Great Britain. * * No one has a natural right to the trade of a money-lender but he who has the money to lend. Let those, then, among us who have a moneyed capital, and who prefer employing it in loans rather than otherwise, set up banks, and give cash, or national bills (United States Treasury notes) for the notes they discount. It is from Great Britain we copy the idea of giving paper in exchange for discounted bills; and while we have derived from that country some good principles of government and legislation, we unfortunately run into the most servile imitation of all her practices, ruinous as they are to her, and with the gulf yawning before us into which these practices are precipitating her."

The dependence of the government upon a medium of exchange for its revenues has contributed largely to the abuses of the banking system, to which we refer, but since the Treasury note, made a legal tender, has been found to answer all the purposes of money, much better than gold, silver, or the bank note, there is no longer any reason for tolerating banks of issue. That this theory in substance finds able advocates, even in England, is manifest from the following extract from an article in the *Westminster Review* of October, 1873, entitled, "The Mint and the Bank of England:"

"In breaking this monopoly of the bank, we should be taking great strides toward the attainment of that ideal system of currency which Sir Robert Peel must have had in heart when he passed his currency laws; a system under which the State shall be the sole fountain of issue; under which no money shall circulate on credit, or if it does, shall circulate on the credit of the State, all bank notes, as well as coins, bearing the image and superscription of the head of the State, and under which all profits upon the issue of money shall form part of the imperial revenue. * * The power of issue, now exercised by the Bank of England, and by the English, Irish and Scotch banks, [all private corporations,] is a relic of feudalism. * * The manufacture of coin has been suppressed long ago, but the manufacture of paper money still remains, and the profits of this manufacture are allowed to remain in private hands, the State taking upon itself the manufacture of the only part of the currency upon which there is, or can be, a loss. It is high time this state of things ceased; that all rights of issue were gathered into the hands of the State; that the debt of the Bank of England was paid off; that all notes but those of the State were suppressed; that the powers of issue, now exercised by the banks, were vested in the royal mint, * * and that the profits upon paper currency were claimed by the State, and appropriated * * * to the reduction of taxation."

Public banks in the United States are conducted solely for private gain, and are free from governmental connection or control. They are, however, as we have already observed, invested with extraordinary privileges and franchises of a public nature, intended for the public good. While they are eminently successful in enabling their corporators and stockholders to secure their own ends, they are far from being beneficial to the public. The languishing condition of the country at the present time demands that the right to make a circulating medium of exchange shall no longer be suffered to remain in private hands, but shall be restored to the nation, to whom it belongs, and by whom alone it can be exercised in a spirit of equal and exact justice to all.

CHAPTER IV.

BANKS OF THE OLD WORLD.

IMPORTANT lessons can be learned from the teachings of experience. A brief glance at the banks of the old world will be found useful at the present time, as well as interesting. The first bank of which history gives an authentic account is the Bank of Venice, established in the year 1171, and which, strange to say, furnishes an example of success that has never been equaled.

THE BANK OF VENICE.

The Bank of Venice was established under peculiar circumstances. The Venetian government, under the Duke Vitale Michel II., was engaged in a war with the Grecian Emperor, on account of an outrage perpetrated in his empire upon Venetian merchants, and also in a war with the Emperor of the West. Standing greatly in need of means, the Venetian government resorted to a forced loan, and required its wealthiest citizens to contribute to the support of the government according to their ability. A chamber of loans was organized, of which the creditors were constituted the managers, books were opened and an inscription of credit entered for the amount paid in by each, on which the State agreed to pay interest at the rate of four per cent. a year. These inscriptions of credit were made transferable in whole or in part on the books of the bank. The government entered into no obligation to repay the money, but, to quote from Colwell, "reimbursement of the loan ceased to be regarded as either necessary or desirable. Every creditor was reimbursed when he transferred his claim on the books of the bank. From being convenient and valuable as an investment readily obtained, and as readily disposed of, it became, by a natural process, a medium of payment in transactions of commerce. That fund, which was desirable to all seeking investment, would be willingly, in many instances, accepted in payment of debts already existing, or for goods just purchased. There is good reason to believe that this fund was largely used in this way for centuries before the final arrangements were made, of which our accounts are more clear. * * There is no question, although we have not the details, that the government had found it perfectly easy to enlarge the amount of the original loan or stock of the bank, as the demand for its funds generally exceeded the supply. All money deposited for the purpose of obtaining a credit in bank was accounted an addition to the original loan, and as such taken into the public treasury as money lent the State. Every such investment increased the stock of the bank, and replenished the treasury of the republic. If individuals could make purchases and pay debts by transfers in bank, the public treasury could well afford to receive, in payment of its dues, credits in bank, as that would only be equivalent to taking up its own obligations. Thus, the more these credits were employed, the more the demand for them increased, the more rapidly money flowed into the treasury, and the more readily the government could afford to receive payment of its revenues in the funds of the bank."

The history of the Bank of Venice is presented by Mr. Colwell, in his able work entitled, "The Ways and Means of Payment," in such a clear light, that we can do no better than to continue to quote from him at length as follows:

"The way was opened, by the experience of two centuries

and a half, for the next chief characteristic of the Bank of Venice. In the year 1423, in the administration of the Doge *Thomas Moncenigo*, it was decreed that all bills of exchange payable in Venice, whether domestic or foreign, should be paid, unless otherwise stipulated and so expressed, in the bank; and that all payments in gross, or in wholesale transactions, should be effected also in bank. This at once brought the mass of the payments of that great commercial city to the bank. Whatever irregularities, and whatever confusion had prevailed, this introduced a uniform and, from long familiarity with the bank, an intelligible system. The endless diversity, and bad condition of the coins circulating in Venice were a sufficient recommendation of the new regulation to all who had not very special reasons, indeed, for disliking it. This measure at once created a great additional demand for the funds of the bank, and brought large sums into the public coffers. The government, however, no longer paid interest for the sums received from the bank. The funds obtained in this way were brought to the bank for the payment of bills of exchange, and were paid in for that purpose, and not with a view to interest. The rapid succession of payments occurring at a point where all the payments of Venetian commerce were accomplished, made the intervals during which the funds remained in the hands of any one merchant too short to make him solicitous about interest on balances or deposits. As all payments of the kind above designated were, by law, to be made in bank, unless otherwise agreed, and as that mode of payment was far more convenient, it became almost the exclusive usage of trade. All who had engagements to meet, found them in the bank: of course, all such provided the bank funds necessary to meet them, or carried to the bank the amount of coins requisite for the purpose. The government continued to take all money paid in as a consideration for allowing an inscription on the books of the bank to the credit of the depositor. The sums which thus flowed through the bank into the treasury would, with the previous bank funds, make up the quantity needful for the convenient discharge of the commercial payments of Venice. As this amount fluctuated from year to year, and during each year, with the course of commerce, a very effective mode of accommodating the supply of bank funds to the exigency of the demand came obviously into use. When the payments in bank were heavy, and the bank funds in great demand, money flowed freely into bank, and the credits were proportionably increased. When an occasional demand for the precious metals arose, the holders of bank funds could readily dispose of them at a slight reduction for coins. The purchasers of bank funds were sure of meeting soon a demand for them; for the demand for a medium in which the ever-recurring payments of debts were made so much exceeded in intensity the occasional demand for specie for exportation, or any other use, that during the whole existence of the bank, with very slight exception, the bank fund was at a large premium over coins, so large that it was finally fixed by law at 20 per cent."

"The republic could well afford to maintain a liberal policy towards an institution so important, both as a fiscal and commercial agent. That the inhabitants of Venice were satisfied, we cannot doubt, as not an objection was ever made to the bank, at least none is extant; neither book, nor speech, nor pamphlet, have we found, in which any merchant or dweller in Venice ever put forth any condemnation of its theory, or its practice. There was no hesitation in carrying money to the bank, so long as it was not doubted that the bank funds would purchase specie without a loss, whenever it might be needed; and the uniform premium of bank funds settled that point. Under such a system, the regular payments of trade would proceed with a rapidity and economy previously unknown, so far as the history of commerce informs us." * *

"It is worthy of remark, that this very efficient mode of adjustment discovered and used so largely. at this early period in the history of commerce, was not dependent for its efficacy on the guarantee of the republic. That guarantee sprung out of the mode in which the bank originated: this convenient method of liquidation sprung from the use of this new substitute for money."

"The facility of payment furnished by the bank, which made it the admiration of Europe, honorable at once to the government and merchants of Venice, and a support to the pride and power of its people, consisted in substituting, as a medium of payment, the debt of the republic for current coin. * * * The government took the coins one time for all, giving therefor a corresponding credit in the bank; and allowed the depositor or lender to transfer his claim upon the republic in payment of his debt, in place of transferring over the coin in each payment. Whatever men can employ in payment of debts, they will be willing to receive in payment, and this independent of any legal compulsion."

"Experience soon evinced the power and convenience of this mode of payment. These bank credits were divisible to every desirable degree, and they could be transferred with a readiness, speed and safety, beyond all comparison, superior to any mode of paying in coin. The same sum or credit might be kept in such rapid circulation, as to effect an amount of payments, in a specified time, far beyond any possible movement of coin. This rapidity became a great economy, for a much less sum of credits was made to effect a given amount of payments with far greater speed than could have been attained with coin. But this economy resulting from an increased speed and power of circulation was still more important, arising from the fact that the coins which were deposited as the basis of the credit were very soon again restored to the usual channels of circulation by the payments of government. Thus the coin was not withdrawn from its proper functions, and the credits remained a perpetual fund, to be employed in large payments. This system of payments was so well adapted to the exigencies of commerce, that it was maintained in full vigor, in the great commercial city of Venice, for almost four hundred years. It was an institution or device of the credit system, for by its aid payments were effected, and that to a vast amount annually, without any use of coins or bullion. It only perished, when the city itself fell, at the conquest of Italy by Napoleon; but the conqueror carried off no coin, no penny of prey. The credits of the bank were crushed under the rude touch of an invading foe. They were lost to the proprietor, but no equivalent passed into the hands of the destroyers. If the holders of these credits suffered, the invaders were not enriched. In assuming the sovereignty of Venice, the conqueror assumed the right and duty of making good these bank credits."

The Venetian government was careful at all times to provide for the wants of the public. In course of time it became necessary to establish in the bank a department for the custody of coin or bullion, which the owner might desire to use. Deposits of this kind were subject to the order of the owner, who could reclaim them at pleasure, or transfer them in the same manner as bank credits. This feature of the bank prove eminently useful to the public, but did not lead to any diminution in the funds of the bank itself, as the demand for inscriptions of credit was always greater than the supply. The original capital of the bank was 2,000,000 ducats, but it rose to about 5,000,000 in the 18th century, and to over 14,000,000 (about $16,000,000) at the close of its long and remarkable career.

The history of the bank of Venice establishes several important facts of deep significance to the American people at the present time. The inscriptions of credit of the bank were simply evidences of indebtedness of the government, bearing no interest, which constituted a medium of exchange. The law which required all bills of exchange payable in Venice to be paid at the bank, unless otherwise expressly stipulated, was apparently an arbitrary requirement, but it worked no injustice; on the contrary it increased the strength of the bank inscriptions, and resulted in greatly promoting the facilities of commerce and in making Venice the commercial metropolis of the world for centuries. The evidences of indebtedness, which the government in the first instance required its creditors to take, it in effect made a legal tender for private debts, which was no more than just. The large premium which these inscriptions bore was not due to any act of the government, but to the value attached to them by the public. It rose to as high as 30 per cent., when the goverment found it necessary to impose a limitation, which was fixed at 20 per cent. This premium on inscriptions of credit in a bank, which were not redeemable or payable in gold, (mere "rag money" they might be styled) which existed for centuries, is inexplicable on any theory which can be advanced by the bullionists. The Venetians were enabled, by the use of their irredeemable inscriptions of credit, to achieve a degree of power and prosperity, which they retained for centuries, that proved a constant source of envy and wonder to the rest of the world; and during the whole time they never once suffered from commercial crashes or money panics, such as are experienced in England and the United States every six to ten years. It has been a matter of surprise that other nations witnessing the prosperity of Venice did not imitate her example, but that is not half so strange as the fact that the people of the United States, having experienced the great advantages of even partial legal tender paper money, should blindly cling to the rotten and disastrous specie basis system of banks of issue.

THE BANK OF GENOA.

The Bank of Genoa was established early in the 13th century, and, like the Bank of Venice, had its origin in the necessities of the State. The loans upon which it was based were not, however, forced, but were the spontaneous offerings of the people. The creditors of the bank became a very powerful body. In the course of time the bank adopted various new devices, and its system became greatly complicated. According to Colwell, the Bank of Genoa was the first to originate the bank note, which has since played so important a part in the affairs of the world. It met with the same fate that befell the Bank of Venice at the time of the French invasion under Napoleon.

THE BANK OF AMSTERDAM.

The Bank of Amsterdam was established in 1609 on the theory that deposits once made could never be withdrawn. For nearly two centuries it enjoyed great credit, and contributed largely to the prosperity of Amsterdam. Coin and bullion were also received on special deposit, and could be reclaimed by the owner at pleasure. The fact that deposits once made could not be withdrawn, resulted in the bank accumulating a vast amount of money, but how much was kept a secret. When the supply of credits based on deposits exceeded the demand, the excess was bought up by the bank, through brokers, at a premium of four per cent. In 1790 it was discovered that, during the preceding fifty years, large loans had been secretly made to the East India Company, the Provinces of Holland and the city of Amsterdam, and that there was but little treasure left in the bank. It consequently failed through the unfaithfulness of its officers.

THE BANK OF HAMBURG.

The Bank of Hamburg was established in 1619 on the model of the Bank of Amsterdam. It is still in existence, and is a useful and flourishing institution.

THE BANK OF ENGLAND.

The next great bank established in the course of time was the Bank of England, an institution which has exercised, from its organization, a powerful influence in the commercial and financial affairs of the world. Its charter was obtained in 1694, and it went into operation January 1, 1695. Its charter conferred on it full authority to borrow or receive money and give security for the same under seal, buy or sell bullion, gold or silver, etc., etc. No special power was granted to issue bank notes, but the authority to do so was assumed as an incident to the general powers with which the bank was invested. It was, in brief, chartered as a bank of deposit, loan, discount, issue and circulation. The whole amount of the capital stock originally subscribed, £1,200,000, was handed over to the government as a special loan, the interest on which was secured by certain taxes designated for that purpose, and the sum of $20,000 a year was allowed by the government to the bank for the management of the loan. The capital stock of the bank is now out

£14,000,000, and the accumulated profits about £3,000,000 —in all about $88,000,000. It can issue bank notes to the amount of $70,000,0000, not under £5 ($25) in denomination, against that amount of government securities, and also to the amount of gold and silver held in its vaults for their redemption.

At an early period in the career of the bank, it took a bold and dangerous step, which introduced a new feature in banking. By its charter the bank was authorized to deal in bills of exchange and promissory notes, and, as has been mentioned, it also assumed the right to issue its own notes. Bills of exchange and promissory notes, then as now, entered largely into all commercial transactions, and usually had some time to run before they were payable. In order to acquire favor with the public and increase its business, the bank adopted the custom of giving its own notes, payable on demand, for discounted paper, payable in the future. This custom was adopted on the theory that the small bills of the bank would pass into circulation, like money, and be dispersed throughout the kingdom; that they would become indispensable in business transactions, which would be greatly increased by the number in circulation, and that consequently they would not be returned suddenly, or in large amounts to the bank for redemption.

The unsoundness of the principles of banking, adopted about this time by the Bank of England, and upon which the specie basis system of banking has been built up, is fully demonstrated by Colwell, from whom we again quote as follows: "Upon such considerations, the bank decided to issue notes payable to bearer on demand, in exchange for individual paper payable at a future day. The bank thus undertook to do an impossibility, in the hope that it would not be called upon to redeem the promise or make the

attempt. What the bank could do was to give its own notes, of convenient denominations for circulation in exchange for individual paper and payable at the same time; and in doing this alone, the bank could have rendered a great service to the public with small risk. The bank had not the money, and could not, therefore, purchase the paper offered; the notes offered by the bank were not money, though a much better substitute for money than the notes of individuals, which could only circulate to a very limited extent as a medium of payment. The bank issued notes payable to bearer, without endorsement, and this certainly added to the facility and convenience of their passing rapidly from hand to hand as a currency. It departed from sound principles, when it made these notes payable on demand in gold or silver; for it must be contrary to sound principles to undertake to do what cannot be done. The bank notes were nothing more, and should not have been held up to the public as anything more, than the mere promissory notes of the bank, convenient in form for circulation among all those who chose to take them, not as money, but as promises to pay money. The promise should have been only such as the bank could perform. Strictly speaking, the bank could only pay in coin when it received in coin. It could exact payment for the note received of every individual only when the note matured and not before. The accommodation between the bank and its customers was mutual in this exchange of notes; the bank received a profit, and the customer received the bank notes, a better medium of payment, one which would be received out of bank as well as in it, in payment of debts or in making of purchases. But it should never have been imagined for a moment, that by this process between the bank and its customers they manufactured money. * *
This advantage, (notes payable on demand,) which the

Bank of England only offered in the first instance to attract business, and to give currency to their notes, has been paid for since by the people of England, in a series of pressures, revulsions, and currency fluctuations, which have inflicted injuries and losses upon the government and people of Great Britain, in comparison with which the present national debt may be insignificant. * * * * * * *

"But the bank was still more daring; it discounted notes largely, and carried the amount of the proceeds to the credit of the party, as so much money deposited; that is, in the same column in which the bank gave its customers credit for gold and silver deposits, it gave them credit for the amounts of notes and acceptances having months to run before maturity, and engaged to pay the amount of these securities on demand. It mingled a process of credit with a process of cash, in a mode as absurd in theory as it was dangerous in practice. The men who had given their notes on time had provided for a regular progression of payments, according to the movements of business and the demands of consumption; but the Bank of England virtually abolished the contract of deferred payment between the parties, and became paymaster on demand of debts not due for months, to an immense amount."

"The bank had no warrant, in principle or practice, for this hazardous engagement. Its only excuse was the same which was given for the issue of bank notes payable on demand, without the money, namely, that the bank would not be asked to pay for them all at one time."

"We regard this error of the Bank of England as the parent of the greater portion of the mischiefs and evils for which banks in more modern times are answerable. The banks from that day to this have continued to issue notes payable on demand, and to grant credits so payable, in exchange for securities payable in from 30 to 120 days. They do this, relying wholly on the forbearance of the public, just as the Bank of England did at first. Sad experience has shown, that there are times when the public is not only not forbearing, but when men rush with frantic haste to demand of the bank payment of both notes and deposits. Nearly every bank in existence, conducted on this plan, has, at some period of its history, felt the power and rashness of the public in seasons of commercial panic. The banks lose their power and usefulness at the very moment when the public most needs their assistance. Friends in sunshine, they become enemies in the storm."

The most notable event in the history of the Bank of England was the suspension of specie payments in 1797. This was caused by the large advances made by the bank to the government, to aid in the prosecution of the wars with France. The specie in the bank had been reduced to a little over £1,000,000, when the directors of the bank became alarmed and brought the matter to the attention of the Privy Council. The council on the 27th of February, 1797, determined "that it is indispensably necessary for the public service, that the Directors of the Bank of England should forbear issuing any cash in payment, until the sense of Parliament can be taken on the subject." On the 3d of May following, the suspension was sanctioned for a limited time by an act of Parliament, and was subsequently continued by repeated acts of Parliament until 1820, when an act was passed providing for the resumption of specie payments by degrees, beginning on the 1st of October, 1820, and reaching full payment on the 1st of May, 1823. The people of Great Britain were obliged, therefore, to carry on their affairs for a period of twenty-five years with an irredeemable bank paper currency. During this period, notwithstanding the vast expenditures of war and the great burdens of taxation, Great Britain increased in wealth and prosperity more rapidly than at any other period in her history. The public revenues were increased from £23,126,000 in 1797 to £72,210,000 in 1815, at the close of the war with France, and stood at £54,282,000 in 1820. The amount raised by loan and taxation, during the time referred to, was never less in any one year than £47,362,000; during nine years it was over £70,000,000 a year; and for the years 1813 and 1814 it was respectively £108,397,000 and £105,698,000. The loans negotiated by the bank for the government during the suspension of specie payments amounted to £350,000,000. During this period the Bank of England was a tower of strength to the government. But what after all enabled Great Britain to surmount all difficulties and come off victorious in one of the greatest contests of modern times, was the wonderful development of her producing forces, occasioned by the abundance of money put in circulation by the war, irredeemable though it was. During this time 3,000,000 of acres of unimproved land were brought under cultivation, and the exportation of manufactured cotton goods increased in amount from £7,000,000 in 1801 to £27,000,000 in 1822. All classes of society participated in the general prosperity which prevailed, and during the entire period the nation never once suffered from a commercial crash or money panic.

The guns of Waterloo, however, had hardly ceased to echo, until the money power became clamorous, just as it is in the United States now, for a return to specie payments. No one was so blind as not to be able to see that Great Britain was enabled, by her paper money alone, to carry on her wars on the Continent, and that by it alone were the people enabled to make such remarkable progress in commerce, agriculture and manufactures; but there were, nevertheless, large numbers who were bitterly hostile to paper currency, and who seemed to imagine that they were being subjected, in some way, to a great wrong. Landlords, for example, in many instances, in contempt of the law which gave their tenants the right to pay in bank notes, compelled them to pay their dues in gold. There were evidently fools and rascals in those days, as well as at the present time. The "political economists," backed by the "cannibals of change alley," were strong in Parliament, and the country gentlemen were led to believe that a return to specie was essential to their interests and safety. Specie payments were accordingly resumed in 1823, and the resumption was accompanied by the most disastrous commercial crash and money panic that ever visited any nation. The era of general prosperity departed to return no more. Real estate depreciated largely in value, and the real estate owners of the kingdom decreased in number from over 150,000 to less than 40,000; business men, merchants, manufacturers, etc., were ruined by the thousand; wages were reduced, and laborers thrown out of employment by the tens of thousands; and the public revenue fell off to such an extent that payments on the public debt ceased, and have never practicably been resumed.*

The bank act of 1844, by which the issue department was separated from the general banking business of the institution, remedied some of the defects of the system which the bank had founded, but suspensions of specie payment are still of frequent occurrence. In 1837 another crash and money panic occurred in England, which also involved this country. Congress, in 1832, had raised the price of gold, as compared with silver, to sixteen to one, and demon-

*See Chapter on Specie Resumption.

etized silver by making it a legal tender only for small sums. Gold thus became the basis of the currency, and when the Bank of England called it away to supply the wants of England, the banks of the United States were obliged to suspend. Business in the United States was brought to a complete stand, and for three years the American people were left without any gold basis, and were consequently obliged to use shinplasters. In England the losses were so enormous and the distress so great, that Parliament at its next session reorganized the bank by separating the issue department from the general business department, as already mentioned.

From September 7, 1844, when the bank was reorganized, to February 4, 1858, it altered its rate of interest fifty-six times, raising it, from time to time, from two to ten per cent., in an effort to retain its specie in its vaults; this, in the meantime, led to great financial embarrassment, and a panic was only averted by the bank suspending specie payments (October 23, 1847) and affording relief by issuing irredeemable paper. In 1857, having ruined the merchants and business of England, it was again obliged to suspend. Eleven changes in the rate of interest were made between April, 1857, and January, 1858. The bank again drew upon the United States for gold, causing the banks to suspend, involving thousands of people in ruin and bankruptcy.

In 1866 the Bank of England suffered another suspension in consequence of the war on the Continent of Europe; but this time the United States escaped. Greenbacks were the medium of exchange, and the nation was no longer at the mercy of foreign banks. Gold was shipped abroad to the amount of $45,000,000, and sold as a commodity at a high price for the use of the Bank of England, without occasioning the slightest ripple in the business affairs of the country.

A distinguished statesman,* in commenting on these facts, says:

"Thus, three times within less than twenty years in this generation, each time in violation of law and without right, has the bank of England suspended, and acknowledged her bankruptcy! what a 'marvel of financial strength and credit' she has been, to be sure! Well may the bullionists sing pæans to this destructionist of all values for their benefit. True, each time her failure was sanctioned by a healing act of Parliament, because her illegal suspensions were necessary to save the credit of the government itself and to prevent the widespread destruction of all values and the overthrow of commerce and manufactures which was then going on."

"Neither of these suspensions took place until she had refused all discount to her customers, even on the best sixty day commercial bills secured by government securities. It will be thus seen that gold was not the regulator of the currency of England, but the price paid for money at her bank, and having provided herself with a currency based on gold, in order to retain that basis whenever it is wanted for foreign loans, or because of a foreign war, she is obliged to increase the value of her unit by changing the rate of discount, or the interest which her people were obliged to pay for their money."

"This is a very important matter to be borne in mind. Indeed it is the root of the whole matter, and in discussing questions of finance has been too often overlooked, because it shows that after all, a currency based on gold must have its value determined by the rate of interest paid for it, and not by the stability in value of gold itself. Because of this necessity of keeping gold in her vaults, the Bank of England could not maintain a steady and permanent rate of interest

*Address of Hon. B. F. Butler, at the request of the Board of Trade of New York City, Oct. 14, 1875.

for money to which her business men could adjust their affairs. Hence come fluctuations of trade, financial depression, ruin of commerce, the stoppage of manufacture. Who can carry on business requiring credit, successfully and without failure, when the rate of interest which he must pay for his accommodations and loans, alters day by day and quintuples in a month, and especially when these changes come from causes that he can neither foresee, guard against, hinder or alleviate?"

"I challenge all the bullionists of the country to show any disasters and losses in trade and commerce, traceable to inconvertible paper, continental money and all, which shall be equal in effect, either as to sums, amounts, disasters or ruin to the business and people of a country, with these I have sketched coming from a currency called 'honest money,' based on gold in the vaults of a bank."

The average bank note circulation of the Bank of England for the past twenty-eight years has been $100,000,000; its average of bullion, $80,000,000; its average rate of discount, 4 per cent.; its average deposits, $100,000,000; its average liabilities, $102,000,000; and its average reserve, $9,500,000.

BANKS OF SCOTLAND.

The first public bank in Scotland was established in 1695, under a charter from the Scottish Parliament before the union with England. The Scotch banking system is similar to that of England, but is conducted very differently. With a population of a little over 3,000,000, Scotland has nearly 400 banks. From Colwell we learn that, "Whilst the Bank of England, from its first conception, was identified with the government, the Bank of Scotland, and those which succeeded it, identified themselves with the whole body of the people, from the laborer who could save five pounds to the richest merchants and manufacturers. They became at once, and have continued to be, the savings banks of the poor but industrious classes. The banks paid one per cent. below the current rate of interest for these deposits, and returned them on demand, or according to stipulation. These savings of the poor help largely to make up the vast sum of deposits which characterize the banks of Scotland. One result has been to give the benefits of these savings to the general customers of the banks, instead of their being invested in the public debt, or lent upon mortgage, as in England. No doubt this has contributed greatly to that progress in wealth and productive industry which has so much distinguished Scotland for more than a century. It had another good effect in begetting that care, caution and prudent management for which the banks of Scotland have so well founded a reputation." Another peculiar feature of the banking system of Scotland consists in the manner of giving cash credits. An applicant deposits approved securities with the bank and is allowed a standing credit on its books. He then draws checks for this amount and makes deposits in the ordinary way. An account is made up every six months, the rate of interest charged on loans being one per cent. more than that allowed on deposits. In commenting upon this feature of banking in Scotland, Colwell says: "In England, the bank which deals in promissory notes and bills of exchange, is dealing in paper which represents business transactions which are past; in Scotland, the bank opens credit for its customers, with reference to business which is to come. In Scotland, the banks give their customers a credit which helps their standing, and upon which they can draw for the purpose of payment, whenever there is need. The theory of the English banks is, that the currency must follow, and be controlled in quantity, by the business transactions which go before. The theory of the Scotch banks is, that these business transactions being all managed by men of business, who decide according to the exigencies of industry and trade what will promote their private interest, and meet the wants of the people, it must prove an important aid to men thus engaged to supply them, in advance of the progress of their business, with a credit upon which they can draw at pleasure. * * In England, they think this will lead to over-trading, by the stimulus it affords to so large a class of dealers: in Scotland, long experience has taught them that this English apprehension is wholly groundless. They know that the dealers who enjoy these cash credits are so immediately brought under the supervision of the banks, and their own sureties, that they are, perhaps, the most prudent and safe men of business in the world. * * There is a prevalent idea among statesmen and writers upon money, that there should be a broad basis of money or gold coin, under and as a support to the paper circulation; * * that a paper currency, to be perfect, should fluctuate as a gold currency would do, if it were the sole medium of payment. To the mind of a Scotch banker, a greater absurdity could not be presented in as many words. He would say: 'What! when a demand springs up for gold, in consequence of some foreign war, must we so regulate the issues of our banks, as to reduce the currency of notes in the same proportion that the currency of gold is carried off! Rather should we increase our issues, and supply the place of the currency that is exported.' They know that bank notes can fully discharge the functions of money, for they see it every day; and not only so, but they are certain that almost no business of Scotland is carried on by means of a currency of gold. The Scottish people can never be made to comprehend why their bank notes, bank deposits, and cash credits, should fluctuate in amount as gold would fluctuate, if exclusively employed. These forms of currency do not come of gold; they are not founded upon it, and they have nothing to do with it. In Scotland they understand, as well as they do in England, the use of gold as money; they know its value as a commodity, but being a costly commodity, they do not incline to employ it as a currency, except so far as their bank currency fails of its object; nor do they wish to purchase or hold it as a commodity, except for such special purpose as may promise adequate advantage. Their system of banking enables them to dispense with it almost entirely. In this, they are far from thinking themselves behind their neighbors, in intelligence or financial skill." The banks of Scotland issue bank notes as low as £1, and the people of Scotland are always amply supplied with a medium of exchange.

THE FRENCH SYSTEM OF FINANCE.

France enjoys a financial system superior to that of any other nation. The fiscal affairs of the government are conducted by a central administration, or Ministry of Finance, and eighty-six branches located in different districts. All transactions between the government and the people are carried on in the forms and methods of the treasury department, without the intervention of banks. The government has no connection with the Bank of France, but deals with it as it does with individuals, except that its notes are made a legal tender whenever the scarcity of specie renders such a step necessary. The treasury department of France in many respects takes the place of banks. It is regarded as a duty by the French government to afford the people all the facilities in the way of domestic exchange that banks could give, instead of allowing it to be furnished exclusively by the banks.

In each district there is a receiver general, in whose office the revenues of the district are paid. When once paid in they are subject to the order of the central administration alone, and abundant precautions exist to insure strict accountability and integrity. The treasury is managed with special reference to the wants and requirements of the public. The manner in which its operations in this respect are conducted is thus set forth by Colwell: "Among its numerous officials, is one in direct relations with the chief minister of finance, who has special charge of the locality of all money in the treasury. He can neither receive nor pay money; but he can transfer the public money from one office of the treasury to another, and place it wherever the exigencies of the government may require. It is in the office of this functionary that is established a direct and very important connection with the current business of the day. His duty requires of him a careful and timely study of the points of public expenditure; he must know not only where the money will be wanted, but he must have it ready when required. To accomplish this important object, it becomes his duty to study the domestic trade of the country, that he may avail himself of the internal exchanges in the necessary distribution of money in the treasury. It is very rare, indeed, that the French treasury ever shifts the locality of gold or silver. It may require many circuitous transfers to move the excess of revenue, in some departments, to the points of expeniture, and to supply the deficiency in other departments. To make these transfers, the officer who has special charge of that duty relies almost wholly on the domestic exchanges. He is well informed where funds are wanted for the purposes of industry or trade; he learns where and when those who reside in the vicinity of each office of the treasury desire to remit funds; and he learns whence and when they wish to draw them. His office becomes the depository of this information, because he intervenes in this business of giving drafts upon the treasury, payable at other points, and giving money at his own office for money received at other offices. His intervention in the transmission of funds assists in balancing the internal exchanges of the country; for, of course, the office is only applied to when the business of individuals requires such accommodation. But this business is not confined to receiving money at an office of the treasury in one place, and paying the amount as may be required at another office, in a different place; that is, to a mere exchange of money between the treasury and individuals at different places; it goes much further. At times and places where large transfers of funds, become necessary, the proper officer of the treasury becomes the receiver of commercial or individual paper to a large amount."

"The receivers-general of the eighty-six departments, and their subordinates, the receivers of the treasuries of the arrondissments and communes, maintain reciprocal business relations by frequent exchanges of money, by drafts upon each other, and by bills upon Paris and other places. The chief officers of the treasury become, by the constant report of this business to them, intimately acquainted with the whole industrial and commercial movement of the population. They regard it as extremely important to these interests, that the money which is necessarily withdrawn from private uses for public purposes, should be retained in the treasury as short a time as possible. Out of 300,000,000 or 400,000,000 of francs annually remitted from the conntry treasuries to Paris, not more than ten per cent., or 30,000,000 or 40,000,000 of francs, are ever at one time in the public treasuries.* This shows that disbursement follows so rapidly upon receipt, that the money taken from the people for taxes does not remain, on the average, more than a month or two out of its proper channels, and that the government has carefully reduced the inconvenience and disadvantage of taxation to the lowest possible point. By this regular and constant communication with men of capital and business, by this constant association with them in the business of transferring funds, the officers of the treasury are able at all times to command, in advance of the regular receipts, large sums of money, which are freely placed in the public treasury at low rates of interest. Money is, in fact, frequently pressed upon the various receivers by those who desire short but safe investments, and by those who would secure, in good season, the aid of the treasury in placing money at particular points. The treasurers of the departments do not lend money, though they receive it in the way of short loans; they transfer money for individuals, and they purchase bills of exchange upon such points as the exigencies of the public may require. Upon one side, then, there are open relations between the public treasuries and the movements of trade, industry and currency; that is, upon the side of the domestic exchanges of the country; the transactions of the treasury, in relation to the distribution of its funds, are blended with the movements of the internal exchanges as conducted by the individuals concerned in it. This constitutes a very broad field of contact between the business of the country, from which the money is withdrawn by taxation, and the public treasury. The public money being retained for the shortest possible time, is so managed, nevertheless, as to render an important service in aiding and regulating the internal exchanges."

*This was prior to 1860.

"Taxation having reached, in France, a point beyond which it cannot be increased without passing the ability of the people to pay, an alleviation of the burden, like that we have just mentioned, is of signal advantage. According to the former revenue system of France, the money remained for many months in the hands of the receivers, who merely made advances, on interest, to the government from time to time, and settled their accounts once a year. Now, all money is held to be in the treasury from the moment it is received into the office of any department; and it is sent into general circulation again with as little delay as posssible. The assistance thus afforded to the adjustment of the domestic exchanges greatly promotes punctuality in commercial and industrial payments and remittances, by diminishing the expense and the disturbances occasioned by paying the balances of the internal trade. These features of the present financial system, by which it is so closely connected with the internal trade and exchanges, are regarded by an eminent French writer upon finance as rendering less necessary in France than in other countries, that development of credit in banking which is so prevalent and so dangerous elsewhere."

Business in France, owing to the abundance of money always kept in circulation, is done mainly with cash, and the credit system, which has wrought so much evil in Great Britain and the United States, has never gained a foothold there. So great is the prejudice of the French people against the system, doubtless because they are not blind to its workings in England, that they cannot be induced to even keep ordinary bank accounts and use checks, in the way of business. M. Pinard, Manager of the *Comptoir d'Escompte*, testified before the French commission of Inquiry of 1865-8, that great efforts had been made by that institution to induce French merchants and shop-keepers to adopt English habits in this respect, but in vain; "it was no use reasoning with them," he said, "they would not do it, because they would not."

Gold and silver are the legal tender money of France, but whenever occasion renders it necessary the notes of the Bank of France are declared a tender in payment of debts; and the channels of trade are thus always supplied with a medium of exchange, to keep the producing forces of the nation at work. The wisdom of this policy has been signally illustrated twice within the past thirty years—in 1848 and in 1870. In 1848, after the revolution, the republic found itself without revenue and the people out of employment. Matters were in a precarious situation, and the Bank of France alone possessed any available money. Instead of looking after its own interests alone, it united with the government in a hearty effort to stimulate industry, by supplying the arteries of trade with a fresh supply of money. To accomplish this end, the government declared the notes of the bank a legal tender—an act which was everywhere denounced by the bullionists as suicidal. The marvelous results of this step are thus depicted by the London *Times*, of February 16, 1849, although less than a year before it had been loud in its denunciation of such a course:

"As a mere commercial speculation, with the assets which the bank held in its hands, it might then have stopped payment, and liquidated its affairs with every probability that a very few weeks would enable it to clear off all of its liabilities. But this idea was not for a moment entertained by M. D'Argout, and he resolved to make every effort to keep alive what may be termed the *circulation of the life blood* of the community. The task was overwhelming. Money was to be found to meet not only the demands of the bank but the necessities, both public and private, of every rank in society. It was essential to enable the manufacturers to work, lest their workmen, driven to desperation, should fling themselves amongst the most violent enemies of public order. It was essential to provide money for the food of Paris, for the pay of the troops, and for the daily support of the *ateliers nationaux.* A failure on any one point would have led to a fresh convulsion. But the panic had been followed by so great a scarcity of the metallic currency, that a few days later, out of a payment of 26 millions fallen due, only 47,000 francs could be recovered in silver."

"In this extremity, when the bank alone retained any available sums of money, the government came to the rescue, and, on the night of the 15th of March, the notes of the bank were by a decree made a legal tender, the issue of these notes being limited in all to 350 millions, but the amount of the lowest of them reduced for the public convenience to 100 francs. One of the great difficulties mentioned in the report, was to print these 100 franc notes fast enough for the public consumption—in ten days the amount issued in this form had reached 80 millions. No sooner was the bank relieved from the necessity of paying away the remnant of its coin, than it made every exertion to increase its metallic rest. About 40 millions of silver were purchased abroad at a high price. More than 100 millions were made over in dollars to the treasury and the executive departments in Paris. In all, taking into account the branch banks, 506 millions of five-franc pieces have been thrown by the bank into the country since March, and her currency was thus supplied to all the channels of the social system."

"Besides the strictly monetary operations, the Bank of France found means to furnish a series of loans to the government—50 millions on exchequer bills on the 31st of

March, 30 millions on the 5th of May, and on the 3d of June, 150 millions, to be paid up before the end of March, 1849; of this last sum only one-third has yet been required by the State. The bank also took a part in the renewed loan of 250 millions, and made vast advances to the City of Paris, to Marseilles, to the department of the Seine, and to the hospitals, amounting in all to 260 millions more. But even this was not all. To enable the manufacturing interests to weather the storm, at a moment when all the sales were interrupted, a decree of the National Assembly had directed warehouses to be opened for the reception of all kinds of goods, and provided that the registered invoice of these goods, so deposited, should be made negotiable by endorsement. The Bank of France discounted these receipts. In Havre alone, 18 millions were thus advanced on Colonial produce, and, in Paris, 14 millions on merchandise—in all, 60 millions were thus made available for the purposes of trade. Thus, the great institution had placed itself, as it were, in direct contact with every interest of the community, from the Minister of the Treasury down to the trader in a distant outport. Like a huge hydraulic machine, it employed its colossal powers to pump a fresh stream into the exhausted arteries of trade, to sustain credit, and to preserve the circulation from complete collapse."

Again, in September, 1870, after France became involved in the war with Germany, the Bank of France suspended specie payments and issued legal tender notes to an immense amount, with like marvelous results. In June, 1870, the circulation of the bank was $275,000,000; in 1871, after the termination of hostilities, it amounted to $420,000,000, and in October, 1873, to $602,000,000. When the first installment of the indemnity of $1,000,000,000 to Germany fell due, gold, for a short period, bore a premium of $2\frac{1}{2}$ per cent., but with this exception the notes of the bank circulated at par with coin, and continue to do so to this day. The amount of irredeemable bank notes in circulation in France at the present time is nearly $500,000,000. The only reason that can possibly be given why French irredeemable bank notes, to the amount of $500,000,000, circulate at par with coin, while United States Treasury notes, less than $400,000,000 in amount, are at a depreciation of over 12 per cent., is that the French notes are a full legal tender for all debts and dues, both public and private, while the United States Treasury notes are only a partial legal tender, not being receivable for duties on imports.

By the free use of irredeemable paper money, the French people, like the people of the United States during the Rebellion, were enabled to rally to the support of their government. But there the parallel ends. After the German war had ended, the circulation of irredeemable bank notes, as we have seen, was increased nearly $200,000,000, and the producing forces of the French people were developed in every way possible, in order to repair the losses sustained during the war, and to enable the government to pay the indemnity to Germany. The wonderful success of this policy is known to all the world. The German indemnity of $1,000,000,000 was paid before it fell due, apparently without an effort, and gold has flowed into France until now the French people have, besides their legal tender bank notes, a specie circulation estimated at $1,200,000,000. It has been the lot of the French people to suffer, in common with other nations, many evils resulting from bad government, but they have great cause to feel profoundly thankful that they have never, in the administration of their finances been cursed with a Hugh McCulloch.

CHAPTER V.

PAPER MONEY AND BANKS OF THE UNITED STATES.

THE trials and tribulations to which the American people have been subjected from the earliest settlement of the country, on account of the want of a proper and well settled system of money, would form a sad but instructive chapter in American history. The limits of this volume, however, preclude more than a cursory view of the subject, but that will be sufficient to establish the fact that when paper money fails to perform the functions of money, it is because it is not based on sound principles, and also that bank notes, nominally redeemable in specie, constitute the worst form of paper money ever devised.

For many generations after the first settlement of the colonies the work of production was slow and laborious, and the surplus products, at least such as could find their way to foreign markets, were hardly sufficient to procure in return the common necessaries of life. The small sums of money brought to the country by the settlers were soon exhausted—sent abroad for merchandise, and trade for the most part had to be carried on by the inconvenient method of barter. The Indians found along the shores of Long Island Sound were more advanced in civilization than those further north, and used a circulating medium of exchange consisting of beads of two kinds, one white, made out of the end of a periwinkle shell, and the other black, made out of the dark part of a clam shell. They were rubbed down and polished, and, when artistically arranged in strings or belts, formed objects of real beauty.* These beads circulated

*Professor Sumner's History of American Currency.

among the Indians as money, one black bead being regarded as worth two white ones, and were known as wampum or wampumpeag. The colonists came to use them, first in their trade with the Indians and then amongst themselves. In Massachusetts they became by custom the common currency of the colony, and were made a legal tender for 12 pence.

Barter currency was established at an early day in the colonies, and products of all kinds were made a tender in payment of debts. "In Connecticut there were four prices: 'Pay,' 'pay as money,' 'money,' and 'trusting.' The merchant asked his customer how he would pay before fixing his price. 'Pay' was barter at the government rates. 'Money' was Spanish or New England coin, also wampum for change. 'Pay as money' was barter currrency at prices one-third less than the government rates. 'Trusting' was an enhanced price according to time. A six-penny knife cost 12d. in pay, 8d. in pay as money, and 6d. in coin."* About the middle of the 17th century the trade with the West Indies began to bring in coin, and a mint was established in Boston, though an infraction of the prerogative of the crown. Laws forbidding the exportation of coin were passed, but it could not be kept in the country. The first issue of paper money made in the colonies was made by Massachusetts in 1690, six years before the establishment of the Bank of England. An expedition had been sent out against Canada, and, returning without spoils and in a state of misery, the soldiers were clamorous for their pay. £7,000 were issued in notes from 5 shillings to £5. The form of these notes or bills was as follows: "This indented bill of ten shillings, due from the Massachusetts colony to the possessor, shall be in value equal to money, and shall be accordingly accepted by the treasurer and receivers subor-

*Professor Sumner's History of American Currency,

dinate to him, in all public payments, and for any stock (cattle) at any time in the treasury." Then followed the date and the signatures of the committee appointed to issue them. They were not a legal tender, but were receivable merely for taxes and property in the treasury. In 1692 it was ordered that these bills be received at 5 per cent. premium over coin in the treasury, and the result was that they circulated at par with coin for twenty years, until redeemed, and barter currency ceased for a time, or at least became less common. In 1703 another issue of bills in the same form, for £15,000, was authorized by act of Parliament, but they were not made a tender. A subsequent act passed in 1712, however, made them a tender for private debts. In 1716 another issue of bills to the amount of £150,000 was authorized by an act of Parliament; to be distributed among the different counties of the province; and to be put into the hands of five trustees in each county, to be appointed by the legislature, to be let out by the trustees on real estate security in the county, in certain specified sums, for the space of ten years, at five per cent. per annum. These bills were not made a tender. Another act for £50,000 in bills was passed in 1720, containing similar provisions. In 1773 Massachusetts was out of debt.

In 1720 bills were issued by the colony of Rhode Island and were made a tender for all debts, except special ones; and similar bills were authorized at different times subsequently, some a tender and others not.

The colony of Connecticut issued similar bills at various times between 1709 and 1731. New York began to issue bills in 1709; Pennsylvania, in 1723; Maryland, in 1733; Delaware, in 1739; Virginia, in 1755; and South Carolina, in 1703. The first emission of bills by Virginia bore interest at 5 per cent., and, according to Jefferson, in a very short time not one of them was to be found in circulation. They were looked up in the chests of executors, guardians, widows, farmers, etc. "We then," says Jefferson, "issued bills bottomed on a redeeming tax, but bearing no interest. These were received, and never depreciated a farthing."* In 1764 Dr. Franklin bore testimony before the British Board of Trade, as we have already mentioned,† to the value and usefulness of the bills issued by Pennsylvania. Just after the Revolution North Carolina issued a large amount of paper money, which was made receivable in dues to her; it was also made a legal tender. Several hundred thousand dollars of this paper money remained in circulation more than twenty years, at par with gold and silver, with no other advantage than being received in the revenues of the State.‡

In 1751 Parliament passed an act forbidding the issue of any more paper money, save in the form of exchequer bills redeemable in a year, except in case of war, when they could be made redeemable in four years; and in 1763 all colonial acts for issuing paper money were declared by act of Parliament to be void. Dr. Franklin protested against the act, but without avail. The English had reached the conclusion that nothing was money but gold and silver, and, animated by that peculiar spirit which has characterized their immediate descendants in this country, were determined that, right or wrong, everybody else should subscribe to the same opinion. In 1773, however, Parliament allowed any bills issued by the colonies to be a tender to their treasury.

CONTINENTAL MONEY.

During the Revolutionary war Congress issued nearly $350,000,000 in bills of credit. The first issue was in 1775, and the confederated colonies were pledged for its redemption. In form these bills were as follows: "This bill entitles the

*See page 56.   †See page 43.   ‡See page 59.

bearer to receive....Spanish milled dollars, or the value thereof, in gold or silver, according to the resolutions of Congress." The last emission was in 1780 under the guarantee of Congress, and was in the following form: "The possessor of this bill shall be paid....Spanish milled dollars by the 31st of December, 1786, with interest, in like money, at the rate of 5 per cent. per annum, by the State of.... according to an act of the legislature of the State of...., the....day of...., 1780." The endorsement by Congress was: "The United States insure the payment of the within bill, and will draw bills of exchange, annually, if demanded, according to a resolution of Congress of the 18th of March, 1780." The bills were required by Congress to issue upon the responsibility of the several States, and the confederated colonies pledged their faith for their payment. They were not made a legal tender, doubtless because Congress did not possess the authority to make them such. They circulated at par with silver for over a year, but after that they began to depreciate rapidly in value, owing to the character of the bills and the excessive amount put in circulation. In March, 1778, they were depreciated to $1.75 for $1, and before the end of the year to $4 for $1; March, 1779, $10 for $1; September, 1779, $18 for $1; March, 1780, $40 for $1. Congress then passed a resolution to fund the whole mass at that rate, but the depreciation continued until it reached $500 for $1, in 1781, and after that they ceased to circulate. In 1791 they were still permitted to be funded at the rate of $100 for $1. Continental money, according to Jefferson, "expired without a single groan. Not a murmur was heard among the people. On the contrary universal congratulations took place on their seeing the gigantic mass, whose dissolution had threatened convulsions which should shake their infant confederacy to its center, quietly interred in its grave. Foreigners, indeed, who do not like the natives feel indulgence for its memory, as of a being which has vindicated their liberties and fallen in the moment of victory, have been loud, and still are loud in their complaints. A few of them have reason; but the most noisy are not the best of them. They are persons who have become bankrupt by unskillful attempts at commerce with America. That they may have some pretext to offer to their creditors, they have bought up great masses of this dead money of America, where it is to be had at five thousand for one, and they show the certificates of their paper possessions, as if they had died in their hands, and had been the cause of their bankruptcy."

As Continental money is the "ghost conjured up by all who wish to give the banks an exclusive monopoly of government credit,"* it may be well to pause a moment to consider its nature. The paper money issued by the several colonies prior to the Revolution had answered the purposes of money admirably, though not issued according to any well settled policy. Whenever it had a fair trial, however, it never failed to succeed. But Continental money was issued under very different circumstances. The colonies had been brought together not out of choice but by necessity. Congress assumed the powers which it exercised through necessity, and its acts were acquiesced in by the people only out of a spirit of patriotism. Congress had no power to lay and collect taxes, and the confederation was without revenue. Whatever was done, had to be done through the States. Even after the adoption of the Articles of Confederation, in 1781, Congress possessed only the semblance of authority. Judge Story describes the situation at the time in the following language: "In the first place there was an utter

*Calhoun, see page 60.

want of all coercive authority to carry into effect its own constitutional measures. This of itself was sufficient to destroy its whole efficiency, as a superintending government, if that may be called a government which possesses no one solid attribute of power. * * In truth, Congress possessed only the power of recommendation. It depended altogether upon the good will of the States whether a measure should be carried into effect or not. * * Even during the Revolution, while all hearts and hands were engaged in the common cause, many of the measures of Congress were defeated by the inactivity of the States; and in some instances the exercise of its powers was resisted. But after the peace of 1783 such opposition became common, and gradually extended its sphere of activity, until, in the expressive language already quoted, 'the confederation became a shadow without the substance.' * * But a still more striking defect was the total want of power to lay and levy taxes, or to raise revenue to defray the ordinary expenses of government. The whole power confided to Congress upon this head was the power to ascertain the sums necessary to be raised for the service of the United States, and to apportion the quota or proportion on each State. But the power was expressly reserved to the States to lay and levy the taxes, and of course the time, as well as the mode of payment, was extremely uncertain. The evils resulting from this source, even during the Revolutionary war were of incalculable extent; and but for the good fortune of Congress in obtaining foreign loans, it is far from being certain that they would not have been fatal. * * Requisitions were to be made upon thirteen independent States, and it depended upon the good will of the legislature of each State, whether it would comply at all; or if it did comply, at what time and in what manner. The very tardiness of such an operation, in the ordinary course of things, was sufficient to involve the government in perpetual embarrassment, and to defeat many of its best measures, even when there was the utmost good faith and promptitude on the part of the States, in complying with the requisitions. But many reasons concurred to produce a total want of promptitude on the part of the States, and, in numerous instances, a total disregard of the requisitions. Indeed from the moment that the peace of 1783 secured the country from the distressing calamities of war, a general relaxation took place; and many of the States successively found apologies for their gross neglect in evils common to all, or complaints listened to by all. Many solemn and affecting appeals were from time to time made by Congress to the States, but they were attended with no salutary effect. Many measures were devised to obviate the difficulties, nay the dangers which threatened the Union; but they failed to produce any amendments in the confederation. An attempt was made by Congress, during the war, to procure from the States an authority to levy an impost of five per cent. upon imported and prize goods, but the assent of all the States could not be procured."*

The population of the thirteen colonies was estimated in 1775 at 2,448,000,† and the entire property of the country at less than $600,000,000. That a paper currency, issued to an excessive amount, by thirteen sparsely settled colonies, in a state of rebellion, under a revolutionary government possessing only a shadow of authority, against the most powerful nation on the earth, should have circulated at all, is one of the most remarkable facts connected with the Revolution, and is to be accounted for only by the patriotism of those engaged in that memorable struggle. But, as we

*Story on the Constitution, Vol. 1. page 171.
†Jefferson's Works, Vol. 9, page 272.

have seen, it circulated for over a year at par with silver, and in 1778, three years after the first emission, it depreciated only to $1.75 for $1. Congress resorted to various measures to sustain the credit of Continental bills, but, as ought to have been expected, without success. Money, as has been fully explained, derives it power to represent value from law, but there must be value in property or products, for which it can be exchanged, for it to represent, and the law must emanate from a responsible source—from a government possessing the right and power to command such property for its uses, otherwise it is only money in name. It is worthy of note, too, that Continental bills were not issued in the form of paper money, such as was first introduced by Massachusetts, and subsequently adopted by many of the other colonies, but in the form of promises to pay specie, at certain specified times, which, under the circumstances, was a manifest impossibility. The gradual depreciation of Continental money, as it passed from hand, inflicted a loss upon each successive holder, which came to be regarded in the nature of a tax or contribution towards the cause of independence. The large sums held by individuals after it ceased to circulate were taken at its greatest depreciation, and no great loss was sustained. When, after it had seen the liberties of the people vindicated, it sank, in the moment of victory, quietly into its grave, no commercial crash or money panic attended its fall. Its ghost has troubled no one since, except the advocates of the British system of bank currency, which, perhaps, is only in accordance with the eternal fitness of things.

BANKS OF THE UNITED STATES.

We come now to a new era in the history of American currency. When the colonies entered the Federal Union, under the Constitution framed in 1787, they surrendered all power or control over the question of money to the Federal Government. The object of this was to secure to the people a uniform and stable medium of exchange, and hence it was that a clause was inserted in the Constitution expressly prohibiting States from coining money, emitting bills of credit, etc.* But this wise provision of the Constitution was soon totally subverted by the money power, through the instrumentality of banks of issue, modeled on the British system of bank currency; and practically the currency of the country has been subject to the control of that power ever since.

About the close of the Revolution four banks of issue were established in the United States; one in each of the States of Pennsylvania, New York, Massachusetts and Maryland. At the time the Federal Constitution was framed, there was a large and formidable party, with aristocratic notions and tendencies, under the leadership of Alexander Hamilton, a statesman of undoubted patriotism and great ability, which was strongly in favor of the formation of what was termed "a strong government." This policy grew out of a want of faith in the people, and the belief that they were incapable of self-government. In a speech on this subject, June 18, 1787, Mr. Hamilton said: "I believe the British government forms the best model the world ever produced, and such has been its progress in the minds of many, that this truth gradually gains ground. This government has for its object public strength and individual security. It is said with us to be unattainable. If it was once formed it would maintain itself. All communities divide themselves into the few and the many. The first are the rich and well born, the other the mass of the people. * * Can a democratic assembly,

*See page 54.

who annually revolve in the mass of the people, be supposed steadily to pursue the public good? Nothing but a permanent body can check the independence of democracy. Their turbulent and uncontrolling disposition requires checks. * * Let one body of the legislature be constituted during good behavior or life. Let one executive be appointed (for life) who dares execute his powers. * * All State laws to be absolutely void which contravene the general laws. An officer to be appointed in each State to have a negative on all State laws. All the militia and the appointment of officers to be under the national government. * * The people are gradually ripening in their opinions of government; they begin to tire of an excess of democracy."* This policy of a strong government, based on an aristocracy of wealth, was rejected by the convention; but it has never been abandoned by the money power of the country. In 1863, in a speech, in the House of Representatives, in support of the National Bank Currency Bill, Hon. E. G. Spaulding, a banker of New York, boldly asserted that, "It is now most apparent that the policy advocated by Alexander Hamilton of a strong central government was the true policy;" and at the present time we have the policy of a third term openly and fearlessly advocated by the money power and its tools.

Hamilton, who was the first Secretary of the Treasury, urged the establishment of a National Bank modeled upon the British system, and upon his recommendation the first Bank of the United States, with a capital of $10,000,000, was chartered by Congress, February 25, 1791, for a period of twenty years. Jefferson, who was then Secretary of State, gave a written opinion denying the power of Congress to incorporate a bank of issue, and Madison, who was in

*Yates' Debates of the Constitutional Convention (1787.)

Congress, opposed it, in a powerful speech, as a violation of the Constitution. In 1811 the bank applied to Congress for a renewal of its charter, but it was not granted. Clay and other leading statesmen opposed its re-charter on the ground that it was "unconstitutional, anti-American, and strictly a British institution."

In the meantime a mania to start banks had sprung up in New England, which subsequently extended to the Middle States, and finally all over the country. In 1815 Jefferson gave the following statement of the number of banks which had been established up to that time:

"In 1781 we had 1 bank, capital,............ $1,000,000
" 1791 " 6 banks, " 13,500,000
" 1794 " 17 " " 18,642,000
" 1796 " 24 " " 20,472,000
" 1803 " 34 " " 29,112,000
" 1804 " 66 " amount of capital not known.

And at this time (1815) we have probably one hundred banks."

Notwithstanding the constitutional prohibition against emitting bills of credit, charters, incorporating private institutions, authorized to emit bills of credit (bank notes), were granted by the legislatures of the several States in large numbers, in utter disregard of the Constitution, as well as of the public good. In Pennsylvania, for example, twenty-five charters, incorporating specie basis banks of issue, were granted during the session of 1813, but were vetoed by the Governor. At the next session of the legislature, in 1814, a bill was passed over the veto of the Governor chartering forty-one banks, with a capital of $17,000,000. Thirty-seven of them went into operation at once, and six months afterwards suspended specie payment. The manner of obtaining a charter was very simple. A petition setting forth "the wants of the people" in the locality where the bank was to be established was all that was required; political influence and intrigue accomplished the rest.

Specie basis banks are always required by law to redeem their notes in specie, but as they are, also, always authorized to issue notes to three times the amount of their capital stock, their redemption in specie becomes an impossibility. This feature in banking, as has been explained,* was originally nothing more than a bold plan on the part of certain ingenious financiers and schemers to acquire favor with the public for the Bank of England and increase its business. As the system in time was found to have a tendency to concentrate wealth in the hands of the few, it commended itself to the aristocratic, or governing class, of that kingdom, and soon became an integral part of the structure of British society. Transplanted to the free atmosphere of America the system was afforded an opportunity to develop its latent evils, greatly to the disadvantage of American society. If banks were authorized to issue only a dollar of paper for a dollar of specie held for its redemption, there would be no advantage in issuing notes; they might as well lend the specie. Individuals obtain charters to carry on the business of banking on the theory that they have capital to employ in that business, but under the specie basis system they are not required to use their capital at all. Bank notes are issued and exchanged for the notes of individuals. These bank notes are based on the credit of the institution which issues them, and represent nothing more; if redeemed, they are good; if not, they are as worthless as the note of an insolvent individual. A bank of issue in effect simply substitutes its notes, of various denominations and otherwise convenient for use in payments, for the notes of its customers. As a large portion of the

*See page 89.

community are constantly having payments to make in bank, the notes of the bank are as good to them as money, and they thus come to perform not only the functions of the individual notes, for which they were substituted, but also the functions of a circulating medium. Whilst in reality they are nothing more than promises to pay, representing credit, (evidences of the indebtedness of the bank,) they at the same time become substitutes for money. In this way a bank of issue enables its corporators and stockholders to force their credit, or evidences of indebtedness, upon the public, at a high rate of interest, and compel its use as a circulating medium, whether the public desires to use it or not. The medium of exchange thus forced upon the public, encumbered with interest, becomes a tax upon the community at large, because its cost enters into the price of commodities.* As bank notes rest entirely upon private credit, they are subject to depreciation in value, which imposes an additional burden upon trade and production. It is, as we have seen,† a part of the specie basis system to treat discounted paper as deposits, and this furnishes the basis for additional loans of credit. By encouraging discounts and lending credit, through the instrumentality of bank notes, to be used as real capital, business becomes active, prices advance and speculation becomes rife. Inflation of bank credit and notes goes on and a huge structure of credit is erected upon an insignificant basis of specie, supposed to be resting in the vaults of the bank, which is toppled over by the first financial breeze that springs up, and the public is buried in its ruins. When the banks are called upon to redeem their promises to pay they are of course unable to do so, for the wit of man has not yet devised a way to redeem several paper dollars with one gold dollar. Like

*See page 49.   †See page 91.

individuals, banks can be thrown into bankruptcy and compelled to go into liquidation, but such a step only aggravates the distress of the public, and is rarely adopted; and the banks are permitted to escape, only to repeat the operation as soon as confidence has been restored through the aid of the Sheriff.* The extent to which banks are enabled to lend their credit by means of the specie basis system of banking will appear from an examination of the following table, which is an abstract of the Commissioners' Report of the banks of Connecticut for a period of twelve years, from 1837 to 1847 inclusive and the year 1849. The banks of Connecticut, it should be mentioned, were conducted during this period with as much safety to the public as those of any other State in the Union:

Year.	Capital.	Circulation.	Total Liabilities.	Specie.	Loans and Discounts.
1837	$8,744,697 50	$3,998,325 30	$15,715,964 59	$415,386 10	$13,246,495 08
1838	8,754,467 50	1,920,552 45	12,302,631 11	535,447 86	9,769,286 80
1839	8,832,223 00	3,987,815 45	14,942,779 31	502,180 15	12,286,946 97
1840	8,878,245 00	2,325,589 95	12,950,572 40	499,032 52	10,428,630 87
1841	8,873,927 50	2,784,721 45	13,866,373 45	454,298 61	10,944,673 35
1842	8,876,317 57	2,555,638 33	13,465,052 32	471,238 08	10,683,413 37
1843	8,580,393 50	5,319,947 02	12,914,124 66	438,752 92	9,798,392 27
1844	8,292,238 00	3,490,963 06	14,472,681 32	455,430 30	10,842,955 35
1845	8,359,743 00	4,102,444 00	15,243,235 79	453,658 79	12,477,196 06
1846	8,475,630 00	3,565,947 06	15,892,685 25	481,367 09	13,032,600 78
1847	8,605,742 00	4,437,631 06	15,784,772 04	462,165 53	12,781,857 43
	$95,273,629 57	$38,549,575 13	$157,550,872 44	$5,168,957 95	$126,292,898 33
1849	8,985,917 00	4,511,571 00		575,676 00	13,740,591 00
	104,259,546 57			$5,744,633 95	$140,033,489 33

Average Capital, — — $8,688,295 55
Average Liabilites, — 13,129,239 37
Average Specie, — 478,719 50
Average Loans and Discounts, 11,669,457 44

Kellogg, who gives this table,† in commenting upon it, says: "By the foregoing table it will be seen that the average amount of the specie held by the banks in the State of Connecticut, for the twelve years, was $478,719, while the average amount of their loans to the public, during the same

*See page 20. †Kellogg's New Monetary System, page 204.

period, was $11,669,457—more than twenty-four and one-third times as much money as the banks had specie. The annual interest on $11,669,457 was $700,167. If they could have loaned only their specie, the interest would have amounted to but $28,723. The banks gained from the public annually $671,444 above the interest on their specie; and, in the twelve years, $8,057,328. They collected this interest in advance, and made their dividends half yearly to their stockholders; therefore, it is proper to compound this interest half yearly, which would swell their gains to nearly $12,000,000, that is to say, $1,000,000 interest annually. These were actual gains, as much realized by these banks as if they had produced and sold annually $700,167 worth of agricultural products." (The statements of the banks of any of the large cities, published from time to time in the newspapers, will disclose a similar inflation of credit at the present time. The fact that the National Banks do not redeem their notes in specie makes no difference. They are banks of issue and belong to the specie basis system all the same.)

The banks of the United States have been compelled to suspend specie payments at various times as follows, to wit: in 1809, 1814, 1819, 1825, 1834, 1837, 1839, 1841, 1857, 1861, and in 1873 currency payment. These suspensions have invariably occasioned great public distress, and in several instances have involved the entire country in bankruptcy and ruin, from which it took years to recover. In March, 1809, a legislative committee of the State of Rhode Island made an examination into the affairs of the Farmers' Exchange Bank of Gloucester, and it was found that the bank had $580,000 of its notes in circulation, and only $86.16 in its vaults for their redemption. Before the end of the year a general suspension of the banks of New England took place, and it was discovered that they were nearly all in the same condition—no specie and nothing to show but the worthless notes of speculators.

CRASH OF 1814.

In 1814 all the banks outside of New England, including the forty-one banks chartered by the Pennsylvania legislature in the early part of the year, were obliged to suspend specie payment, occasioning great distress. The people were helpless, and could do no better than to use their depreciated notes. This condition of affairs lasted for years. The following table shows the depreciation of the notes of the banks of the cities of Baltimore, New York and Philadelphia during the suspension:

		Baltimore. Per cent.	Philadelphia. Per cent.	New York. Per cent.
1814—	September	20	..	..
	October	15	..	..
	November	10	..	..
	December	14	..	..
1815—	January	20	..	15
	February	5	..	2
	March	5	..	5
	April	10	..	$6\frac{1}{2}$
	May	14	5	5
	June	16	9	11
	July	20	11	14
	August	19	11	$12\frac{1}{2}$
	September	20	15	13
	October	$21\frac{1}{2}$	15	16
	November	15	16	12
	December	18	14	$12\frac{1}{2}$
1816—	January	15	14	$12\frac{1}{2}$
	February	13	14	9
	March	18	$12\frac{1}{2}$	$12\frac{1}{2}$
	April	23	$14\frac{1}{2}$	$10\frac{1}{4}$
	May	20	14	$12\frac{1}{4}$
	June	20	16	$12\frac{1}{4}$
	July	15	15	6
	August	12	10	5
	September	10	$7\frac{1}{2}$	3
	October	8	$9\frac{1}{2}$	2
	November	9	7	$1\frac{3}{4}$
	December	9	7	$2\frac{1}{2}$
1817—	January	2	$4\frac{1}{2}$	$2\frac{1}{2}$
	February	$2\frac{1}{2}$	4	$2\frac{1}{4}$

On the first of January, 1817, the second Bank of the United States began business, and on the 20th of February following specie payments were nominally resumed. The extent and character of the resumption that took place may be gathered from the following case cited by Sumner, in his History of American Currency: "In 1817 a case at Richmond, after specie payments were resumed, gave an insight into the state of things. A man having presented ten one hundred dollar notes for redemption was refused. He could not get a lawyer to take a case against the bank for a long time. Finally having obtained judgment, the Sheriff was sent to collect. The president of the bank was taken before the court, but refused to pay. The bank was closed by the Sheriff, but soon after opened and went on."

The specie basis system had now been in operation long enough to produce its legitimate fruits, and accordingly we find that here and there the people were becoming alarmed at its encroachments upon their rights, as well as at the evils which it inflicted upon the public. The following is an extract from a report of a legislative committee of the State of New York in 1818:

"Of all aristocracies, none more completely enslave a people than that of money; and, in the opinion of your committee, no system was ever better devised so perfectly to enslave a community as that of the present mode of conducting banking establishments. Like the siren of the fable, they entice to destroy. They hold the purse-strings of society, and, by monopolizing the whole of the circulating medium of the country, they form a precarious standard, by which all property in the country—homes, lands, debts and credits, personal and real estate of all descriptions—are valued, thus rendering the whole community dependent upon them; proscribing every man who dares to expose their unlawful practices. If he happens to be out of their reach, so as to require no favors from them, his friends are made the victims; so no one dares complain. The committee, on taking a general view of our State, and comparing those parts where banks have been, for some time, established with those that have none, are astonished at the alarming disparity. They see, in the one case, the desolation they have made in societies that were before prosperous and happy; the ruin they have brought on an immense number of the more wealthy farmers, and they and their families suddenly hurled from wealth and independence into the abyss of ruin and despair. If the facts stated in the foregoing be true, (and your committee have no doubt they are,) together with others equally reprehensible and to be dreaded, such as that their influence too frequently, nay, often already, begins to assume a species of dictation altogether alarming, and, unless some judicious remedy is provided by legislative wisdom, we shall soon witness attempts to control all selections to offices in our counties—nay, the elections to the very legislature. Senators and members of assembly will be indebted to the banks for their seat in this capitol; and thus the wise end of our civil institutions will be prostrated in the dust of corporations of their own raising."

THE CRASH OF 1819.

In 1818 the bank of the United States had discounted to the amount of $43,000,000, and had $2,000,000 in specie. It had established eighteen branches, and its notes could not be signed fast enough for the public. To increase its reserve of specie it had bought $7,000,000 of bullion abroad, at a cost of $800,000 for expenses, but it was exported as fast as it was imported. The Bank of England, which had been in suspension since 1797, was preparing to resume specie payments, and was drawing specie from every source that was available. In April, 1818, less than fifteen months after the Bank of the United States started, it was believed to be insolvent. A committee, appointed by Congress to investigate its affairs, reported a resolution requiring the bank to show cause why its charter should not be forfeited, but the resolution was lost, forty members of Congress being stockholders in the bank. The bank now resorted to vigorous measures to save itself from bankruptcy, and in a little over two months was once more solvent. It had, however, ruined the country. The amount of bank note circulation in 1813–14 was about $45,000,000; in 1817–18, $100,000,000; and in 1819 about $45,000,000. Contraction had done its work, and the ruin which it had accomplished was deep and widespread. In August, 1819, 20,000 persons were seeking employment in Philadelphia, and a similar condition of affairs prevailed in New York, Baltimore and other cities. The distress was least severe in New England. In the Western States it was intense. In the South the banks still pretended to pay specie, but the following account of the manner in which they did business in some localities would hardly justify the pretension: One who presented a bill had to make oath in the bank that the bill was his own and that he was not an agent for any one. He was required to make this oath before the cashier and five directors, and had to pay $1.37½ expenses on each bill.

Stagnation and distress lasted throughout the year 1820. Wheat was 20 cents per bushel in Kentucky. At Pittsburgh flour was $1 per barrel, boards, $2 per thousand, etc., etc., while imported goods remained at their old prices. One and a half bushels of wheat would buy a pound of coffee; a barrel of flour would buy a pound of tea, and twelve and a half barrels of flour would buy a yard of broadcloth. But a better idea of the condition of affairs may be formed, perhaps, from a report of a committee of the Senate of Pennsylvania, of which the distinguished Condy Raguet was chairman, made on the 20th of February, 1820. It is as follows:

"In ascertaining the extent of the public distress, your committee has had no difficulties to encounter. Members of the legislature from various quarters of the State, have been consulted in relation to this subject, and their written testimony in answer to interrogatories submitted to them by the committee, has agreed, with scarcely a single exception, on all material points. With such respectable weight of evidence, added to that which has been derived from the prothonotaries, recorders and sheriffs of the different counties, from intercourse with numerous private citizens residing in different parts of the state, as well as from the various petitions presented to the legislature, your committee can safely assert that a distress unexampled in our country since the period of its independence, prevails throughout the commonwealth. This distress exhibits itself under the various forms of—

"1. Ruinous sacrifices of landed property at sheriff's sales, whereby, in many cases, lands and houses have been sold at less than a half, a third, or a fourth of their former value, thereby depriving of their homes, and of the fruits of laborious years, a vast number of our industrious farmers, some of whom have been driven to seek, in the uncultivated forests of the west, that shelter of which they have been deprived in their native State.

"2. Forced sales of merchandise, household goods, farming stock and utensils, at prices far below the cost of production, by which many families have been deprived of the common necessaries of life, and of the implements of their trade.

"3. Numerous bankruptcies and pecuniary embarrassments of every description, as well among the agricultural and manufacturing as the mercantile classes.

"4. A general scarcity of money throughout the country, which renders it almost impossible for the husbandman or other owners of real estate to borrow at a usurious interest, and where landed security of the most indubitable character is offered as a pledge. A similar difficulty of procuring on loan had existed in the metropolis previous to October last, but has since then been partially removed.

"5. A general suspension of labor, the only legitimate source of wealth, in our cities and towns, by which thousands of our most useful citizens are rendered destitute of the means of support, and are reduced to the extremity of poverty and despair.

"6. An almost entire cessation of the usual circulation of commodities, and a consequent stagnation of business, which is limited to the mere purchase and sale of the necessaries of life, and of such articles of consumption as are absolutely required by the season.

"7. A universal suspension of all manufacturing operations, by which, in addition to the dismissal of the numerous productive laborers heretofore engaged therein, who can find no other employment, the public loses the revenue of the capital invested in machinery and buildings.

"8. Usurious extortions, whereby corporations instituted for banking, insurance and other purposes, in violation of law, possess themselves of the products of industry without granting an equivalent.

"9. The overflowing of our prisons with insolvent debtors, most of whom are confined for trifling sums, whereby the community loses a portion of its effective labor, and is compelled to support families by charity who have thus been deprived of their protectors.

"10. Numerous law-suits upon the dockets of our courts and of our justices of the peace, which lead to extravagant costs and loss of a great portion of valuable time.

"11. Vexatious losses arising from the depreciation and fluctuation in the value of bank notes, the imposition of brokers and the frauds of counterfeiters.

"12. A general inability in a community to meet with punctuality the payment of debts even for family expenses, which is experienced as well by those who are wealthy in property as by those who have hitherto relied upon their current engagements. With such a mass of evils to oppress them, it cannot be wondered at that the people should be dispirited, and that they should look to their representatives for relief. Their patient endurance of suffering, which can only be imagined by those who have habitually intermingled with them at their homes and by their firesides, merits the commendation of the legislature and prefers a powerful claim to their interference."

The people of the United States had not been without warning as to the evils and dangers of the specie basis system, but they had supinely allowed the money power to gain control of the monetary affairs of the country, precisely as they are doing now. January 16, 1814, previous to the crisis of that year, Jefferson wrote as follows: "Everything predicted by the enemies of the banks in the beginning is now coming to pass. We are to be ruined by the deluge of bank paper, as we were formerly by the old Continental paper. It is cruel that such revolutions in private fortunes should be at the mercy of avaricious adventurers, who, instead of employing their capital, if any they have, in manufactures, commerce, and other useful pursuits, make it an instrument to burthen all the interchanges of property with their swindling profits, profits which are the price of no useful industry of theirs. * * I am an enemy to all banks discounting bills or notes for anything but coin." And again, January 6, 1816 he wrote as follows: "The American mind is now in that state of fever which the world has so often seen in the history of other nations. We are under the bank bubble, as England was under the South Sea bubble, France under the Mississippi bubble, and as every nation is liable to be, under whatever bubble, design or delusion may puff up in moments when off guard. We are now taught to believe that legerdemain tricks upon paper can produce as solid wealth as hard labor in the earth. It is vain for common sense to urge that *nothing* can produce but *nothing;* * * Not Quixot enough, however, to attempt to reason Bedlam to rights, my anxieties are turned to the most practicable means of withdrawing us from the ruin into which we have run. Two hundred millions of paper in the hands of the people, (and less cannot be from the employment of a banking capital known to exceed one hundred millions,) is a fearful tax to fall at hap-hazard on their heads. * * And what have we purchased with this tax of two hundred millions, which we are to pay by wholesale, but usury, swindling and new forms of demoralization." As we have seen, the bubble burst, as predicted by Jefferson, in 1819. The stagnation and distress continued during 1821 and 1822. In 1823 there was a large creation of banks in New York, and the Bank of the United States began to expand. In 1824 all the banks began to expand. Pennsylvania rechartered the banks of 1814. In the spring of 1825 petitions were presented in New York for fifty-two charters for banks and insurance companies. "In Kentucky there was anarchy. Alabama and Tennessee notes were at a discount. Indiana, Illinois and Missouri were still suffering from the 'relief' system (stay laws against the collection of debts, etc.) The New York and Boston banks were fighting the country issues. * * The bank of the United States increased its issues over $3,000,000."*

CRASH OF 1825.

In the latter part of 1824 and beginning of 1825 the Bank of England found it necessary to curtail its discounts, in order to check the outflow of bullion. This occasioned another terrible crisis in that country. Seventy banks failed and nearly two thirds of the merchants and manufacturers stopped payment, causing great distress among the working classes. Gold began to flow from the United States, and the banks were obliged to suspend specie payments. Fifty failures occurred in New York before December, and banks went under all over the country. The crisis, however, was not felt so severely in the United States as it was in England, because the banks had not yet had sufficient time to inflate their credit and circulation to the greatest extent. Here and there throughout the country industrial activity was stimulated somewhat during the next few years by the high tariff of 1824 and 1828, and by the building of railroads, which began in 1830; but business generally continued to suffer from the rotten monetary system which had been fastened upon the country, and distress was more or less common.

THE WAR WITH THE UNITED STATES BANK.

The fight between President Jackson and the United States Bank, which occupied the attention of the people for years, now began. The specie basis system had been in operation for over a quarter of a century, and during the whole time the country had never once enjoyed the advan-

*Sumner's History of American Currency.

tages of a sound currency. Pecuniary distress, periodical returns of expansion and contraction, deranged currency, ruined exchanges, and panics and convulsions had characterized the entire period. The banks, although based on "hard money," and professing to pay coin, were in a state of chronic suspension. The press of the country was completely subsidized; Congress, as well as State legislatures, bowed in abject submission to the mandates of the money power; and even the Supreme Court of the United States did not escape its contaminating influence. The people were perfectly helpless, and the outlook of American freedom and independence was dark indeed. It is worthy of mention that Pitt, in 1791, when Hamilton brought forward his funding and banking scheme, said: "Let the Americans adopt their funding system and go into their banking institutions, and their boasted independence will be a mere phantom." But fortunately for the country the election of 1828 resulted in the choice of Andrew Jackson as President of the United States, and the people found in him a leader, as fearless as he was patriotic. In his first message to Congress, December 8, 1829, in language of extreme moderation, he called public attention to the United States Bank, and expressed himself as unfavorable to its continued existence. He said:

"The charter of the Bank of the United States expires in 1836, and its stockholders will probably apply for a renewal of their privileges. In order to avoid the evils resulting from precipitancy in a measure involving such important principles, and such deep pecuniary interests, I feel that I cannot, in justice to the parties interested, too soon present it to the deliberate consideration of the legislature and the people. Both the constitutionality and expediency of the law creating this bank are well questioned by a large portion of our fellow citizens; and it must be admitted by all that it has failed in the great end of establishing a uniform and sound currency."

The bank immediately began preparations for war. Through its branches and its control over State banks, its power extended into every part of the country. Millions of dollars (belonging, as it subsequently appeared, to depositors and stockholders) were squandered for the purpose of corrupting the people. Statesmen, Congressmen, brawling politicians, editors, all succumbed to its influence, very much in the same way as they are seen bowing to the power of the National Banks at the present day. After a careful survey of the field and a thorough canvass of Congress, it was determined by the bank that a renewal of its charter should be applied for during the session of Congress immediately preceding the next general election in 1832. The bill passed Congress by a majority of eight in the Senate and twenty-two in the House. As was expected, it was returned with the President's veto, on the 10th of July, 1832. The contest was then transferred to a wider field and carried on with excessive virulence. The money power everywhere went to work to defeat Jackson. In Philadelphia, for example, "the bank would order the business men to hold public meetings in its behalf in order that it might ascertain who were its friends, and who were courageous enough to stand by the government in its efforts to redeem the people, and then, in turn, would appoint places for the assembling of the different trades, in order that the employers might see who of their workmen had opinions which they dared maintain."* The masses, however, rallied to the support of the President, and the capacity of the American people for self-government was triumphantly vindicated. President

*From Speech of Hon. W. D. Kelley, at Indianapolis, Aug., 1875.

Jackson was re-elected, defeating Mr. Clay by a vote of 228 to 49 in the electoral college. Upon examination it will be found that the principles involved in the contest between General Jackson and the United States Bank are precisely identical with those which underlie the impending contest between the people and the National Banks. The subject is, therefore, worthy of more than a passing notice. Benton, in his "Thirty Years in the United States Senate," in commenting upon some errors of Mons. de Tocqueville "in relation to the Bank of the United States, the President and the people," gives a clear and comprehensive analysis of the principles and purposes involved in the contest, from which we quote as follows:

"This passage* was the grand feature of the message, rising above precedent and judicial decisions, going back to the Constitution and the foundation of party on principle; and risking a contest at the commencement of his administration, which a mere politician would have put off to the last. The Supreme Court had decided in favor of the constitutionality of the institution; a democratic Congress, in chartering a second bank, had yielded the question, both of constitutionality and expediency. Mr. Madison, in signing the bank charter in 1816, yielded to the authorities without surrendering his convictions. But the effect was the same in behalf of the institution, and against the Constitution, and against the integrity of party founded on principle. It threw down the great landmark of party, and yielded a power of construction which nullified the limitations of the Constitution, and left Congress at liberty to pass any law which it deemed *necessary* to carry into effect any granted power. The whole argument for the bank turned upon the word 'necessary' at the end of the enumerated

*See page 134.

powers granted to Congress; and gave rise to the first division of parties in Washington's time—the federal party being for the construction which would authorize a national bank; the democratic party (republican, as then called,) being against it.

"It was not merely the bank which the democracy opposed, but the latitudinarian construction which would authorize it, and which would enable Congress to substitute its own will in other cases for the words of the Constitution, and do what it pleased under the plea of 'necessary'—a plea under which they would be left as much to their own will as under the 'general welfare' clause. It was the turning point between a strong and splendid government on one side, doing what it pleased, and a plain economical government on the other, limited by a written Constitution. The construction was the main point, because it made a gap in the Constitution through which Congress could pass any other measures which it deemed to be 'necessary;' still there were great objections to the bank itself. Experience had shown such an institution to be a political machine, adverse to free government, mingling in the elections and legislation of the country, corrupting the press, and exerting its influence in the only way known to the moneyed power—by corruption. General Jackson's objections reached both heads of the case—the unconstitutionality of the bank and its inexpediency. It was a return to the Jeffersonian and Hamiltonian times of the early administration of General Washington, and went to the words of the Constitution, and not to the interpretations of the administrators for its meaning.

"Such a message, from such a man—a man not apt to look back when he had set his face forward—electrified the democratic spirit of the country. The old democracy felt as if they were to see the Constitution restored before they died—the young, as if they were summoned to the reconstruction of the work of their fathers. It was evident that a great contest was coming on, and the odds entirely against the President. On the one side, the undivided phalanx of the federal party (for they had not then taken the name of whig); a large part of the democratic party, yielding to precedent and judicial decision; the bank itself, with its colossal money power—its arms in every State by means of branches—its power over the State banks—its power over the business community—over public men who should become its debtors or retainers—its organization under a single head, issuing its orders in secret, to be obeyed in all places and by all subordinates at the same moment. Such was the formidable array on one side: on the other side a divided democratic party, disheartened by division, with nothing to rely upon but the goodness of their cause, the *prestige* of Jackson's name, and the presidential power;—good against anything less than two-thirds of Congress on the final question of the re-charter; but the risk to run of his non-election before the final question came on.

"Under such circumstances it required a strong sense of duty in the new President to commence his career by risking such a contest; but he believed the institution to be unconstitutional and dangerous, and that it ought to cease to exist; and there was a clause in the Constitution—that Constitution which he had sworn to support—which commanded him to recommend to Congress, for its consideration, such measures as he should deem expedient and proper. Under this sense of duty, and under the obligation of this oath, President Jackson had recommended to Congress the non-renewal of the bank charter, and the substitution of a different fiscal agent for the operations of the government—if any such agent was required. And with his accustomed frankness, and the fairness of a man who has nothing but the public good in view, and with a disregard of self which permits no personal consideration to stand in the way of a discharge of a public duty, he made the recommendation six years before the expiration of the charter, and in the first message of his first term; thereby taking upon his hands such an enemy as the Bank of the United States, at the very commencement of his administration. That such a recommendation against such an institution should bring upon the President and his supporters, violent attacks, both personal and political, with arraignment of motives as well as of reasons, was naturally to be expected; and that expectation was by no means disappointed. Both he and they, during the seven years that the bank contest (in different forms) prevailed, received from it—from the newspapers and periodical press in its interest, and from the public speakers in its favor of every grade—an accumulation of obloquy, and even of accusation, only lavished upon the oppressors and plunderers of nations—a Verres, or a Hastings."   *   *

"He impugned neither the integrity nor the skill of the institution, but repeated the objections of the political school to which he belonged, and which were as old as Mr. Jefferson's cabinet opinion to President Washington, in the year 1791, and Mr. Madison's great speech in the House of Representatives in the same year. He, therefore, made no attack upon the bank, either upon its existence, its character, or any one of its rights. On the other hand, the bank did attack President Jackson, under the lead of politicians, and for the purpose of breaking him down. The facts were these: President Jackson had communicated his opinion to Congress in December, 1829, against the renewal of the charter; near three years afterwards, on the 9th of January, 1832, while the charter had yet above three years to run, and a new Congress to be elected before its expiration, and the presidential election impending—(General Jackson and Mr. Clay the candidates)—the memorial of the president and directors of the bank was suddenly presented in the Senate of the United States, for renewal of its charter.

"Now, how came that memorial to be presented at a time so inopportune? so premature, so inevitably mixing itself with the presidential election, and so encroaching upon the rights of the people, in snatching the question out of their hands, and having it decided by a Congress not elected for the purpose—and to the usurpation of the rights of the Congress elected for the purpose? How came all these anomalies? all these violations of right, decency and propriety? They came thus: the bank and its leading anti-Jackson friends believed that the institution was stronger than the President—that it could beat him in the election—that it could beat him in Congress (as it then stood), and carry the charter—driving him upon the *veto* power, and rendering him odious if he used it, and disgracing him if (after what he had said) he did not. This was the opinion of the leading politicians friendly to the bank, and inimical to the President. But the bank had a class of friends in Congress also friendly to Gen. Jackson; and between these two classes there was vehement opposition of opinion on the point of moving for the new charter. It was found impossible, in communications between Washington and Philadelphia, then slow and uncertain, in stage coach conveyances, over miry roads and frozen waters, to come to conclusions on the difficult point. Mr. Biddle and the directors were in doubt, for it would not do to move in the matter, unless all the friends of the bank in Congress acted together. In this state of uncertainty, General Cadwallader, of Philadelphia, friend and confidant of Mr. Biddle, and his usual envoy in all the delicate bank negotiations or troubles, was sent to Washington to obtain a result; and the union of both wings of the bank party in favor of the desired movement. He came, and the mode of operation was through the machinery of *caucus*—that contrivance by which a few govern many. The two wings being of different politics, sat separately, one headed by Mr. Clay, the other by Gen. Samuel Smith of Maryland. The two caucuses disagreed, but the democratic being the smaller, and Mr. Clay's strong will dominating the other, the resolution was taken to proceed, and all bound to go together." * *

"The prudential counsels of such men as Mr. Dallas did not prevail; political counsels governed; the bank charter was pushed—was carried through both Houses of Congress—dared the veto of Jackson—received it—roused the people—and the bank and all of its friends were crushed. Then it affected to have been attacked by Jackson; and Mons. de Tocqueville has carried that fiction into history, with all the imaginary reasons for a groundless accusation, which the bank had invented.

"The remainder of this quotation from Mons. de Tocqueville is profoundly erroneous, and deserves to be exposed, to prevent the mischiefs which his book might do in Europe, and even in America, among that class of our people who look to European writers for information upon their own country. He speaks of the well informed classes who rallied round the bank; and the common people who had formed no rational opinion upon the subject, and who had joined General Jackson. Certainly the great business community, with few exceptions, comprising wealth, ability and education, went for the bank, and the masses for General Jackson; but which had formed the rational opinion is seen by the event. The 'well informed' classes have bowed not merely to the decision, but to the intelligence of the masses. They have adopted their opinion of the institution—condemned it —repudiated it as an 'obsolete idea;' and of all of its former advocates, not one now exists. All have yielded to that instinctive sagacity of the people, which is an overmatch for book-learning; and which being the result of common sense, is usually right; and being disinterested, is always honest. I adduce this instance—a grand national one—of the succumbing of the well informed classes to the instinctive sagacity of the people, not merely to correct Mons. de Tocqueville, but for the higher purpose of showing the capacity of the people for self-government. The rest of the quotation, 'the independent existence—the people accustomed to make and unmake—startled at this obstacle— irritated at a permanent institution—attack in order to shake and control;' all this is fancy, or as the old English wrote it, fantasy—enlivened by French vivacity into witty theory, as fallacious as witty."   *   *

"Now, while Mons. de Tocqueville was arranging all this fine ecomium upon the bank, and all this censure upon its adversaries, the whole of which is nothing but a French translation of the bank publications of the day, for itself and against President Jackson—during all this time there was a process going on in the Congress of the United States, by which it was proved that the bank was then insolvent, and living from day to day upon expedients; and getting hold of property and money by contrivances which the law would qualify as swindling—plundering its own stockholders —and bribing individuals, institutions, and members of legislative bodies, wherever it could be done. Those fine notes, of which he speaks, were then without solid value. The salutary restraint attributed to its control over local banks was soon exemplified in its forcing many of them into complicity in its crimes, and all into two general suspensions of specie payments, headed by itself. Its solidity and its honor were soon shown in open bankruptcy—in the dishonor of its notes—the violation of sacred deposits—the disappearance of its capital—the destruction of institutions connected with it—the extinction of fifty-six millions of capital (its own, and that of others drawn into its vortex);—and the ruin or damage of families, both foreign and American, who had been induced by its name, and by its delusive exhibitions of credit, to invest their money in its stock. Placing the opposition of President Jackson to such an institution to the account of base and personal motives—to feelings of revenge because he had been unable to seduce it into his support—is an error of fact manifested by all the history of the case; to say nothing of his own personal character. He was a senator in Congress during the existence of the first national bank, and was against it; and on the same grounds of unconstitutionality and of inexpediency. He delivered his opinion against this second one before it had manifested any hostility to him. His first opposition was abstract—against the institution—without reference to its conduct; he knew nothing against it then, and neither said, or insinuated anything against it. Subsequently, when misconduct was discovered, he charged it; and openly and responsibly. Equally unfounded is the insinuation in another place, of subserviency to local banks. He, the instrument of local banks! he who could not be made the friend, even, of the great bank itself; who was all his life a hard money man—an opposer of all banks—the denouncer of delinquent banks in his own State; who, with one stroke of his pen, in the recess of Congress, and against its will, in the summer of 1836, struck all their notes from the list of land office payments! and whose last message to Congress, and in his farewell address to the people, admonished them earnestly and affectionately against the whole system of paper money (bank currency)—the evils of which he feelingly described as falling heaviest upon the most meritorious part of the community, and the part least able to bear them—the productive classes."

The United States Bank continued its war upon the administration until the last moment of its existence. Its charter expired by limitation in 1836, but it was entitled to two years in which to wind up its affairs. Instead of preparing to close up its business it resorted to new and desperate measures to prolong its powers. In January, 1836, a bill was "snaked" through the legislature of Pennsylvania, by means of bribery and corruption, entitled "An Act to repeal the State tax, and to continue the improvement of the State by railroads and canals, and for other purposes;" and under the vague generality of "other purposes," was found a charter for the United States Bank, adopting it as a State Bank. The people of Pennsylvania were astounded, and met in masses to denounce the act and demand its repeal; and at the next session of the legislature an investigation was ordered, but, as is usual in such cases, it came to nothing. Rotten and corrupt as the institution subsequently proved to be, it went on for several years, and exerted great influence in the commercial and political affairs of the country. The two general suspensions of specie payments, headed by the United States Bank, referred to in the foregoing extracts from Benton, were the suspensions of 1837 and 1839, in the latter of which the bank closed its doors upon its creditors October 9th, 1839, never really to open them again. A report of its affairs was made by a committee of stockholders, and disclosed, to quote again from Benton, " such an exhibition of waste and destruction, and of downright plundering and criminal misconduct, as was never seen before in the annals of banking. Fifty-six and three-quarter millions of capital out of eighty-two and one-quarter millions, (including its own of thirty-five,) were sunk in the limits of Philadelphia alone; for the great monster, in going down, had carried many others along with her; and, like the strong man in scripture, slew more in her death than in her life. Vast was her field of destruction—extending all over the United States—and reaching to Europe, where four millions sterling of her stock was held, and large loans had been contracted. Universally on all classes the ruin fell—foreigners as well as citizens—peers and peeresses, as well as the ploughman and the wash-woman—merchants, tradesmen, lawyers, wards and guardians; confiding friends who came to the rescue; deceived stockholders who held on to their stock, or purchased more; the credulous masses who believed in the safety of their deposits, and in the security of the notes they held— all—all saw themselves the victims of indiscriminate ruin. An hundred millions of dollars was the lowest at which the destruction was estimated; and how such ruin could be worked, and such blind confidence kept up for so long a time, is the instructive lesson for history; and that lesson the report of the stockholders' committee enables history to give. From this authentic report it appears that from the year 1830 to 1836—the period of its struggles for a· re-charter—the loans and discounts of the bank were about doubled—its expenses trebled. Near thirty millions of these loans were not of a mercantile character—neither made to persons in trade or business. * * To whom were they made? To members of Congress, to editors of newspapers, to brawling politicians, to brokers and jobbers, to favorites and connections; and all with a view to purchase a re-charter, or to enrich connections and exalt himself, (Nicholas Biddle,

10

President of the Bank.) The importance of the destruction of the United States Bank cannot be overestimated. In no other way could the government have been rescued from the domination of the money power, which was sparing no pains to subvert the liberties of the people. John Randolph warningly said: "Charter a bank with thirty-five millions of capital; let it establish and learn its power; and then find, if you can, means to 'bell the cat.' It will be beyond your power; it will overawe your Congress, and laugh at your laws." His words were fully verified. Even Clay, who had said, in 1811, "I conceive the establishment of this bank (National Bank) as dangerous to the safety and welfare of this republic," and Webster, who had declared his hostility to bank currency repeatedly, as "one of the greatest of political evils," and "a contrivance for cheating the laboring classes of mankind," were both dragooned into the support of the United States Bank, in its application for a renewal of its charter; and all this power over the monetary and political affairs of the country was developed by the bank while it was yet in its infancy and rotten, financially, to the core.

We have dwelt at some length upon the subject of the United States Bank, because the country is now undergoing a similar ordeal. The money power is seeking to again secure control of the monetary and political affairs of the country through the instrumentality of the National Banks. The monster is now hydra-headed. Its political tools of both parties, in and out of Congress, pretend to be in favor of specie circulation—of "hard money," "honest money," etc. It is a mere pretense. If they were honestly for "hard money," and opposed to "paper money," their first step would be to suppress the paper money of the banks, because, of all forms of paper money, that is the worst and most dangerous. Benton, the great champion of hard money, could tolerate United States Treasury notes, and even voted for a bill authorizing their issue; but, unlike these hypocritical champions of hard money of the present day, he left no one in doubt in regard to his views upon the question of banks of issue. In his speech, on the Divorce of Bank and State, in 1837, he said: "Banks of circulation are banks of hazard and of failure. It is an incident of their nature. Those without circulation rarely fail. That of Venice has stood seven hundred years; those of Hamburg, Amsterdam, and others, have stood for centuries. The Bank of England, the great mother of banks of circulation, besides an actual stoppage of a quarter of a century, has had her crisis and convulsion in average periods of seven or eight years, for the last half century—in 1783, '93, '97, 1814, '19, '25, '36— and has only been saved from repeated failure by the powerful support of the British government, and profuse supplies of exchequer bills. Her numerous progeny of private and joint stock banks of circulation have had the same convulsions; and not being supported by the government, have sunk by hundreds at a time. All the banks of the United States are banks of circulation; they are all subject to the inherent dangers of that class of banks, and are, besides, subject to new dangers peculiar to themselves. From the quantity of their stock held by foreigners, the quantity of other stocks in their hands, and the current foreign balance against the United States, our paper system (bank currency) has become an appendage of that of England. * * The power of a few banks over the whole presents a new feature of danger in our system. It consolidates the banks of the whole Union into one mass, and subjects them to one fate, and that fate to be decided by a few, without even knowledge of the rest. (This was strikingly illustrated by the almost general suspension of the National Banks in 1873.) An unknown divan of bankers sends forth an edict which sweeps over the empire, crosses the lines of States with the facility of a firman, prostrating all State institutions, breaking up all engagements, and leveling all laws before it. This is a kind of consolidation which the genius of Patrick Henry had not even conceived. But while this firman is thus potent and irresistible for prostration, it is impotent and powerless for resurrection. It goes out in vain, bidding the prostrate banks to rise. A *veto* power intervenes. One voice is sufficient to keep all down; and thus we have seen one word from Philadelphia* annihilate the New York proposition for resumption and condemn the many solvent banks to the continuation of a condition as mortifying to their feelings as it is injurious to their future interests. Again from the mode of doing business among our banks—using each others notes to bank upon, instead of holding each other to weekly settlements, and liquidation of balances in specie, * * our banks have all become links of one chain, the strength of the whole being dependent on the strength of each. A few govern all. Whether it is to fail, or to resume, the few govern; and not only the few but the weak. A few weak banks fail; a panic ensues, and the rest shut up; many strong ones are ready to resume; the weak are not ready, and the strong must wait. Thus the principles of safety, and the rules of government, are reversed. The weak govern the strong; the bad govern the good; and the insolvent govern the solvent. This is our system, if system it can be called, which has no feature of consistency, no principle of safety, and which is nothing but the floating appendage of a foreign and overpowering system." Who can doubt as to where Jackson and Benton would stand to-day, if they were alive, in regard to the issue now pending, whether the government and people of the United

*See page 150.

States shall use United States Treasury notes, or National Bank notes, nominally redeemable in gold, for their circulating medium? It was impossible in Jackson's time for the administration to suppress State banks of issue, so deeply had they become rooted in the structure of American society, but everything possible was done to curtail their power for mischief. The first step taken in this direction was the publication, July 11, 1836, of the famous "specie circular," ordering agents for the sale of public lands to take nothing in payment but specie. This circular was based on a law passed in 1816, requiring the Secretary of the Treasury to take nothing but specie, Treasury notes, or the notes of specie paying banks. The notes of eastern banks at this time were sent West for a "good circulation," and "coon-box banks" were set up in the Western States, which issued notes in easy loans to land speculators.* The title to land was passing rapidly to speculators, and the treasury was being filled with worthless paper. Ten millions of bank currency of this sort was arrested by the circular on its way to the land office at Washington. The money power was highly indignant, and Congress, then as now its suppliant tool, at its next session passed a bill rescinding the circular, but it was not signed by the President and failed to become a law. This led to the establishment of the Independent Treasury system, of which more will be said hereafter. The number of specie basis banks in existence during this period were as follows:

Years.	Number.	Years.	Number.	Years.	Number.
1820	308	1835	558	1838	663
1830	330	1836	567	1839	840
1834	506	1837	634	1840	901

The country was flooded with a depreciated currency, based on "hard money," and commercial crashes and money

*History of American Currency.

panics occurred with almost as much regularity as the ebb and flow of the tides.

THE CRASH OF 1837.

In the latter part of 1836 several large failures occurred in Great Britain. This was the beginning of a crisis which convulsed both Europe and America. Early in May one bank in New York City and three in Buffalo failed. On the 10th of May all the banks in New York suspended specie payments, under a law passed by the legislature allowing them to suspend for one year. The banks throughout the country soon followed their example. The distresses of the year were aggravated by a failure of the wheat crop. The New York banks being required by law to resume May 10, 1838, contracted their circulation as rapidly as possible. It was reduced over $12,000,000, or one-half, during the year 1837. The banks of New England were in a bad condition, the best of them having only $1 in specie to redeem $11 in notes. A meeting of bank delegates in New York was called for November 27, 1837, to confer in regard to resumption, but the United States Bank refusing, the convention did not meet. The New York Banks resumed on the 10th of May, 1838, and nearly all the banks throughout the country soon followed, at least nominally, except those of Philadelphia. Towards the end of the year the Bank of England again became involved in trouble, producing the usual effect in America.

CRASH OF 1839.

On the 10th of October, 1839, the Bank of the United States closed its doors, and was followed by nearly all the banks in the South and West. The banks in New York and New England made a show of holding out, but to no purpose. According to Sumner, 343 out of 850 banks closed entirely, and 62 partially, and the government lost over $2,000,000 in deposits.

CRASH OF 1841.

An attempt was made to resume specie payments in 1841. But a run was made on the United States Bank, which had again opened, and it was compelled to finally close February 4, 1841. This led to another general suspension, followed by great distress.* Specie payments were not again resumed until March, 1842.

During all these years of banking on the specie basis system, banking operations had been carried on in the most reckless manner, without regard to personal integrity, or the laws of banking. Every possible device was resorted to by banks to put their notes in circulation, in such a way as would prevent their speedy return for redemption. Judge Kelley, in an able speech on the subject of banking, delivered at Indianapolis, in August, 1875, thus felicitously describes the manner in which this was frequently done:

"Do you know where the phrase 'carpet-bagger' came from? The younger men of our day think it was invented to describe a man from the North who went South and got an office. Oh, no; not at all. The older members of my audience will attest the truth of what I say when I state that the phrase 'carpet-bagger' arose from the fact that nearly every specie basis bank had its carpet-bagger—a fellow it sent with notes by the carpet-bag full into some distant State to get them into circulation there. If he could not buy cattle, corn, hogs or something else in which there might be a profit, he was to enter into a treaty with the carpet-bagger or other officer of some bank out there for an exchange of notes. For instance: The Frogtown bank—for I am told there were banks located occasionally in

*How this distress was relieved in Pennsylvania, see page 44.

almost impenetrable swamps, and in those days, you must remember, there were no telegraphs and but few railroads —the fellow from Frogtown would get way out into Skunktown, another almost inaccessible place, and he would effect an exchange of ten, twenty, or thirty thousand dollars of Frogtown bank notes for a like amount of Skunktown bank notes, and the Skunktown bankers would put off the Frogtown notes on their customers, and the Frogtown bankers would put off the Skunktown bank notes on theirs, and thus they would go on with this legitimate business to their common advantage. I am giving you a historic fact when I tell you that I first became acquainted with that term in designating those fellows who were traveling from one out-of-the-way place to another with a carpet-bag full of notes to exchange, so that the notes put in circulation in Skunktown couldn't find their way back to Frogtown, because the people in Skunktown didn't know where Frogtown was, and the people in Frogtown didn't know where Skunktown was —and if they did they couldn't get there; the people in one place couldn't get to the other to get the specie on which the notes were based. Then after the bank at Frogtown had paid out the Skunktown notes, the bank at Frogtown would refuse to receive the Skunktown notes, but it would send the holder, who was its debtor, around the corner to a broker, who would buy them at seven or nine per cent. discount, and then the broker and the bank would divide the proceeds of this gold basis transaction. That is a specimen of what was going on all over the country."

In referring to this period, in the same speech, Judge Kelley forcibly says: "It is usual to speak of the great crisis of 1837, but from 1832 to 1843 was one unbroken period of individual suffering, resulting from the alternating expansions and contractions of a banking system based on what it could not get, and could not have retained if it had got—gold coupled with permission to issue notes and lend money deposited for safe keeping."

In 1840 the Independent Treasury act was passed, which took from the banks the custody of the funds of the government. This act excited great indignation amongst the banks and their tools, and the next year, a new administration coming into power, Harrison having been elected President, the first step taken by Congress was to repeal it. It was re-enacted, however, in 1846, and remained in force until 1861, when it was suspended to enable the Secretary of the Treasury to deposit the funds of the government with "specie paying banks." (The Secretary of the Treasury was about to negotiate a loan of $150,000,000 from the banks of New York, Boston and Philadelphia, and the Independent Treasury act was suspended at their instance, so as to enable them to retain their gold and pay the government in bank currency; but the Secretary of the Treasury unexpectedly required the loan to be paid in specie, and, after that, there were no "specie paying banks" left in which to deposit government funds.)

The stimulus of the tariff of 1842, a great demand for breadstuffs from abroad, the introduction of foreign capital, the discovery of gold in California, and other causes combined to carry the country through from 1841 to 1857 without a commercial crash or money panic.

CRASH OF 1857.

In 1857, however, the people of Great Britain were overtaken by another of their periodical crises, which, as usual, involved the banks of the United States. The Ohio Life and Trust Company failed August 24, 1857, with liabilities to the amount of $7,000,000. Sumner says, "at this period no rule seems to have governed issues save to keep one-third of the circulation in specie, and in some States even this dwindled down to one-tenth or one-twelfth. Such a rule, however, is entirely fallacious, as any other arbitrary rule of reserve must be, and it proved in the time of trial that there was no strength to endure any shock." The New York banks, as an example of the contraction which followed, curtailed their loans from $116,000,000, August 29, 1857, to $94,500,000, November 28, 1857. The banks of Philadelphia, Washington, Baltimore, and interior towns, suspended in September, and those of New York, Boston and of the country generally, in October. Stocks fell 40 or 50 per cent., and 20,000 persons were thrown out of employment in New York City within a fortnight.* But it is unnecessary to go into details. It was the same old story over again. The people were accused of "extravagance," "over production," etc., and after "confidence" had been restored by the Sheriff, the banks started afresh.

SUSPENSION OF 1861.

In the beginning of 1861, when the great Rebellion broke out, the number of banks in the United States was about 1,600, with a circulation of over $200,000,000. Of this circulation, about three-fourths belonged to the Northern States. The specie reserve of the banks of the Northern States, kept on hand for the purposes of redemption, amounted to probably some $60,000,000. The necessities of the government becoming urgent, two loan acts were passed by Congress, during the extra session of 1861, one approved July 17th and the other August 5th. By the act of July 17th Congress authorized loans to the amount of two hundred and fifty millions of dollars, in bonds running twenty years, at not over 7 per cent. interest; in 7-30 notes running three years;

*Sumner, page 183.

or fifty millions of the amount could, at the discretion of the Secretary, be issued in the form of Treasury notes, payable on demand, without interest.* The act of Congress of August 5th authorized the Secretary of the Treasury to issue 6 per cent. bonds, running twenty years, for the purpose of funding the Treasury notes, etc., and also suspended the provision of the sub-Treasury act of 1846, "so far as to allow the Secretary of the Treasury to deposit any of the moneys obtained on any of the loans now authorized by law, to the credit of the United States, in such solvent specie paying banks as he may select." Then, to quote from Spaulding's Financial History of the War, "the banks in New York, Boston and Philadelphia most patriotically came forward and made arrangements in several negotiations with Secretary Chase to loan the government $150,000,000 under the provisions of the two loan acts passed at the extra session. Of this sum $105,000,000 was apportioned to the associated banks of New York, payable in installments. The banks were in good condition, * * and the loan to the government was made with the expectation that the money would be checked out under the direction of the Secretary, in pursuance of the sixth section (suspending the sub-Treasury act) above referred to. The Secretary of the Treasury refused to use the discretionary power conferred upon him by that section, and would not check on the banks for the expenses of the war, so that current bank notes could be paid or balances settled through the clearing house, but insisted that the banks should pay the money loaned into the sub-Treasury in gold or gold Treasury notes. * * The banks having been committed to making the loans, and having made partial advances on account of the same, were obliged to complete the loan, notwithstanding the Secretary

*These notes (known afterwards as old demand notes) were subsequently made a full legal tender and circulated at par with gold. See Chapter VI.

of the Treasury deemed it incompatible with his views of duty, and the traditions of the sub-Treasury law to use such banks as disbursing agents of the government, even under the extraordinary exigency under which the loans were made." From this it appears that when the banks "most patriotically came forward" to lend the government the sum of $150,-000,000, they confidently expected that they would be permitted to exchange bank currency for the bonds of the government, and in effect to become factors between the government and the people, in exchanging the bonds of the government for the products of industry. Had this arrangement been carried out, it is not difficult, in the light of sixty years experience with the specie basis banking system, to conjecture what would have been the result. The banks would have taken the loans of the government as fast as they were offered, and inflated their circulation to a corresponding degree. Sooner or later the inflation would have ended in a commercial crash and money panic; the banks would have suspended specie payments as usual, and the people would have found themselves with some hundreds of millions of dollars of worthless or depreciated paper on their hands—in a state of bankruptcy. Secretary Chase undoubtedly became entangled in the toils of the money power, but his action in this particular, in refusing to take anything but specie from the banks on account of their loan of $150,000,-000, was a fortunate circumstance, which led to important results. When urged to check upon the banks, instead of requiring them to pay specie, he said, "however harmless or beneficial it might be, if confined to the New York banks, it would inevitably result in a general payment and receipt for public dues of bank notes, which in turn would lead to expansion, which in turn would terminate in suspension and vast injuries to the sound banks."*

*Letter of J. E. Williams to Hon. S. P. Chase.

The banks accused the Secretary of the Treasury of acting in bad faith with them, not only in the matter of requiring them to pay specie, but in continuing to issue Treasury notes (demand notes under the act of July 17, 1861) after he had given assurances to the contrary, and a general suspension of specie payments took place on the 28th of December, 1861. A prominent banker* in speaking of this period says: "Even with all these unfavorable circumstances surrounding them (the banks), it was an encouraging fact observed by those who were anxiously watching the practical operation of this great and novel experiment, that while the circulating notes in the country were restricted, the disbursements of the government for the war were so rapid, and the consequent internal trade movement was so intense, that the coin paid out upon each installment of the loan came back to the banks, through the community, in about one week. The natural effect of this general commercial activity upon the circulating medium being to quicken its flow. After taking the third amount of fifty millions by the associated banks, those in New York who had at that time paid in of their proportion over eighty millions in all found themselves in this position:

Their aggregate coin, which on the 17th of August, before
   the first payment into the Treasury, was.....$49,733,990
Was on December 7th...................... 42,318,610

A reduction of only........................ $7,415,380
and the other two cities in like proportion."

In the latter part of 1861 gold began to flow towards Europe. This, together with the issue of demand notes, caused the specie reserve of the banks to diminish rapidly. The drain upon the New York banks in December went on at the following rate:

*Letter of Geo. S. Coe to E. G. Spaulding, Financial History of the War.

December 7, 1861, the banks had in specie.....$42,300,000
"   14,   "   "   "   39,000,000
"   21,   "   "   "   36,800,000
"   28,   "   "   "   29,300,000

After a final conference with Secretary Chase, in which he refused to abandon the course he had thus far pursued, the banks decided that it was expedient to suspend specie payments, and accordingly, as already mentioned, a general suspension took place on December 28, 1861. From this time on the specie in the New York banks began to increase again, and March 8, 1862, was $30,000,000.

The State banks continued to circulate their notes until after the National Banks were put in operation, when they were driven out of circulation by taxation. The National Banking bill became a law on the 25th of February, 1863, and on the 3d of March following an act of Congress was passed imposing a tax of one per cent. each half year, on a graduated scale, of State bank circulation, according to the capital stock of each bank. This was done for the purpose of getting the State banks of issue out of the way of the National Banks, and proved successful. Thus, after an eventful career of over half a century, during which they had inflicted incalculable injury and suffering upon the American people, the specie basis banks of issue, organized under State authority, passed away, not in a merited storm of public indignation, but quietly and stealthily at the command of the money power, to enable it to erect in their stead a more powerful and dangerous development of the same system of banking.

NATIONAL BANKS.

The National Banking system was planned shortly after Secretary Chase entered upon the duties of his office, and was recommended by him in his first annual report to Congress, December 10, 1861. It was found impossible to put the system into operation soon enough to meet the necessities of the government, and it became necessary to issue Treasury notes (greenbacks.) There is abundant reason to believe that the instigators of the National Banking system were in no particular hurry to have it put into operation. As the circulation of the National Banks was to be based on government bonds, it became an object to these conspirators, chief among whom was the Hon. John Sherman, United States Senator from Ohio, to so shape legislation as to depreciate the paper of the government and enable them to secure the bonds necessary to establish the National Banking system at the lowest possible figure. The National Banking bill, therefore, was not pressed until 1863. It was then foisted upon the country at a time when National Banks could render no possible service to either government or people—in fact, were a disadvantage, for their circulation differs in no material respect from the circulation of specie basis banks of issue, and is a breeder of inflation. The National Banking system was conceived in fraud, and its promoters, who found it to their advantage to first depreciate by legislation and then decry, as they are still doing, the paper of the government, were more dangerous, because more subtle enemies of the government, than Jefferson Davis and all his hosts. The last step in the scheme, planned by Secretary Chase and certain capitalists and politicians, is now in process of consummation. We refer to the retirement of the greenback and the resumption of specie payments, January 1, 1879. When this is accomplished the National Banks will hold the purse strings of society, and, by monopolizing the whole of the circulating medium of the country, by which all property in the country—homes, lands, debts and credits, personal and real estate of all descriptions—are valued, will render the whole community dependent upon them. John Randolph predicted, and his prediction was verified, that if a National Bank was established with a capital of $35,000,000, it would "overawe Congress and laugh at its laws." Now we have 2,000 National Banks with a capital of nearly $400,000,000. Benton characterized the unity of interest of the old State banks of issue as "a consolidation of a kind which the genius of Patrick Henry had not even conceived." The National Banking system constitutes "a consolidation" besides which the one denounced by Benton is a mere pigmy. Hamilton when he sought to found a strong government, based on an aristocracy of wealth, and to that end urged the establishment of a United States Bank modeled on the British system, never dreamed of such a consolidated power as that now constituted by 2,000 National Banks, modeled on that (the British) system.

But, apart from the dangerous power over the property and political affairs of the country, which such a system confers upon a comparatively small class of people, why should all other classes be compelled to pay the banking class interest on $400,000,000, more or less, of paper money based on bonds of the government, for which the people are responsible, when they can have a better circulating medium, *without interest*, based on precisely the same security?

The history of the National Banking system can be more clearly set forth in connection with the history of the legal tender acts, passed during the war, and with that will form the subject of the next chapter. The details of the system will be duly explained in a subsequent chapter (Chapter VII.)

CHAPTER VI.

HISTORY OF THE PAPER MONEY ISSUED DURING
THE REBELLION.

MONEY, as has been fully explained, is an important element in the production and distribution of wealth in all its forms. Without it production is slow and laborious, and the distribution of the products of industry difficult and expensive. Hence the necessity of an abundance of money based on sound principles—that is money that is free to obey the natural laws of trade, and not subject to the control of private corporations, as is the case with bank currency— to fill the channels of circulation. With a sound currency in circulation the production and accumulation of wealth would go on gradually and steadily, and commercial crashes and money panics would be unknown. Individuals would succeed or fail, as now, but it would be through natural causes. That a people can carry on commercial operations of great magnitude for centuries, by means of an enlightened system of money, without being visited once by such crises and convulsions as have marked the history of Great Britain and the United States, since the adoption of the specie basis (banks of issue) system of money, is fully demonstrated by the history of the Venetians,* and the experience of other European nations in more recent times. The weakness of the specie basis system has been most signally illustrated, however, in times of war, when great activity in both production and distribution became absolutely imperative. In the war with France, from 1793 to 1815, Great Britain was obliged to abandon a medium of exchange based on

*See Chapter IV.

specie altogether. By means of irredeemable paper money she was enabled to carry on successfully one of the most tremendous wars of modern times, and at its close the people of Great Britain were, individually and collectively, prosperous. Ignoring the teachings of experience she waded back through individual bankruptcy and ruin to the old system, and has had her commercial crashes and money panics since with the same regularity as before. If paper money is found to be so invaluable in the production and distribution of the products of industry, under the most disadvantagous circumstances, in time of war, what is to hinder it from being equally invaluable in time of peace, when no uncertainty in regard to its ability to represent value can attend its use? That the use of paper money during war is a matter of compulsion, is the merest sophistry. During the Revolutionary war, when Continental money, which can hardly be said to have been based on anything, began to grow worthless, Congress declared that those who refused to take it should be regarded as public enemies. The public smiled, and barbers papered their shops with it.* Paper money, however, undoubtedly becomes an acknowledged necessity during war especially in countries whose medium of exchange belongs to the specie basis system. In Great Britain business affairs in times of peace have to be conducted almost entirely, as we have seen,† by means of devices of the credit system, on account of the limited amount of money in circulation, and when an emergency arises, requiring great rapidity of production and distribution, both government and people find themselves without any adequate means to accomplish the ends desired.

When the Rebellion broke out in 1861, the people of the United States were in the enjoyment of unusual prosperity.

*Sumner's History of American Currency. †See page 47.

The crops had been more than ordinarily good, and the country generally was rapidly recovering from the crash of 1857. The cotton crop of 1860 had reached the enormous amount of 5,387,052 bales (of 400 lbs. each.)

The state of the banks and the currency from 1857 to 1863 was as follows:

	Circulation.	Deposits.	Loans.	Specie.
1857—	$214,700,000	$230,309,000	$684,400,000	$58,300,000
1858—	155,200,000	185,900,000	583,100,000	74,400,000
1859—	193,300,000	259,500,000	657,100,000	104,500,000
1860—	207,100,000	253,800,000	691,900,000	83,500,000
1861—	202,000,000	257,200,000	696,700,000	87,600,000
1862—	183,700,000	296,300,000	646,300,000	102,100,000
1863—	238,600,000	393,600,000	648,600,000	101,200,000

Preparations for war were begun by the Federal Government on a scale of great magnitude, with an empty Treasury. The real and personal property of the country, according to the census report of 1860, amounted to $16,159,616,068, or, leaving out the States in rebellion, to $10,957,450,961. The people of the States which sustained the Federal Government possessed ample resources and were inspired by a sincere feeling of patriotism. The only question, therefore, was as to the means by which the resources of the people could be rendered available to the government. It could of course be done only through the instrumentality of a medium of exchange.* Taxation was impracticable at the outset, because the government did not possess the machinery for laying and collecting taxes, and funds were required at once; and besides the amount of money in circulation was insignificant as compared with the wants of the government. There was manifestly but one of two courses to pursue. Either to adopt the machinery of the banks and through them exchange the credit of the government for the products of industry, or deal directly with the

*Read in this connection page 62, also pages 70, 71, 72 and 73.

people by issuing legal tender Treasury notes, based on and representing the wealth of the country and redeemable in the revenues of the government. Neither course, however, was pursued, or rather the Secretary of the Treasury attempted to use both plans in part, and with the most wretched results.

THE FIRST LOAN ACTS.

During the extra session of Congress in July and August, 1861, two important loan acts were passed, which are deserving of special notice, one approved July 17th and the other August 5th. By the act of July 17th the Secretary of the Treasury was authorized to borrow $250,000,000, for which he was authorized to issue coupon bonds or registered bonds or Treasury notes in such proportions of each as he might deem advisable. The bonds were to bear interest not exceeding seven per cent. per annum, payable semi-annually, and to run for twenty years, when they would be redeemable at the pleasure of the United States; and the Treasury notes were to be issued in denominations of not less than $50, payable three years after date, with interest at 7 3-10 per cent., payable semi-annually, and exchangeable at any time for twenty years six per cent. bonds. Or, at his option, the Secretary of the Treasury might issue $50,000,000 of the above loan in Treasury notes, payable on demand, in denominations of not less than ten dollars each, without interest, and made payable for salaries and other dues from the United States Treasury (afterwards known as old demand notes); or he might issue Treasury notes, payable in one year from date, bearing interest at 3 65-100 per cent. per annum, exchangeable at any time in sums of $100, or upwards, for three year Treasury notes bearing 7 3-10 interest. By the act of August 5th, which was supplementary to the act of July 17th, the Secretary of the Treasury was authorized to issue bonds bearing interest at six per cent. per annum, payable after twenty years from date, which, in denominations not less than $500, might be exchanged for Treasury notes bearing 7 3-10 per cent. interest. The act of July 17th, fixing the denomination of the Treasury notes without interest (demand notes) at not less than ten dollars was modified so as to fix the limit at not less than five dollars, and these notes (demand notes) were *made receivable in payment of public dues.* By the sixth section of this act the Sub-Treasury act of 1846 was "suspended so far as to allow the Secretary of the Treasury *to deposit any of the moneys* obtained on any of the loans now authorized by law, to the credit of the Treasurer of the United States, *in such solvent specie paying banks as he may select.*' By an act of Congress approved February 12, 1862, the Secretary of the Treasury was authorized to issue $10,000,000 of Treasury notes, payable on demand, not bearing interest, in addition to the $50,000,000 of like notes authorized by acts of July 17th and August 5th, 1861, which should be deemed part of the loan of $250,000,000 authorized by said acts. And by the act of March 17, 1862, it was enacted that these demand notes ($60,000,000 in all) *shall, in addition to being receivable in payment of duties on imports, be receivable, and shall be lawful money and a legal tender*, in like manner and for the same purposes and to the same extent as the notes (greenbacks) authorized by the act approved February 25, 1862. These demand notes were the only notes issued during the war that were made a full legal tender, that is, receivable for all public dues (including duties on imports) and a tender for private debts. After they were made a full legal tender they circulated at par and went up with gold to a premium of $2.85, or in other words it cost $2.85 in greenbacks to buy a dollar in gold or demand notes.

From these acts of Congress it appears that Secretary Chase was clothed with the most ample powers to borrow money. He immediately proceeded to New York and, on the 9th of August, 1861, held a consultation with a number of leading bankers and capitalists of the cities of New York, Boston and Philadelphia, whom he met there by appointment. It was suggested on the part of the banks, that the banks of the North should form an "organization that would combine them into an efficient and inseparable body, for the purpose of advancing the capital of the country upon government bonds in large amounts, and through their clearing house facilities and other well known expedients, to distribute them in smaller sums among the people in a manner that would secure active co-operation among the members in this special work, while in all other respects each bank could pursue its independent business. This suggestion," says Mr. Coe, from whom we quote,* "met the hearty approbation of the assembled company, and arrested the earnest attention of the Secretary. At his request it was presented to the consideration of the banks at a meeting called for that purpose at the American Exchange Bank on the following day, and was so far entertained as to secure the appointment of a committee of ten bank officers, to give it form and coherence. The committee convened at the Bank of Commerce, whose officers zealously united in the effort, and a plan was reported unanimously. It may be found, with the names of the committee, in the Bankers' Magazine of September, 1861. This report was cordially accepted and adopted by the banks in New York, those in Boston and Philadelphia being represented at the meeting and as zealously and cordially united in the organization. It was greatly desired to include also the banks of the West,

*Letter of Geo. S. Coe, Esq.: Spaulding's Financial History of the War. Apx. p. 90.

but it was found impracticable to secure the co-operation of the State banks of Ohio and Indiana, and the State banks of Missouri, the only other organization under a compacted system, were surrounded by combatants. It was at once unanimously agreed that the associated banks of the three cities would take fifty millions of 7 3-10 notes at par, with the privilege of an additional fifty millions in sixty days, and a further amount of fifty millions in sixty more, making $150,000,000 in all, and offer them to the people of the country at the same price, without change."

The amount of specie held by the banks of the three cities at this time was as follows:

Banks of New York	....	$49,733,990
" Boston	....	6,665,929
" Philadelphia	....	6,765,120
		$63,165,039

The Treasury notes could not be delivered at once, as time was required for their preparation and execution. It was manifestly impossible, therefore, for the banks to advance the several amounts of the loan, in specie, without danger of exhausting their reserve. The Sub-Treasury act, as we have seen, however, had been suspended, evidently at the instance of the banks, with a view to enabling them to handle the bonds and securities of the government, in return for bank currency. "Accordingly," says Mr. Coe, from whom we have just quoted, "it was at once proposed to the Secretary that he should suspend the operations of the Sub-Treasury act in respect to these transactions, and following the course of commercial business, that he should draw checks upon some one bank in each city representing the association, in small sums as required, in disbursing the money thus advanced. By this means his checks would serve the purpose of a circulating medium, continually redeemed, and the exchange of capital and industry be best promoted. * * To the astonishment of the committee, Mr. Chase refused." It was urged by the bankers that the Sub-Treasury act had been suspended for this very purpose, but Mr. Chase thought differently, declaring that it had no such meaning or intent. Another subject of discussion between the banks and the Secretary was the issue of demand notes. A small amount of these notes had already been emitted, and a resolution requesting the Secretary to refrain from issuing any more, until all other means had been exhausted, had been adopted by the associated banks. Mr. Coe says that the Secretary gave assurances of his acquiescence in this suggestion, but refused "to openly pledge himself not to exercise a power conferred by law," and "that with this understanding the banks began their work, paying into the treasury in coin $150,000,000, in sums at the rate of about $5,000,000 at intervals of six days." The rapid disbursements by the government, and the intense activity of the movements of trade, as we have seen,* brought the coin nearly all back to the banks within a week after it was issued, so that in December the banks of New York, after paying to the government over $80,000,000, found their specie reserve reduced only from $49,733,990, August 17th, to $42,318,619, December 7th. The banks undoubtedly expected that sooner or later Secretary Chase could be induced to accede to their plan, but, as he continued to issue the demand notes, it became apparent in the latter part of December, 1861, after the banks had paid in a large portion of their loan, that the Secretary was determined to adhere to his own course; and after a conference, in which he expressed himself to that effect, the banks decided that it was expedient to suspend specie payments

*See page 157.

forthwith, and did so on the 28th of the month. The balance of the loan was paid by the banks principally in Treasury notes, and was finally closed on the 3rd of February, 1862.

The patriotism of the banks oozed out as soon as they found that they could not control Secretary Chase in their interests. After they had succeeded in paying the greater part of their loan without any material diminution of their specie, there was manifestly no good reason why they should suspend specie payments, other than on account of the inherent weakness of the specie basis system. Their circulation did not exceed $140,000,000, and their specie reserve was unusually large, about $60,000,000. The suspension complicated matters greatly. With irredeemable bank paper and demand notes of the government promising to pay specie, when it had no specie, filling the channels of circulation, gold of course began to command a premium.* Had Secretary Chase adopted the plan of the banks, the securities of the government could unquestionably have been handled by them during the first part of the war with advantage to the government. In that event the government should have issued no paper currency. But the result would undoubtedly have been disastrous in the end. The expenses of the government soon reached $2,000,000 a day. To meet the necessities of the government, the banks would have been obliged to inflate their circulation to an alarming extent. The first financial breeze that sprung up would have occasioned a panic; the banks would have been obliged to suspend, as they had done nine times before during their brief existence, and most probably, too, at a critical period of the war, which could not fail to have resulted in great distress and general demoralization, to the great peril of the government. Secretary Chase seemed to apprehend the danger of adopting

*A table showing the monthly range of gold, from 1862 to 1876, will be found in the Appendix.

the plan suggested by the associated banks, but in all other respects he proved himself utterly incompetent as a Minister of Finance. When he renounced the machinery of the banking system, instead of urging upon Congress the necessity of adopting at once the full legal tender money system, and devising a judicious system of taxation, *he recommended the establishment of the National Banking system.* The inconsistency of his action in this respect cannot fail to strike the reader, when it is considered that the National Banking system differs in no essential particular from the State Banking system, which he had just rejected, except that its notes instead of being secured by State bonds, as in the case of the banks of New York, were to be secured by bonds of the Federal Government.

When Congress convened, December 2, 1861, the paramount question was that relating to the finances of the Federal Government. The people of the Northern States possessed unlimited resources, were animated by feelings of devoted patriotism, and were willing to assume any burdens in the shape of taxation, or otherwise, that Congress might deem necessary to impose for the legitimate prosecution of the war for the preservation of the Union. It simply devolved upon Congress to devise the ways and means to render the resources of the nation available to the government. As this could be done only through the instrumentality of a medium of exchange, it was the first duty of Congress to see that the channels of trade were supplied with a sufficient amount of money to develop the producing forces of the nation to their utmost capacity, and enable the people to respond to the requirements of the government. It was manifest that the banks could not be relied upon for that purpose with any degree of certainty or safety. There was, therefore, no other alternative but for Congress, by virtue of the sovereign prerogative inherent in the people, and as their representative duly authorized by the Constitution, to issue full legal tender Treasury notes, not bearing interest. The reason of this is obvious. The chief end desired was *to create a circulating medium of exchange*, and this end could be accomplished only by issuing Treasury notes in a form that would enable them to perform the functions and serve the purposes of money.

TREASURY NOTE BEARING INTEREST AND NOT A LEGAL TENDER.

And here it is proper to call attention to the difference between an ordinary Treasury note, bearing interest and not a legal tender, and a full legal tender Treasury note, not bearing interest. They are both based on the wealth and credit of the nation, but there the similitude ends. A Treasury note, bearing interest and not a legal tender, is simply an evidence or security of indebtedness, and differs from a bond only in form. It does not possess the attributes, nor can it perform the functions, of money. A creditor of the government may be obliged to take it at its face value or wait an indefinite time for his money; but, as it is not a legal tender, no one else is obliged to receive it at the value inscribed on its face. By its nature it is nothing more than a security in which to invest money, and is not designed or calculated to serve the purposes of a medium of exchange. The fact that it bears interest is a disadvantage to it as a medium of exchange, because in the ordinary transactions of life people cannot stop to reckon interest every time it changes hands; and the fact that it is a partial legal tender (payable for certain dues or taxes to the government) leads those who have such duties to pay to decry its value in order that they may purchase it at a depreciation. It is on the same principle that the greenback is decried by the bullionists, because they have gold to sell, and it is to their advantage to buy greenbacks (with gold) as cheaply as possible.

FULL LEGAL TENDER TREASURY NOTE, NOT BEARING INTEREST.

On the other hand a Treasury note, not bearing interest, cannot be used as a security in which to invest money. Like money (made of gold or silver) it is of no use to the possessor until it is parted with.* If only a partial legal tender (receivable for certain dues to the government), it is to the interest of many, as already mentioned, to decry its value, in order to obtain it as cheaply as possible. If the government obliges its creditors to take it at its face value, and it is not a legal tender in payment of debts, no one else is obliged to receive it at the same value, or indeed to receive it at all. While it is then the same as money as between the government and its creditor, it is quite a different thing between the creditor and the public. This is manifestly unjust. Treasury notes are issued by the people in their collective capacity, through the agency of the government, and, unless simply intended as an interest bearing security, not designed to perform the functions of money, ought clearly to be made a legal tender for private debts as well as public dues, otherwise it places it in the power of the public to repudiate individually what they have done collectively, and the people do not all stand on the same platform with respect to the government or to each other. The Treasury note, therefore, in this form (a legal tender and not bearing interest) constitutes a peculiar form of indebtedness or credit, which serves all the purposes of a medium of exchange and enables the government to draw upon the resources of the people in *advance of taxation*,

*See page 30.

bearing equally upon every individual in the nation. The bullionists and their organs, in their efforts to decry the legal tender Treasury note and deceive the public, are constantly asserting that it costs the government nothing more than the expense of printing, and is, therefore, worthless. This is not a mere fallacy—it is a willful perversion of the truth. Every dollar of legal tender paper money issued by the government costs the people precisely one dollar's worth of property or labor. A dollar greenback is put in circulation by the government for value received in property or services; it passes from hand to hand, commanding a dollar's worth of property or services every time it is used as a medium of exchange; until finally it is returned to the Federal Treasury in the shape of taxation or revenue.

On the 5th of December, 1861, the Committee of Ways and Means was organized as follows:

THADDEUS STEVENS, of Penn., Chairman.
JUSTIN S. MORRILL, of Vt.   JOHN S. PHELPS, of Mo.
E. G. SPAULDING, of N. Y.   V. B. HORTON, of Ohio.
ERASTUS CORNING, of N. Y.   SAMUEL HOOPER, of Mass.
HORACE MAYNARD, of Tenn.   J. L. N. SHATTON, of N. Y.

SECRETARY CHASE'S REPORT.

On the 10th of December, 1861, the Secretary of the Treasury submitted his annual report to Congress. He set forth in strong terms the weakness and disadvantages of the banking system of the country, and expressed the belief that the emission of bills of credit by state banks was in violation of the spirit, if not the letter, of the Constitution. He said: "It has been well questioned by the most eminent statesmen whether a currency of bank notes, issued by local institutions under State laws, is not in fact prohibited by the national Constitution. Such emission certainly falls within the spirit, if not within the letter, of the constitutional prohibition of the emission of 'bills of credit' by the States, and of the making by them of anything except gold and silver coin a legal tender in payment of debts. However this may be, it is too clear to be reasonably disputed, that Congress, under its constitutional power to lay taxes, to regulate commerce, and to regulate the value of coin, possesses ample authority to control the credit circulation which enters so largely into the transactions of commerce, and affects in so many ways the value of coin. In the judgment of the Secretary, the time has arrived when Congress should exercise this power. * *   Two plans for effecting this object are suggested. The first contemplates the gradual withdrawal from circulation of the notes of private corporations, and for the issue, in their stead, of United States notes, payable in coin on demand, in amounts sufficient for the useful ends of a representative currency. The second contemplates the preparation and delivery, to institutions and associations, of notes prepared for circulation under national direction, and to be secured, as to prompt convertibility into coin, by the pledge of United States bonds and other needful regulations."

The Secretary then proceeds to say, that the first of these plans was partially adopted by Congress during the extra session in July and August, in authorizing the issue of $50,000,000 of demand notes, and after suggesting some of the advantages and disadvantages of the plan, concludes by declaring "that he feels himself constrained to forbear recommending its adoption." The principal features of the second plan are presented by the Secretary as follows: "First, a circulation of notes bearing a common impression and authenticated by a common authority: Second, the redemption of these notes by the associations and institutions to which they may be delivered for issue; and, third, the security of that redemption by the pledge of United States stocks, and an adequate provision of specie." After eulogizing the plan,* he adds: "The Secretary entertains the opinion that if a credit circulation in any form be desirable, it is most desirable in this."

THE LEGAL TENDER ACTS.

The Committee of Ways and Means appointed a sub-committee, consisting of Messrs. Spaulding, Hooper and Corning, on the proposed National Bank currency, the issue of Treasury notes and bonds, and the mode of raising means to carry on the war. The chairman of the sub-committee, Mr. Spaulding, prepared a National Bank currency bill by the end of the month (December), and also drafted a legal tender Treasury note section, to be added to the bank bill, for the issue of Treasury notes to be used while the bank bill was being put in operation throughout the country. In his Financial History of the War, Mr. Spaulding says that, "upon more mature consideration and further examination, he came to the conclusion that the bank bill, containing sixty sections, could not, with the State Banks opposed to it, be passed through both Houses of Congress for several months, and that so long a delay would be fatal to the Union cause. * * He, therefore, changed the legal tender section intended originally to accompany the bank bill into a separate bill, with alterations and additions, and on his own motion introduced it into the House by unanimous consent on the 30th of December, 1861." The bill was duly considered by the Committee of Ways and Means, and, on the 7th of January, 1862, was reported from the committee to the House.

The original bill offered by Mr. Spaulding authorized the Secretary of the Treasury "to issue on the credit of the

*See Chapter VII. on National Banks.

United States $100,000,000 of Treasury notes, not bearing interest, payable generally, without specifying any place or time of payment, and of such denominations as he may deem expedient, not less than five dollars each; and such notes, and all other Treasury notes payable on demand, not bearing interest, that have been heretofore authorized to be issued, shall be receivable for all debts and demands due to the United States, and for all salaries, dues, debts and demands owing by the United States to individuals, corporations and associations within the United States; and shall also be lawful money, and a legal tender in payment of all debts, public and private, within the United States, and shall be exchangeable in sums not less than one hundred dollars, at any time, at their par value, at the Treasury of the United States, * * for any of the six per cent. twenty years coupon or registered bonds which the Secretary of the Treasury is now, or may hereafter be, authorized to issue; and such Treasury notes shall be received the same as coin at their par value, in payment for any bonds that may be hereafter negotiated by the Secretary of the Treasury; and such Treasury notes may be re-issued from time to time, as the exigency of the public service may require."

This bill was no sooner made public, than delegations of bankers from New York, Boston and Philadelphia hurried to Washington to oppose it. They organized in a formal manner by the selection of a chairman (S. A. Mercer, of Philadelphia), and invited the Finance Committee of the Senate, and the Committee of Ways and Means of the House, to meet them at the office of the Secretary of the Treasury, January 11, 1862. The invitation was accepted. At the meeting which followed, the bankers spoke in opposition to the bill, and submitted the following plan for raising money:

"1. A tax bill to raise $125,000,000 over and above duties on imports by taxation.

2. Not to issue any demand Treasury notes, except those authorized at the extra session in July last.

3. Issue $100,000,000 Treasury notes at two years, in sums of five dollars and upwards, to be receivable for public dues to the government, except duties on imports.

4. A suspension of the Sub-Treasury act, so as to allow the banks to become depositories of the government of all loans, and to check on the banks from time to time as the government may want money.

5. Issue six per cent. twenty year bonds, to be negotiated by the Secretary of the Treasury, and *without any limitation as to the price he may obtain for them in the market.*

6. That the Secretary of the Treasury be empowered to make temporary loans to the extent of any portion of the funded stock authorized by Congress, with power to hypothecate such stock, and if such loans are not paid at maturity, *to sell the stock hypothecated for the best market price that can be obtained.*"

Mr. Spaulding says that "these propositions having been read, the Secretary and Finance Committees of the Senate and House expressed themselves favorable to the first proposition to raise by taxation $125,000,000 a year, over and above duties on imports. It will be observed that this plan did not include the national currency bank bill recommended by the Secretary of the Treasury in his annual report, and was not, therefore, in this respect satisfactory to him. The meeting was somewhat conversational in character, but there appeared to be a general dissent by the Secretary and committees from all other propositions. * * The only remarks that I (Mr. Spaulding) can find reported as being made by any member of the committees of the Senate and House are in the New York *Tribune*, January 13, 1862, in substance as follows:

"'The Sub-Committee of Ways and Means, through Mr. Spaulding, objected to any and every form of "shinning" by government through Wall or State streets, to begin with; objected to the knocking down of government stocks to seventy-five or sixty cents on the dollar, the inevitable result of throwing a new and large loan on the market, *without limitation as to price;* claimed for Treasury notes as much virtue of par value as the notes of banks which have suspended specie payments, but which yet circulated in the trade of the North; and finished with firmly refusing to assent to any scheme which should permit a speculation by brokers, bankers, and others, in the government securities, and particularly any scheme which should double the public debt of the country, and double the expenses, by damaging the credit of the government to the extent of sending it to "shin" through the shaving shops of New York, Boston and Philadelphia. He affirmed his conviction as a banker and legislator, that it was the lawful policy, as well as the manifest duty of the government in the present exigency, to legalize as tender its fifty million issue of demand Treasury notes, authorized at the extra session in July last, and to add to this stock of legal tender immediately, etc.'" The conference adjourned without agreeing upon any plan or arrangement. The bank delegates, however, remained in Washington, and held further consultations with Secretary Chase, extending through several days, which resulted in an arrangement with him to the effect, amongst other things, that Congress should be urged to pass the National Bank bill, and that the amount of the demand notes should not be increased beyond the

$50,000,000 authorized by the act of July, 1861, and also that Congress should be urged to extend the provisions of the existing loan acts, so as to enable the Secretary of the Treasury to exchange interest bearing Treasury notes for the demand notes, not bearing interest, and get them out of the way.

Thus while the masses were exerting every energy to sustain the government, the money power was plotting to get control of its finances, in order that it might be enabled to prey upon the people in the hour of their extremity. How well it succeeded will duly appear.

On the 22d of January the legal tender bill was again reported from the Committee of Ways and Means, with an additional section authorizing the Secretary of the Treasury to issue, on the credit of the United States, coupon bonds or registered bonds to an amount not exceeding $500,000,000, and redeemable at the pleasure of the government, after twenty years from date, and bearing interest at six per cent. per annum, payable semi-annually, to enable the Secretary of the Treasury to fund the Treasury notes and floating debt of the United States; and it was made the special order for the 28th day of the month. The debate on the bill accordingly began on that day, and was opened by Mr. Spaulding in an able argument in its favor. The debate, which continued until the 6th day of February, when the bill passed the House, with some slight modifications, was characterized by unusual ability. It had never before, in the history of the government, been deemed necessary to issue Treasury notes, in the legal tender form, not bearing interest, to enable them to circulate as a medium of exchange and perform the functions of money, and there was naturally a great diversity of opinion upon the subject. Several substitutes and amendments were offered, most of them in the interest of the money power. The views held by those who advocated the use of Treasury notes, but honestly opposed the legal tender feature, as an infraction of the Constitution, were embodied in a substitute offered by Mr. Vallandigham, and were supported by able speeches, especially that delivered by Mr. Pendleton, of Ohio. Mr. Vallandigham's substitute provided for the same issue of notes as the original bill, but not made a legal tender, and instead of making them payable in coin on demand, they were to be simply receivable for all public dues. In this particular (making them receivable for public dues instead of payable in coin on demand), the substitute was preferable to the original bill. A Treasury note, properly understood, is "a promise to receive" and not "a promise to pay,"* and making it redeemable in coin could add nothing to its value, but under the circumstances was calculated only to depreciate its value, because it misled the public, especially professors of political economy. The following extracts from the speech of the Hon. Thaddeus Stevens in support of the bill, will sufficiently explain the nature and character of the substitutes and amendments offered, and, also, of the arguments employed for and against them, as well as the bill itself. Mr. Stevens said:

"The Secretary of the Treasury, in his report, recommended a scheme to produce a uniform national currency, and furnish a market for government bonds. It proposes that the banks shall receive their circulation from the government to the amount of government bonds pledged, with the Treasury for their security; and that no more notes should be issued than the par value of such bonds, and should be redeemed by the banks. As a general system of banking in ordinary times, it might be very useful in regulating the currency, and by the sale of bonds the govern-

See pages 52 & 58.

ment might command coin. But while the banks are in suspension, it is not easy to see how it would relieve the government. If the notes were procured it must be by accepting payment by the government in depreciated circulation. How would that be any better than the government's own notes? The security of the government is equal to that of the banks, and would give as much currency. To the banks I can see its advantage. They would have the whole benefit of the circulation without interest, and at the same time would draw interest on the government bonds from the time they got the notes. Now, it is very plain, that if the United States issued those notes direct, they would have the benefit of the whole circulation. In other words, it would be equal to a loan, without interest, to the full amount of the circulation. This project, therefore, however desirable as a banking system, could afford no immediate relief, especially as it would afford no sale for additional bonds, as the banks have already as many as would form the basis of their operations. Having, as I think, shown the impossibility of carrying on the government in any other way, let us briefly notice some of the objections to it. First, is it constitutional?

"The power to emit bills of credit and make them a legal tender is nowhere expressly given in the Constitution; but it is known that but few of the acts which government can perform are specified in that instrument. It would require a volume larger than the Pandects of Justinian or the Code of Napoleon to make such enumeration, whereas our Constitution has but a few pages. But everything necessary to carry out the granted powers of the government is not only implied but expressly given to Congress. If nothing could be done by Congress except what is enumerated in the Constitution, the government could not live a week.

"The States are prohibited from making anything but 'gold and silver coin a tender in the payment of debts;' but such prohibition does not extend to Congress. The Constitution is silent as to the power of Congress over that subject. The whole question of the right to emit bills of credit by Congress was considered in the convention that framed the Constitution. It was reported as a part of the power to 'borrow money.' It was objected to as tending to make a paper currency with legal tender, and a motion was made to strike it out and insert an express prohibition. This was resisted, because, as Mr. Mason said, 'it could not be foreseen what the necessities of the government might at some time require.' 'The late war,' he said, 'could not have been carried on had such prohibition existed.' It was finally agreed to strike out the express power, and not insert the prohibition, leaving it to the exigencies of the times to determine its necessity." * *

"If constitutional, is it expedient? It is objected by the gentleman from Ohio that the legal tender clause would depreciate the notes. All admit the necessity of the issue. But some object to their being made money. It is not easy to perceive how notes issued without being made immediately payable in specie can be made any worse by making them a legal tender. And yet that is the whole argument so far as expediency is concerned. Other gentlemen argued that this would impair contracts by making a debt payable in other money than that which existed at the time of the contract, and would so be unconstitutional. Where do gentlemen find any prohibition on Congress against passing laws impairing contracts? There is none, though it would be unjust to do it. But this impairs no contract. All contracts are made not only with a view to present laws, but subject to the future legislation of the country. We have more than once changed the value of coin. Neither our gold nor silver coin is as valuable as it was fifty years ago. Congress in 1853, I believe, regulated the weight and value of silver. They debased it over seven per cent. and made it a legal tender. Who ever pretended that that was unconstitutional? The gentlemen from Vermont [Mr. Morrill] and Ohio [Mr. Pendleton] think it an *ex post facto* law. It is not wonderful that my distinguished colleague, not being a professional lawyer, should not be aware that the *ex post facto* laws prohibited by the Constitution refer only to crimes and misdemeanors, and not to civil contracts. The gentleman from Ohio no doubt knew but forgot it." * *

"I know the danger of granting to irresponsible institutions or individuals the right to issue paper currency not immediately convertible, because their avarice would always abuse the privilege and over issue. But when the government thus issues, the fault and the crime is theirs if they do not restrain it within proper bounds. Is the proposed issue of $150,000,000 too much? It is believed that the ordinary business of the country, especially now, requires a circulation of $400,000,000. The bank circulation has been about $200,000,000, with coin to the amount of $250,000,000. The bank paper, now in suspension, would largely disappear before this par paper; and during suspension, which means during the war, there will be but little coin circulation. If the whole $150,000,000 of United States notes could be kept circulating, I do not think the surviving bank paper would furnish a sufficient currency for commercial purposes —some coin must be added. But it is not probable that it could all be kept out; much would rest in banks, in the pockets of private individuals, or await investment temporarily, at least, for a while.

"But my distinguished colleague from Vermont fears that

enormous issues would follow to supply the expenses of the war. I do not think any more would be needed than the $150,000,000. The notes bear no interest. No one would seek them for investment. In the rapid circulation of money, $100 in a year is turned so often as to purchase ten times its value. This money would soon lodge in large quantities with the capitalists and banks, who *must* take them. But the instinct of gain, perhaps I may call it avarice, would not allow them to keep it long unproductive. A dollar in a miser's safe unproductive is a sore disturbance. Where could they invest it? In United States loans at six per cent., redeemable in gold in twenty years, the best and most valuable permanent investment that could be desired. The government would thus again possess such notes in exchange for bonds, and again reissue them. I have no doubt that thus the $500,000,000 of bonds authorized would be absorbed in less time than would be needed by the government; and thus $150,000,000 would do the work of $500,000,000 of bonds. When further loans are wanted, you need only authorize the sale of more bonds; the same $150,000,000 of notes will be ready to take them.

"I contend that this currency will be better than any this country can produce. Bank notes are merely local. The holder of them in St. Louis, wishing to transmit to New York, must pay a discount of from one to ten per cent. If he has gold, the cost of transportation is considerable. If he travel, it is cumbersome. But if he has United States par notes, he can send them without cost all over the Union.

"Gentlemen are clamorous in favor of those who have debts due them, lest the debtor should the more easily pay his debt. I do not much sympathize with such importunate money lenders. But widows and orphans are interested, and in tears lest their estate should be badly invested. I pity no one who has his money invested in United States bonds, payable in gold in twenty years, with interest semi-annually.

"But while these men have agonized bowels over the rich man's cause, they have no pity for the poor widow, the suffering soldier, the wounded martyr to his country's good, who must receive these notes without legal tender or nothing, and who must give half of it to the Shylocks to get the necessaries of life. Sir, I wish no injury to any, nor with our bill could any happen; but if any must lose, let it not be the soldier, the mechanic, the laborer, and the farmer.

"Let me restate the various projects. Ours proposes United States notes, secured at the end of twenty years to be paid in coin, and the interest raised by taxation, semi-annually; such notes to be money, and of uniform value throughout the Union. No better investment, in my judgment, can be had; no better currency can be invented.

"The amendment of the gentleman from Ohio [Mr. Vallandigham] proposes the same issue of notes, but objects to a legal tender; but does not provide for their redemption on demand in coin. He fears our notes would depreciate. Let him who is sharp enough to see it instruct me how notes that every man must take are worth less than the same notes that no man need take, and few would, being irredeemable on demand. But he doubts its constitutionality. He who admits our power to emit bills of credit, nowhere expressly authorized by the Constitution, is a sharp and unreasonable doubter when he denies the power to make them a legal tender.

"The proposition of the gentleman from New York [Mr. Roscoe Conkling] authorizes the issuing of seven per cent. bonds, payable in thirty one years, to be sold ($250,000,000 of it) or exchanged for the *currency* of the banks of Boston, New York and Philadelphia.

"Sir, this proposition seems to me to lack every element of wise legislation. Make a loan payable in irredeemable currency, and pay that in its depreciated condition to our contractors, soldiers, and creditors generally! The banks would issue unlimited amounts of what would become trash, and buy good hard money bonds of the nation. Was there ever such a tempation to swindle?

"He further proposes to issue $200,000,000 United States notes, redeemable in coin in one year. Does not the gentleman know that such notes must be dishonored, and the plighted faith of the government broken? No one believes that we could then pay them, and it would run down at once. If we are to use suspended notes to pay our expenses, why not use our own? Are they not as safe as bank notes? During the suspension the government would have the benfit of the whole circulation, without interest, until they were funded—that is, the interest of all we could keep out would accrue to the government. If the $150,000,000 were constantly afloat, it would be a loan to the government, without interest, to that amount, $9,000,000 a year. But if we used the suspended paper of the banks our bonds would bear interest from the instant we got their notes—a good thing for the suspended banks. Besides, government would have the benefit of all the lost and destroyed notes—a considerable item.

"Last comes the substitute of the minority of the committee. I look upon it as a curiosity. It proposes to issue United States notes, not a legal tender, bearing an interest of three and sixty-five hundredths per cent., and fundable into seven and three-tenths per cent. bonds, but not payable on demand, but at the pleasure of the United States. This gives one and three-tenths per cent. higher interest than our loan, and not being redeemable on demand, would fare the fate of all non-specie paying notes not a legal tender. But the ingenious minority have invented a kind of currency never before known—*a circulation bearing interest*. Bonds or notes intended for investments bear interest, but no one expects they will be used as currency; whether in the shape of bonds or notes they will be used only as investments, or as pledges on which to procure loans. Suppose a tailor, shoemaker, or other mechanic or laborer, were to take one of these bills, and in a week he should wish to use it in market, or store, or elsewhere, he must sit down and calculate the interest on the days he has had it to find its value. This would be rather inconvenient in a frosty day. This currency would make it necessary for every man to carry an arithmetic or interest table with which to gauge the value of the circulating medium. Gentlemen must see how ridiculous, if not impracticable, this scheme is.

"Here, then, in a few words lies your choice. Throw bonds at six or seven per cent. on the market between this and December, enough to raise at least $600,000,000—about this sum is already appropriated, $557,000,000—or issue United States notes, not redeemable in coin, but fundable in specie paying bonds at twenty years; such notes either to be made a legal tender, or to take their chance of circulation by the voluntary act of the people.

"I maintain that the highest sum you could sell your bonds at would be seventy-five per cent., payable in currency itself at a discount. That would produce a loss which no nation or individual doing a large business could stand a year.

"I contend that I have shown that such issue, without being made money, must immediately depreciate, and would go on from bad to worse. I flatter myself that I have demonstrated, both from reason and undoubted authority, that such notes, made a legal tender and not issued in excess of the demand, will remain at par and pass in all transactions, great and small, at the full value of their face; that we shall have one currency for all sections of the country and for every class of people, the poor as well as the rich.

"Some gentlemen are as much frightened as if this were an unwonted apparition, for the first time prowling forth to swallow the rich creditor and nurse the poor debtor. No nation, it is said, has ever tried anything like it."   *   *

"Mr. Chairman, let me say in conclusion that unless this bill is to pass with the legal tender clause in it, it is not desirable to its friends or to the administration that it should pass at all, and those who think as I do will have to vote against it if it shall be thus mutilated and emasculated. If it is to be defeated, I should be glad if we had the power which they have in the British Parliament—to resign our places on the Committee of Ways and Means and leave it to those who oppose this bill to mature some other measure. So far as I am concerned, I shall be modest enough not to attempt any other scheme. The Committee of Ways and Means have labored in the preparation of this measure anxiously and to the best of their poor abilities. We are not infallible. We do not come near it. I am but poorly qualified for anything of this kind. But we have given it our most anxious consideration, and have consulted those whom we believed to be the best qualified to advise us. We have sought to harmonize conflicting views in the substitute which the majority of the committee have prepared, and we hope it will pass. We believe that the credit of the country will be sustained by it, that under it all classes will be paid in money which all classes can use, and that it will confer no advantage on the capitalist over the poor laboring man.

If this bill shall pass, I shall hail it as the most auspicious measure of this Congress; if it should fail, the result will be more deplorable than any disaster which could befall us."

Mr. Stevens' speech closed the debate, and the bill came up for final action in the House, February 6, 1862, and was adopted by a vote of 93 to 59.

THE LEGAL TENDER BILL IN THE SENATE.

On the 10th day of February, 1862, Mr. Fessenden, Chairman of the Committee on Finance in the Senate, reported the House bill from the Finance Committee with amendments. The important amendments were as follows:

1. That the legal tender notes should be receivable for all claims and demands against the United States of every kind whatever, "*except for interest on bonds and notes, which shall be paid in coin.*"

2. That the Secretary might dispose of United States bonds "*at the market value thereof, for coin or Treasury notes.*"

3. A new section, No. 4, authorizing deposits in the Sub-Treasuries at five per cent., for not less than thirty days, to the amount of $25,000,000, for which certificates of deposit might be issued.

4. An additional section, No. 5, "that all duties on imported goods, and proceeds of the sale of public lands," etc., should be set apart to pay coin interest on the debt of the United States; and one per cent. for a sinking fund, etc.

On the 12th day of February, 1862, the debate in the Senate was opened by Mr. Fessenden in a lengthy speech. A motion was made by Mr. Collamer to strike out the legal tender clause, which was lost. On the 14th inst. the bill, as amended, passed the Senate by a vote of 30 to 7, and was returned to the House.

THE BILL AGAIN IN THE HOUSE.

On the 18th, Mr. Stevens reported the bill, as amended by the Senate, from the Committee of Ways and Means to the House, and said, "I have no purpose of considering the bill at this time. I desire that it shall be referred to the Committee of the Whole, and be made the special order for to-morrow at one o'clock. I hope gentlemen of the House will read the amendments. *They are very important, and, in my judgment, very pernicious*, but I hope the House will examine them."

On Wednesday, the 19th, Mr. Spaulding opened the debate in opposition to some of the amendmets of the Senate. We quote as follows:

"Mr. Chairman, I desire especially to oppose the amendments of the Senate which require the interest on bonds and notes to be paid *in coin* semi-annually, and which authorizes the Secretary of the Treasury to sell six per cent. bonds at the market price for coin to pay the interest.

"The Treasury note bill, as reported first from the Committee of Ways and Means as a necessary war measure, was simple and perspicuous in its terms, and easily understood. It was so plain that everybody could understand that it authorized the issue of $150,000,000 of legal tender demand notes, to circulate as a national curreucy among the people in all parts of the United States, and that they might, at any time, be funded in six per cent. twenty years' bonds. The passage of the measure in this house was hailed with satisfaction by the great mass of the people all over the country. It received the hearty endorsement of such bodies as the Chambers of Commerce of New York, Cincinnati, St. Louis, Chicago, Buffalo, Milwaukee, and other places. I have never known any measure receive a more hearty approval from the people.

"Nearly every amendment to the bill since it was matured has rendered it more complex and difficult of execution. I regret to say that, some of the amendments of the Senate render the bill incongruous, and tend to defeat its great object, namely—to prevent all forcing of the Government to sell its bonds in the market to the highest bidder for coin. It might be very pleasant for the holders of the seven and three-tenths Treasury notes and six per cent. bonds, to receive their interest in coin semi-annually, but very disastrous to the government to be compelled to sell its bonds, at ruinous rates of discount, every six months to pay them gold and silver, while it would pay only Treasury notes to the soldier, sailor, and all other creditors of the government.

"I am opposed to all those amendments of the Senate which make unjust discriminations between the creditors of the government. A soldier or sailor who performs service in the army or navy is a creditor of the government. The man who sells food, clothing, and the material of war, for the use of the army and navy, is a creditor of the government. The capitalist who holds your seven and three-tenths Treasury notes, or your six per cent. coupon bonds, is a creditor of the government. All are creditors of the government on an equal footing, and all are equally entitled to their pay in gold and silver.

"I am opposed to all those amendments of the Senate which discriminate in favor of the holders of bonds and notes by compelling the government to go into the streets every six months to sell bonds at the 'market price,' to purchase gold and silver in order to pay the interest 'in coin' to the capitalists who now hold United States stocks and Treasury notes heretofore issued, or that may hold bonds and notes hereafter to be issued; while all persons in the United States (including the army and navy and all who supply them with food and clothing) are compelled to receive legal tender Treasury notes in payment of demands due them from the government.

"Why make this discrimination? Who asks to have one class of creditors placed on a better footing than another class? Do the people of New England, the Middle States, or the people of the West and Northwest, or anywhere else in the rural districts, ask to have any such discrimination made in their favor? Does the soldier, the farmer, the mechanic, or the merchant ask to have any such discrimination made in his favor? No, sir; no such unjust preference is asked for by this class of men. They ask for the legal tender note bill pure and simple. They ask for a national currency which shall be of equal value in all parts of the country. They want a currency that shall pass from hand to hand among all the people in every State, county, city, town and village in the United States. They want a currency secured by adequate taxation upon the whole property of the country, which will pay the soldier, the farmer, the mechanic, and the banker alike for all debt due. They ask that the government shall stand upon its own responsibility, its own rights, and exert its vast powers, preserve its own credit, and carry us safely through this gigantic rebellion, in the shortest time, and with the least possible sacrifice. They intend to foot all the bills, and ultimately pay the whole amount, principal and interest, in gold and silver.

"Who, then, are they that ask to have a preference given to them over other creditors of the government? Sir, it is a very respectable class of gentlemen, but a class of men who are very sharp in all money transactions. They are not generally among the producing classes—not among those who, by their labor and skill, make the wealth of the country; but a class of men that have accumulated wealth, men who are willing to lend money to the government if you will make the security beyond all question, give them a high rate of interest, and make it payable in coin. Yes, sir, the men who are asking these extravagant terms, who want to be preferred creditors, are perfectly willing to lend money to the government in her present embarrassments, if you will only make them perfectly secure, give them extra interest, and put your bonds on the market at the 'market price,' to purchase gold and silver to pay them interest every six months. Yes, sir, entirely willing to loan money on these terms! Safe, no hazard, secure, and the interest payable 'in coin!' Who would not be willing to loan money on such terms? Sir, the legal tender Treasury note bill was intended to avoid all such financiering and protect the government, and people who pay the taxes, from all such hard bargains. It was intended as a shield in the hands of the patriotic people of the country against all forced sales of bonds, and all extravagant rates of interest.

"The legal tender note bill is a great measure of equality. It proposes a currency for the people which is based upon the great faith of the people and all their taxable property. All are obliged to receive and pass it as money, and all are obliged to submit to heavy taxation to provide for its ultimate redemption in gold and silver. Every attempt on the part of any class of citizens to create distinctions and secure a legal preference, mars the simplicity and success of the whole plan. The very discrimination proposed carries on its face notice to everybody, that although the notes are declared to be 'lawful money and a legal tender in payment of debts,' yet that there is something of higher value, that must be sought after at a sacrifice to the government, to pay a peculiar class of creditors to whom it owes money—a kind of absurdity and self-stultification which does not appear well on the face of the bill. It is an unjust discrimination which does not appear well now, and will not look well in history. You will, if the Senate's amendment is adopted, depreciate, by your own acts, your own bonds and notes, and effectually destroy the symmetry and harmonious workings of the whole plan."

* (Mr. Spaulding, in his Financial History of the War, calls attention to the fact that "at the time the above remarks were made by him *the duties on imports* were, as the bill then stood, payable in legal tender notes; but this was afterwards changed in the committee of conference, making those duties payable *in coin*, so that the interest might be paid in coin, without being obliged to force the bonds on the market to obtain coin for that purpose.")

During the discussion in the Committee of the Whole an amendment to the Senate amendment requiring interest on bonds and notes to be paid in coin, was offered by Mr. Pendleton to the effect, "that the officers, soldiers, seamen and marines, engaged in the military service of the United States," should also be paid in coin, which was not agreed to.

On the 20th the House resumed consideration of the Senate amendments. Mr. Stevens closed the debate. We quote from his speech as follows:

"Mr. Speaker, I have a very few words to say. I approach the subject with more depression of spirits than I ever before approached any question. No personal motive or feeling influences me. I hope not, at least. I have a melancholy foreboding that we are about to consummate a cunningly devised scheme, which will carry great injury and great loss to all classes of the people throughout this Union, except one. With my colleague, I believe that no act of legislation of this government was ever hailed with as much delight throughout the whole length and breadth of this Union, by every class of people, without any exception, as the bill we passed and sent to the Senate. Congratulations from all classes—merchants, traders, manufacturers, mechanics and laborers—poured in upon us from all quarters. The Board of Trade from Boston, New York, Philadelphia, Cincinnati, Louisville, St. Louis, Chicago and Milwaukee approved its provisions, and urged its passage as it was.

"I have a dispatch from the Chamber of Commerce of Cincinnati, sent to the Secretary of the Treasury, and by him to me, urging the speedy passage of the bill as it passed the House. It is true there was a doleful sound came up from the caverns of bullion brokers, and from the saloons of the associated banks. Their cashiers and agents were soon on the ground, and persuaded the Senate, with but little deliberation, to mangle and destroy what it had cost the House months to digest, consider, and pass. They fell upon the bill in hot haste, and so disfigured and deformed it, that its very father would not know it. Instead of being a beneficent and invigorating measure, it is now positively mischievous. It has all the bad qualities which its enemies charged on the original bill, and none of its benefits. It now creates money, and by its very terms declares it a depreciated currency. It makes two classes of money—one for the banks and brokers, and another for the people. It discriminates between the rights of different classes of creditors, allowing the rich capitalist to demand gold, and compelling the ordinary lender of money on individual security to receive notes which the government had purposely discredited.

"Let us examine the principal amendments separately, and see their effect. The first important one (being the fifth) makes the notes issued under the law of July 17th a legal tender, equally with those authorized by this bill.

There can be but little wisdom in putting these two classes on an equality. The notes of July bear seven and three-tenths per cent. interest, and are payable in three years. This gives them a sufficient advantage over notes bearing no interest and payable virtually in twenty years, with six per cent. interest. Why give them this additional advantage? Simply because the $100,000,000 issued are all held by the associated banks, and this is their amended bill. They would displace $100,000,000 of this money in the circulation, and render it impossible to use any considerable amount of these United States notes as a currency. These notes have served their purpose. Why allow them to block up the market against further relief to the government?

"The banks took $50,000,000 of six per cent. bonds, and shaved the government $5,500,000 on them, and now ask to shave the government fifteen or twenty per cent. half yearly, to pay themselves the interest on these very bonds. They paid for the $50,000,000 in demand notes, not specie, and now demand the specie for them. Yet gentlemen talk about our making other loans in these times. They are crazy or sleeping, one or the other, I do not know which." * *

"The notes, by another amendment, are authorized to be invested in notes or bonds payable in two years, and bearing an interest of seven and three-tenths. One of the great objects was to induce capitalists to invest in six per cent. bonds or lose their interest, and thus to furnish a continually recurring currency by the sale of these six per cent. bonds. This provision would effectually prevent the funding a dollar in those bonds. They would all go in preference into seven and three-tenths bonds, due in two years, when no one believes we can pay them.

"But this is not the worst. The tenth amendment provides that any holder of the United States legal tender notes, if he have $100 and upwards, shall draw five or six per cent. interest on them until he choses to use them. The poor who have less than $100 shall draw no interest. It is plain that, by these two contrivances, not one dollar of these United States notes will ever be funded in six per cent. bonds.

"But now comes the main clause. All classes of people *shall* take these notes at par for every article of trade or contract unless they have money enough to buy United States bonds, and then they shall be paid in gold. Who is that favored class? The banks and brokers, and nobody else. They have already $250,000,000 of State debt, and their commissioners would soon take all the rest that might be issued.

"But how is this gold to be raised? The duties and public lands are to be paid for in United States notes, and they or bonds are to be put up at auction to get coin for these very brokers who would furnish the coin to pay themselves, by getting twenty per cent. discount on the notes thus bought.

"Now, in less than a year, taking the public debt at what my colleague makes it—I make it more—$1,200,000,000, what will the interest be upon it at seven and three-tenths per cent., for it will all center in that rate of interest? It will be $87,000,000, and one-half of that amount, $43,500,000, must be raised every six months for the paying of this interest, and is to be raised in coin, which nobody holds but the large capitalists. Does anybody suppose that they are going to give that coin for such notes as we are now about to issue, at par? They will sell the gold for what their conscience will allow, and they will compel the government to give anything they choose, unless the government consents to become dishonored. The first purchase of gold by the government will fix the value of these notes which we issue and declare to be a legal tender. That sale will fix their value at ten, fifteen, or twenty-five per cent. discount, and then every poor man, when he buys his beef, his pork, and his supplies, must submit to this fifteen or twenty-five per cent. discount, because you have said that that shall be the value of the very notes which you have made a legal tender to him, but not a legal tender to those who fix the value of these very notes. Does any one believe that anybody but bankers and brokers fixes the depreciation of currency? So you will thus have fixed the market value of your notes at seventy-five or eighty per cent., and yet they are a legal tender to the poor of the country, while they are no legal tender to those who hold the coin of the country.

"By the original bill the Secretary of the Treasury was allowed to sell these bonds at their value for lawful money —that is, for these legal tender notes. But now, by the provisions of this bill, after the market value has been fixed and they are depreciated, the Secretary of the Treasury is authorized to go into the market and sell them for coin, not at par, but at the market value therefor. Was there ever a more convenient contrivance got up, into which blind mice run, to catch them? Was ever before such a machine got up for swindling the government and making the fortunes of the gold bullionists in one single year?

"But as if this accumulated folly were not quite enough, another amendment provides that these notes, when presented in sums not less than $100, may be transferred into seven and three-tenths notes payable in two years. Parties may buy these notes at a discount and put them into notes payable in bullion at two years, at seven and three-tenths interest, for that is a part of the whole system.

"Now, sir, does any man here believe that, notwithstanding the victories we are gaining, the government will be able to redeem these notes in two years? If not, they will be shoved upon the market and sold for coin at whatever discount may be demanded."

Mr. Stevens also offered an amendment to pay the army and navy in specie, the same as the bondholders' interest in coin, which was voted down. The Senate amendments were concurred in only in part, which rendered the appointment of a committee of conference necessary. The conference committee appointed by the Senate consisted of Messrs. Fessenden, Sherman and Carlisle, and the conference committee of the House of Messrs. Stevens, Horton and Sedgwick. The conference committee were in session two or three days, and finally reported the bill with several alterations, the most important of which was that *the duties on imports should be paid in coin*,* so as to do away with the necessity of forcing the bonds on the market to procure coin *to pay interest in coin on the bonded debt* of the government.

On the 24th of February, 1862, the action of the conference committee was agreed to by the House by a vote of 97 to 22. On the 25th the Senate concurred in the action of the conference committee, and the same day the legal tender act was approved by the President.†

THE GREENBACK.

Thus were the most sacred interests of the people, especially of the producing classes—the farmer, the mechanic, the manufacturer and the laboring man, grossly and wickedly betrayed into the hands of the money power by the Senate of the United States. The Senate at that time was a small body, but twenty-four States being represented, with but three or four members whose ability rose above mediocrity.

*See speech of Hon. Thaddeus Stevens in the Appendix.
†The Legal Tender Act as finally passed will be found in the Appendix.

The occupants of seats once filled by statesmen, whose ability and eloquence had made the Senate of the United States famous throughout the world, they became puffed up with ideas of self-importance, which, with the venality of the Shermans of the body, rendered them easy prey for the sharks of Wall street. It will be observed that the points contended for, so strenuously and successfully, by the conference committee of the Senate, which represented the sentiment of the majority of that body, were, in substance and effect, the same as those contained in the plan of the bankers, offered at their meeting, which convened in Washington immediately after the introduction of the legal tender bill in the House.* That the Senate was controlled, in its action in regard to the legal tender bill, by improper influences is not a matter of conjecture, but of history. In his speech at Philadelphia, January 15, 1876, Judge Kelley says: "I remember the grand 'Old Commoner' (Thaddeus Stevens) with his hat in his hand and his cane under his arm, when he returned to the House after the final conference, and shedding bitter tears over the result. 'Yes,' said he, 'we have had to yield; the Senate was stubborn. We did not yield until we found *that the country must be lost or the banks be gratified*, and we have sought to save the country in spite of the cupidity of its wealthier citizens."

Here begins one of the darkest chapters in American history. It will be found that every step taken by Congress from this on, in matters pertaining to the finances of the nation, has been dictated by the money power. Foreign capitalists, such as the Rothschilds, became deeply interested in the scheme of robbery inaugurated by the passage of the first legal tender act, and through their agents, such as August Belmont, banker and whilom chairman of the Dem-

*See page 177.

ocratic National Committee, have aided the money power here materially in controlling the policy of both of the great political parties. The amount stolen from the people during the war by the financial policy then adopted, and which now encumbers the nation in the shape of a bonded debt, payable principal and interest in gold, is estimated by such writers upon the subject of finance as J. S. Gibbons (contributor to Johnson's Universal Cyclopædia) at over one thousand millions of dollars,* to say nothing of the thousands of millions of which the people have been robbed indirectly, by means of the pernicious monetary system then foisted upon the country.

The first legal tender notes (greenbacks) issued under the act of Congress of February 25, 1862, were issued bearing date March 10, 1862, and on the back of them was printed these words:

"This note is a legal tender for all debts, public and private, except duties on imports and interest on the public debt, and is exchangeable for United States six per cent. bonds, redeemable at the pleasure of the United States after five years."

Notwithstanding the mutilated form in which the greenbacks were sent out by the Treasury department, they performed a marvellous work. The producing forces of the nation were set at work, and there was no longer any difficulty in rendering the resources of the people available to the government. In speaking of this period, Judge Kelley, in his Philadelphia speech of January last, thus graphically and eloquently pictures the wonderful change which followed the passage of this legal tender act. He says: "But the patriots, (Lincoln, Stevens, etc.,) to whom I have referred, had studied the Constitution of the United States. They

*Letter of J. S. Gibbons: Spaulding's Financial History of the War.

knew that it imposed upon them the duty of saving the nation. They knew that money is the sinew of war, and that it must be had. They knew that the Constitution authorized the coining of the public credit into money. They 'smote the rock of public credit,' and power and prosperity gushed forth. 'Smote the rock of public credit!' What does that mean? Why, they called into existence 'the rag-baby!' They said to every man that would work— 'Here are wages for you; this rag-baby will pay you.' They said to ship-owners, 'unfurl your rotting sails and open your hatchways; we have brought you grain from the farm, carry it abroad to buy us clothing and arms; for our industries have been stricken, and we cannot provide clothing or arms for the army that is to sustain the Union.' The 'rag-baby" showered greenbacks upon them, and the ships spread their sails, and carried rich cargoes to foreign lands, which were exchanged for clothing, arms and munitions of war. Industry was rife throughout the land. The farmers, who had been without an adequate or remunerative market for years, were getting good prices for their grain, were paying their debts to the local merchant, who in turn paid his to those of the great cities. A marvellous child was that 'rag-baby.' While not yet a month old, its name, 'greenback,' not yet familiar to the people, it lighted the fires in every forge and furnace of the country; it hired ships, and bought others; it blockaded the whole southern coast; it rallied an army of 75,000 men, and we soon after heard ringing through the streets the shout of well paid and well clad soldiers, 'we're coming, Father Abraham, three hundred thousand more! The 'rag-baby' was welcomed by every commissary, quartermaster and paymaster. It furnished transportation; it met all demands, and the American people—at least those of the free States—with the great war on their hands, were prosperous as they had never been before, thanks to the marvellous power of the 'rag-baby.' * * I name it not the 'rag-baby;' I take the derisive term from the door of the Presidential mansion. I cannot imply a want of respect for the constitutional legal tender money of the country, the Treasury note, which did all that I have attributed to the 'rag-baby.'"

The premium on gold, which was 3½ per cent. when the legal tender act was passed, February 25, 1862, immediately began to decline, and did not go up again until the latter part of May. United States bonds immediately went up from 90 to 102.

TEMPORARY DEPOSITS IN THE SUB-TREASURY.

By the fourth section of the legal tender act, the Secretary of the Treasury was authorized to receive deposits in the Sub-Treasury to the amount of $25,000,000, in sums of not less than $100, at five per cent. interest, with the privilege of drawing it out again on ten days' notice after thirty days. On the 17th day of March, 1862, the authority to receive these deposits was increased to $50,000,000. On the 11th of July, 1862, it was still further extended to $100,000,000; and by the act of January 30, 1864, to $150,000,000, and the Secretary was authorized to pay as high as six per cent. interest. These deposits reached the sum of $120,176,196.

CERTIFICATES OF INDEBTEDNESS.

By the act of March 1, 1862, the Secretary of the Treasury was authorized to issue to public creditors "who may be desirous to receive the same in satisfaction of audited and settled demands against the United States," certificates of indebtedness in sums not less than $1,000 each, payable in one year, with interest at six per cent. And by the act of March 17, 1862, this power was enlarged, so as to embrace checks drawn in favor of creditors by disbursing officers upon sums placed to their credit on the books of the Treasurer. These certificates were issued in the form of bank notes and circulated to a large extent as currency. The amount of certificates of indebtedness in circulation November, 1864, was $238,593,000.

THE SECOND LEGAL TENDER ACT.

On the 7th day of June, 1862, Secretary Chase sent a communication to the Committee of Ways and Means of the House asking for authority to issue $150,000,000 more legal tender Treasury notes, and that $35,000,000 of this sum should be of a less denomination than five dollars. On the 11th of June a bill was reported to the House from the Committee of Ways and Means. The bill was made the special order for the 17th inst. On that day the debate was opened by Mr. Spaulding in a speech in favor of the bill. A vote was reached June 24th, when the bill passed, substantially as recommended by the Secretary, by a vote of 76 to 47.

On the 28th of June the Finance Committee of the Senate reported it to that body with amendments. On the 2d of July it passed the Senate, as amended, by a vote of 22 to 13. The House refused to agree to the amendments; the farce of a conference committee was again gone through with; the report of the conference committee was agreed to on the 8th of July, and on the 11th the bill was approved by the President.

SECOND ANNUAL REPORT OF SECRETARY CHASE.

Congress convened in regular session December 1, 1862. On the 4th Secretary Chase submitted his second annual report. After an elaborate review of the revenues and expenditures of the government, he discussed the financial affairs of the nation at large. He reiterated his objections to the State banks and declared that, as between a currency furnished by numerous and unconnected banks in various States and a currency furnished by the government, he unhesitatingly gave his "preference for a circulation authorized and issued by national authority."

He took issue with those who entertained the opinion that the rise in the price of gold was due to the redundancy of the currency, and supported his views with great force,* but it did not occur to him to suggest the true reason, viz: because coin was the only currency that was a full legal tender. He again took occasion to renew his recommendation of the National Banking system. He said:

"While the Secretary thus repeats the preference he has heretofore expressed for a United States note circulation, even when issued directly by the government and dependent on the action of the government for regulation and final redemption, over the note circulation of the numerous and variously organized and variously responsible banks now existing in the country; and while he now sets forth, more fully than heretofore, the grounds of that preference, he still adheres to the opinion expressed in his last report, that a circulation *furnished by the government, but issued by banking associations* organized under a general act of Congress, is to be preferred to either."

The amount to be provided for by Congress for the current year he estimated at about $300,000,000, and for the next fiscal year, (beginning July 1st,) $600,000,000, and recommended that the chief dependence of the government to secure that amount be placed on the negotiation of bonds.

Congress was then urged by the Secretary to repeal that portion of the act of Congress of February 25, 1862, which *restricted the sale of bonds to their market price*, and

*See Report of the Secretary of the Treasury: Appendix to the Congressional Globe, 1862-'63.

also the *clause providing for the convertibility of bonds and Treasury notes, (greenbacks.)* In conclusion he said: "The general views of the Secretary may, therefore, be thus briefly summed: He recommends that whatever amount may be needed beyond the sums supplied by revenue and through other indicated modes, be obtained by loans, without increasing the issue of United States notes beyond the amount fixed by law, unless a clear public exigency shall demand it. He recommends, also, the organization of banking associations for the improvement of the public credit, and for the supply to the people of a safe and uniform currency. And he recommends no change in the law providing for the negotiation of bonds except the necessary increase of amount, and the *repeal of the absolute restriction to market value and of the clauses authorizing convertibility at will.*"

THE THIRD LEGAL TENDER ACT—$900,000,000 LOAN ACT.

Early in the session the Hon. Thaddeus Stevens introduced a bill "to provide means to defray the expenses of the government," which, in his own language, "produced a howl among the money changers as hideous as that sent up by their Jewish cousins when they were kicked out of the temple." This bill was in substance the same as the legal tender bill, as it originally passed the House and before it was mutilated by the Senate in the manner above explained. It was intended to bring the government back to the full legal tender money system, "the simplicity and harmony of which had been mangled and destroyed by the Senate." In a brief, but powerful speech, (December 23, 1862) Mr. Stevens pointed out the injustice and danger of the financial policy which was then being pursued, and closed with this prophetic warning: "But I ought perhaps to say, before I close, to my country banking friends that they need not be alarmed. There is no great prospect that we shall return to the system I have indicated, nor do much to protect the people from their own eager speculations. *When a few years hence, the people shall have been brought to general bankruptcy* by their unregulated enterprise, I shall have the satisfaction to know that I attempted to prevent it." (Mr. Stevens' speech will be found in full in the Appendix.)

On the 8th of January, 1863, the Committee of Ways and Means reported a bill entitled, "A bill to provide Ways and Means for the Support of the Government," afterwards known as the $900,000,000 loan act. The bill reported contained no provision for the repeal of the clause in the act of February 25, 1862, restricting the Secretary of the Treasury in the sale of bonds to their "market value," or of the clause allowing the holders of legal tender notes to convert them at any time into 5-20 six per cent. bonds.

On the 12th of January the bill was taken up in the House, and Mr. Spaulding opened the debate in a lengthy speech in support of the bill, in which he discussed the National Banking scheme, recommended by the Secretary, arguing in its favor. On the 17th of January, 1863, a joint resolution was passed "to provide for the immediate payment of the army and navy of the United States," authorizing the Secretary of the Treasury to issue $100,000,000 legal tender Treasury notes, to be covered by the bill then pending ($900,000,000 loan act.) On the 26th of January, 1863, the bill was passed—a substitute offered by Mr. Hooper, and one by Mr. Stevens, having been first decided in the negative—without a division. On the 13th of February, 1863, the bill, after being amended, passed the Senate by a vote of 32 to 4. The usual routine of a conference committee was gone through with, with the usual result, and the bill was finally agreed to as amended by the Senate, and approved by the President March 3, 1863. The following is a synopsis of the bill as given by Mr. Spaulding:*

"1. The first section authorizes a loan of $300,000,000 for the then current year, and $600,000,000 for the then next fiscal year, and to issue bonds therefor at not less than ten nor more than forty years, at not exceeding six per cent. interest, in coin, not exceeding in all $900,000,000.

"2. By section second of the same act the Secretary, in lieu of an equal amount of said bonds, was authorized to issue $400,000,000 of Treasury notes, bearing interest not exceeding six per cent., payable in lawful money, which notes, payable at periods expressed on their face, *might be made a legal tender at their face value.*

"3. By the third section $150,000,000 in amount of United States notes, made a legal tender, might be issued. The restriction in the sale of bonds to '*market value* was repealed. '*And the holders of United States notes issued under former acts, shall present the same for the purpose of exchanging them for bonds as therein provided, on or before the first of July,* 1863, *and thereafter the right to exchange the same shall cease and determine.*'

"4. This section imposed a tax of one per cent. each half year, on a graduated scale of *State bank circulation*, according to the capital stock of each bank."

Making the interest of the bonds payable in gold and declaring that the legal tender Treasury note (greenback) should not be receivable for duties on imports, was a gross betrayal of the interests of the people by the Senate of the United States. But that body was capable of still greater perfidy. It will be observed by the synopsis of the $900,-000,000 loan act, given above, that the convertibility of the

*Financial History of the War, page 155.

greenback with United States six per cent. bonds, as provided by the act of February 25, 1862, was repealed

By the terms of the act of February 25, 1862, under which the greenback was issued, the right to exchange it for United States bonds was distinctly guaranteed, and was *in the nature of a contract*, made by the government with the holder, and to abrogate this right was an act of repudiation. The motive which inspired the act, was to still further depreciate the paper of the government. It is a fact worthy of note, that when Congress perpetrated this act of repudiation, "no doleful sound came up from the caverns of the bullion brokers or the saloons of the associated banks," nor was there any howl heard from the gentlemen of the press, who were so quick to detect repudiation in Mr. Stevens' bill to restore the legal tender act to the condition in which it first passed the House.*

NATIONAL BANK BILL.

On the 2d of February, 1863, the National Bank bill, as prepared by Mr. Spaulding in December, 1861, was reported, with alterations and amendments, from the Finance Committee to the Senate by Mr. Sherman. The debate upon it began in the Senate on the 9th, and on the 12th (three days after) the bill passed by a vote of 23 to 21. It was taken up in the House on the 19th, and passed *the next day* by a vote of 78 to 64; and received the President's signature March 25, 1863. (See Chapter on National Banks.)

The money power now had matters all its own way, and was in a situation to prey upon the government and people at its pleasure. Duties on imports were payable in gold; interest on the bonds of the United States were payable in gold; the exchangeability of the greenback with bonds had

*See Speech of Hon. Thaddeus Stevens in the Appendix.

14

been abrogated; the country was flooded with evidences of indebtedness of the government in all forms and shapes, such as demand notes, Treasury notes bearing interest, mutilated legal tender notes, certificates of deposit, certificates of indebtedness, etc.; and a banking bill, authorizing the issue of $300,000,000 in bank notes had been passed.

The following statement of the public debt (January 2, 1863) will show exactly the amount and character of the indebtedness of the government at this time:

Loan of 1842............................	$2,883,364 11
" 1847............................	9,415,250 00
" 1848............................	8,908,341 80
" 1858............................	20,000,000 00
" 1860............................	7,022,000 00
" 1861, act of February 8, 1860.....	18,415,000 00
" 1861, act of July 18, 1861........	50,002,000 00
" 1862, five-twenty six per cent......	25,050,850 00
Texas indemnity........................	3,461,000 00
Oregon war debt........................	1,026,600 00
Texas debt.............................	112,092 69
Old funded and unfunded debt...........	114,115 48
Treasury notes under acts prior to 1857....	104,561 64
" " " subsequent......	2,750,350 00
Treasury notes seven-thirty per cent. interest	139,998,000 00
Temporary deposits at four per cent.......	38,458,008 50
" " five per cent........	41,777,628 16
United States notes, legal tender and receivable for customs.....................	14,913,315 25
United States notes, legal tender..........	223,108,000 00
Postal currency less than one dollar......	6,844,936 00
Certificates of indebtedness, six per cent...	110,321,241 65
Requisitions on the Treasurer for soldiers' pay and other creditors, due but not paid	59,117,597 46
Total funded and unfunded debt to January 2, 1863, according to the books in the Treasury Department................$783,804,252 64	

The time had now arrived to put the $500,000,000 of

United States bonds authorized by the act of February 25, 1862, on the market. Notwithstanding the urgent need of the government during this time, Secretary Chase had held these bonds back for over a year on the pretence that the restriction to a sale at "market value" prevented him from negotiating their sale to any considerable amount. Mr. Gurley, of Ohio, effectually disposed of this plea in the course of his speech on the nine hundred million loan act. He said: "He did not agree with the Secretary in several things contained in his report; the banking scheme, which the Secretary admits would not afford any immediate relief, should be rejected; we need a sensible, practicable plan that will furnish immediate means to pay the army and navy. He insisted that Congress, by the act of February 25, 1862, authorized the Secretary to sell $500,000,000 six per cent. 5-20 bonds at 'the market value thereof,' *which he had not done, as intended by Congress*, and the consequence was that the soldiers and sailors were not paid, as they ought to have been before this time. * * The words 'market value' do not mean par value, nor any specified time or sums. The market value was the price they would bring when offered in the market. There has been no business day or week since the law was passed, when any of the many agents of the Secretary in New York could not have placed one million, or several millions, in the market, and sold them somewhere near par, to raise money to pay the army and navy."

In May, 1863, Jay Cooke, "an enterprising banker" of Philadelphia, was employed to dispose of the five-twenty bonds. The Secretary of the Treasury, up to this time, had put out only about $25,000,000, leaving $475,000,000 yet to be sold. No effort was made by Mr. Cooke to negotiate these bonds with bankers or capitalists, but (to quote from

Spaulding), "the editors of newspapers and others were enlisted to bring the advantages of the loan before the *people*, in order to make it a great popular loan, to be taken by them in large and small sums in all the loyal States. Mr. Cooke succeeded admirably in this undertaking. The loan became very popular, and was taken extensively by farmers, mechanics and laboring people, in all the towns, villages and cities over the country. By the first of July, 1863, the amount of $168,880,250 of these bonds were taken; and by the first of October following, $278,511,500 had been taken up; and by the 21st of January following the whole sum of $500,000,000 had been taken *at par*, and the rush was so great near the closing out of the loan, that nearly $11,000,000 extra had been subscribed and paid for before notice could be given to sub-agents that the amount authorized by that act had been taken up. Congress, however, soon after authorized this extra sum to be issued."

Hugh McCulloch also bears testimony as to what class of people took the 5-20 bonds. In a letter to the New York *Tribune*, dated at London in September last, he said: "I recollect the time when subscribers for United States bonds were regarded as patriots, and I happen to know to what class they belonged. With rare exception they were not capitalists. * * The purchasers of our bonds were the patriotic men of all parties, chiefly men of moderate means, who were resolved that the Union should be saved, no matter at what cost of money or blood." It may be interesting to state that Mr. McCulloch was not one of those who were resolved that the Union should be saved, no matter at what cost, etc. At the time he refers to, he was a country banker "of moderate means," somewhere in the State of Indiana, and was solicited, we believe, by the Sub-

Treasurer of the United States, Mr. Cisco, to have his bank take and dispose of some of "our bonds." He treated the request with contempt. This matter was so well known at the time of his appointment as Secretary of the Treasury, as to be talked of on the streets of Washington, and was hushed up by his friends only with great difficulty.

The partial legal tender Treasury note (greenback), issued by the government, now constituted the medium of exchange of the nation. Its legal tender property gave it the power and functions of money, to measure and exchange values. The legal tender money of a country is the measure of all values and the basis of all money contracts among its people; consequently prices in the United States came to be regulated by the greenback and not by gold. Any one can satisfy himself on this point by comparing the market prices of any of the leading products of the country for a given time with the fluctuations in the price of gold. Secretary Chase referred to this fact in his second annual report, in which he said: "That such is the case (no redundancy of the currency) may be reasonably inferred from the fact that the prices of many of the most important articles of consumption have declined or not materially advanced during the year. Wheat, quoted at $1.38 to $1.45 per bushel on the first of November, 1861, was quoted at $1.45 to $1.50 on the first of November, 1862. Prime mess pork on the first of November, 1861, was quoted at $15 to $15.50 per barrel, and on the first of November, 1862, at $12.50 to $13. Corn sold on the first of November, 1861, at 62 to 63 cents per bushel, and on the first of November, 1862, at 71 to 73 cents. A comparison between the prices of hay, beef, and some other staples of domestic produce, at the two dates, exhibits similar conditions of actual depression in price or moderate rise." Products rise and fall in price according to the laws of supply and demand. Foreign goods, however, the duties on which have to be paid in gold, are subject to a different standard of payment, and are governed in price largely by the price of gold. The price of gold is regulated by the laws of supply and demand, supplemented by the arts and efforts of speculators and gold gamblers. As long as the greenback was convertible at the will of the holder into a six per cent. gold interest bond, there was no danger of its becoming redundant, or in any way affecting the price of domestic products. But, as we have seen, this convertibility was taken away, in the face of the plighted faith of the government, after July 1, 1863.

On March 3, 1864, an act of Congress was passed giving Secretary Chase still further discretionary power. It authorized him to issue $200,000,000 of bonds, bearing date March 1, 1864, or any subsequent date, redeemable after five years and payable in forty years, in coin, bearing interest not exceeding six per cent., subsequently known as 10-40 bonds. Under authority of this act, Secretary Chase, immediately after the 5-20 bonds bearing *six* per cent. interest had been disposed of, put 10-40 bonds bearing only *five* per cent. interest on the market. Very naturally the loan did not prove a success, and by the 1st of July, 1864, the sum realized from 10-40 bonds amounted to only $73,337,750. In order to defray the expenses of the government, the Secretary continued to issue evidences of indebtedness of the government in various forms calculated to circulate as a currency. By this time National Bank notes began to swell the volume of the currency. The following statement shows the amount and kinds of paper in circulation June 30, 1864:

U. S. notes, greenbacks................ $431,178,670 84
Postal, fractional currency.............. 22,894,877 25
Interest bearing legal tender Treasury notes 168,571,450 00
Certificates of Indebtedness............. 160,720,000 00
National Bank notes.................... 25,825,695 00
State Bank circulation about............ 135,000,000 00
Seven-thirty Treasury notes............. 109,356,150 00
Temporary deposits for which certificates
  were issued...................... 72,330,191 44

$1,125,877,034 53.

From the above table it will be seen that the country was flooded with paper securities of the government of every description, mostly bearing interest and issued in a form to circulate as currency. Now take into consideration the fact that over $700,000,000 of bonds bearing interest payable *in gold* had just been issued, and also that the military situation was very critical, and no one can fail to see into what a wretched condition the finances of the country had been brought. The "bulls" and "bears" of Wall street fairly rioted in the speculation and gold gambling which ensued. The premium on gold began to go up. On the 15th of January, 1864, it was 1.55; on the 15th of February, 1.59; on the 15th of April, 1.78; on the 15th of June, 1.79; on the 30th of June, 2.50; and on the 11th of July, 2.85½. The business affairs of the country were of course greatly deranged, and distrust became general. The credit of the government suffered enormously—worse than if it had sustained a dozen defeats in the field. But the game had been carried too far, and it was no longer possible to deceive the public, so something had to be done to allay public feeling and restore confidence. Secretary Chase was compelled to resign June 30, 1864. No change, however, was made in the policy of the Treasury Department, and matters went on from bad to worse.

BONDS, ETC., EXEMPTED FROM TAXATION.—GREENBACKS LIMITED TO $400,000,000.

By the act of June 30, 1864, the amount of greenbacks issued or to be issued, was limited to $400,000,000, and "such additional sum, not exceeding $50,000,000, as may be temporarily required for the redemption of temporary loans." The Secretary was authorized to issue $200,000,000 legal tender Treasury notes bearing interest, payable in three years. By the same act all bonds, coupons, national currency, United States notes, Treasury notes, fractional notes, certificates of indebtedness, certificates of deposit, etc., were declared *to be exempt from taxation* by or under State or municipal authority.

SENATOR FESSENDEN APPOINTED SECRETARY OF THE TREASURY.

William P. Fessenden, United States Senator from Maine, was appointed to succeed Secretary Chase, and entered upon the duties of his office July 5, 1864. Secretary Fessenden raised the means to carry on the government to March 4, 1865, by issuing greenbacks, 7-30 Treasury notes, interest bearing Treasury notes, certificates of indebtedness, 5-20 bonds, etc. Secretary Fessenden, while in the United States Senate, had played a conspicuous part in mutilating the greenback, and the following paragraph from his annual report, in December, 1864, in view of his course, cannot fail to strike the reader as a singular admission. He said: "The experience of the past few months cannot have failed to convince the most careless observer that, whatever may be the effect of a redundant circulation upon the price of coin, other causes have exercised a greater and more deleterious influence. In the course of a few days the price of this article rose from $1.50 to $2.85 in paper for $1.00 in specie, and subsequently fell, in as short a period, to $1.87, and then again rose as rapidly to $2.50; and all *without any assignable cause, traceable to an increase or decrease in circulation of paper money*, or an expansion or contraction of credit or other similar influence on the market, tending to occasion a fluctuation so violent. It is quite apparent that the *solution of the problem may be found in the unpatriotic and criminal efforts of speculators*, and probably of secret enemies, to raise the price of coin, regardless of the injury inflicted upon the country,—or desiring to inflict it." No man living, except John Sherman of Ohio, was better able to explain how and through whose instrumentality these rascally speculators were enabled to prosecute their "unpatriotic and criminal efforts" than Mr. Fessenden himself. Under the circumstances Mr. Fessenden did not find the position of Secretary of the Treasury a very comfortable one; and at the beginning of Mr. Lincoln's second term he surrendered it with feelings of great relief.

M'CULLOCH APPOINTED SECRETARY OF THE TREASURY.

Immediately after President Lincoln entered upon his second term of office Hugh McCulloch, a banker, of the State of Indiana, was appointed Secretary of the Treasury. Mr. McCulloch was unknown to the public, but it was hoped that, being a banker and of course familiar with the manner in which the government and people were being robbed by the money power, and not identified with the corrupt political ring at Washington through which it operated, he would endeavor to restore the finances of the country to a more healthy condition. Never were a people doomed to be more bitterly disappointed. McCulloch only entered into the designs of the money power, became its most subservient tool, and retired with the re tation of being the first Secretary of the Treasury of United States who had ever prostituted his high office for purpose of enriching himself and his associates. Henry Carey, who had a conversation with him immediately a his accession to office, says that he expressed himself t as unfavorable to contraction, and quotes him as saying he "should gladly see it (gold) at 1.75," meaning that would not favor contraction for the purpose of reducing premium on gold. "Three months later," says Mr. Ca "he was instructing his representatives abroad to g assurances that we should have resumed specie payme before the 7-30's became due. Two months yet later ca the destructive Fort Wayne decree (a letter from McCull in which he expressed himself in favor of the policy of c traction), and from that hour did the Secretary persis the absurd and injurious policy therein announced."

Mr. McCulloch, at the same time that he was giv instructions to his representatives abroad that we sho have resumed specie payments before the 7-30's became c was issuing 7-30 Treasury notes and compound inte bearing Treasury notes, made a tender at their face va to an enormous amount. The payment of the army, wh was mustered out of service during this period, al required an immense sum, which was obtained by sel 7-30 Treasury notes through the agency of Jay Cooke. ' amount of 7-30 Treasury notes outstanding October, 1: which were convertible in less than three years into 5-20 per cent. bonds, was $830,000,000.

The following is a statement of the debt and circula of the United States, as it stood October 31, 1865:

Bonds, 10-40's, five per cent., due in 1904 .. $172,770,100 00
Bonds, Pacific R. R., 6 per cent., due in 1895   1,258,000 00
Bonds, 5-20's, 6 per cent., due in 1882, '84, '85   659,259,600 00
Bonds, 6 per cent., due in 1881..........   265,347,400 00
Bonds, 5 per cent., due in 1880..........   18,415,000 00
Bonds, 5 per cent., due in 1874..........   20,000,000 00
Bonds, 5 per cent., due in 1871..........   7,022,000 00
Bonds, 6 per cent., due in 1868..........   8,908,341 80
Bonds, 6 per cent., due in 1867..........   9,415,250 00
Bonds, Texas indemnity, part due........   760,000 00
Bonds, Treasury notes, etc., part due......   613,920 09

  Total Bonds....................$1,163,769,611 89

Compound interest notes,
 due in 1867-'68.......$173,012,141 00
7-30 Treasury notes, due
 in 1867 and 1868...... 830,000,000 00
Temporary loans, 10 days'
 notice................   99,107,745 46
Certificates of indebted-
 ness, due in 1866......   55,905,000 00
Treasury notes, 5 per cent.,
 Dec. 1, 1865..........   32,536,901 00
United States notes..... 428,160,569 00
Fractional currency.....   26,057,469 20—1,644,779,825 66

  Total debt October 31, 1865......$2,808,549,437 55

National Bank notes issued............. $185,000,000 00
State Bank notes issued................   65,000,000 00
Treasury notes, greenbacks, etc........   1,644,779,825 66

  Total circulation*..............$1,894,779,825 66

M'CULLOCH'S CONTRACTION POLICY.

Secretary McCulloch, in his first annual report, December 4, 1865, argued that the legal tender acts were war measures and only temporary in character, and "ought not to remain in force a day longer than would be necessary to enable the people to prepare for a return to the gold standard; and that

*See table of circulation, Sept. 1, 1865, page 16.

the work of retiring the notes which have been issued should be commenced without delay, and carefully and persistently continued until all are retired." On the 18th of December, 1865, Congress adopted a resolution "cordially concurring in the views of the Secretary of the Treasury, in relation to a contraction of the currency," by a vote of 144 to 6. This was followed by an act of Congress, approved April 12, 1866, authorizing the Secretary to sell 5-20 bonds, and with the proceeds to retire six per cent. compound interest notes and legal tender notes (greenbacks), and other evidences of indebtedness of the government, but not to retire more than four millions of dollars of greenbacks a month, or forty-eight millions of dollars in a year, but without restriction as to the amount of compound sixes and seven-thirties. This act gave Secretary McCulloch unlimited control over the monetary affairs of the country.

The banks and sharks of Wall street and their kind, at home and abroad, held hundreds of millions of securities of the government, which they had purchased at various prices ranging from thirty-five cents on the dollar upwards. During the war whilst these securities were being emitted, it was the policy of the money power to depreciate their value in every way possible, in order that they might be bought in at a sacrifice. Hence it was that interest on the bonds and duties on imports were made payable in gold, and subsequently, that the convertibility of legal tender notes into bonds was abrogated. It was for the same reason, too, that Congress, instead of adopting a plain, simple system, easily understood by the public, such as the legal tender Treasury note sustained by an interest bearing bond, persisted in authorizing the Secretary of the Treasury to issue government securities, bearing interest, and mostly payable in three years, in all sorts of forms and shapes. Government obligations were issued during the war by the Treasury Department in *fifteen different* forms. It was of course impossible for the general public to keep the run of, much less to understand, all these various forms of indebtedness, nor was it designed that they should. It need scarcely be added, that issuing the securities of the government in these peculiar forms furnished the banks an additional opportunity to prey upon the people.

As soon as the last batch of 7-30 Treasury notes was disposed of by McCulloch to raise means to pay off the army on the eve of its disbandment, the money power changed its policy. It was now to the advantage of the holders of government securities to do everything in their power to enhance their value. Accordingly from this time on the efforts of the money power will be found turned in that direction. Secretary McCulloch, who had informed Mr. Carey that he would like to see gold stay at $1.75, as we have seen, was soon brought to terms, and was now a zealous champion of contraction, for the purpose of bringing the country back to "honest money." The Treasury notes, purposely made payable in three years, and which were convertible into 5-20 bonds, constituted the greater part of the public debt held at home. These notes were payable in lawful money (greenbacks), and it became an important object to have them converted into long time bonds, so that the money power might have ample time to secure such legislation as would result in the principal as well as the interest being paid in gold. Mr. McCulloch entered into this method of liquidating the outstanding obligations of the government with great zeal. The following items taken from his report of December, 1866, exhibit the character and extent of the contraction which took place (by substituting 5-20 bonds for Treasury notes, etc.,) from August 31, 1865, to October 31, 1866:

Temporary loan, 4, 5 and 6 per cent., acts of
February 25, 1862, and June 30, 1864... $62,146,714 27
Certificates of indebtedness, 6 per cent., acts
of March 1, 1862, and March 3, 1863.... 84,911,000 00
Treasury notes, 5 per cent., one and two
years, act of March 3, 1863............ 31,000,000 00
Treasury notes, 7-30, act of July 17, 1861.. 295,100 00
Compound interest notes, 6 per cent., act of
July 30, 1864....................... 68,512,020 00
Treasury notes, 7-30, acts of June 30, 1864,
and March 3, 1865................... 105,985,700 00
United States notes, acts of July 17, 1861,
and February 12, 1862............... 134,610 00
United States notes (greenbacks), acts of
February 25, 1862, and March 3, 1863... 42,830,174 00

Amount retired first year.......... $395,815,318 27

This policy was persisted in until all evidences of indebtedness of the government bearing currency interest, and having but a short time to run, were converted into gold interest long bonds. The following synopsis of the public debt statement contained in Secretary McCulloch's annual report of December 1, 1868, will exhibit the progress made by him on the 1st day of July, 1868:

DEBT BEARING COIN INTEREST.
5 per cent. bonds...... $221,588,400 00
6 per cent. bonds......1,848,415,241 80
Navy Pension fund.... 13,000,000 00—$2,083,003,641 80

DEBT BEARING CURRENCY INTEREST.
6 per cent. bonds...... $29,089,000 00
3 year comp'nd int. notes 21,604,890 00
3 year 7-30 notes...... 25,534,900 00
3 per cent. certificates.. 50,000,000 00— $126,228,790 00

MATURED DEBT NOT PRESENTED FOR PAYMENT.
Treasury notes, compound int'st notes, etc. 20,527,302 64

DEBT BEARING NO INTEREST.
U. S. notes (greenbacks) $356,141,723 00
Fractional currency.... 32,626,951 75
Gold certific's of deposit 17,678,740 00— $406,447,414 75

Total debt............ $2,636,207,149 19

In the meantime contraction had done its work. Business men began to suffer and the industries of the country to decline. "Hugh McCulloch had tapped a great artery and let nearly all the blood flow from the body politic." Besides the hundreds of millions of evidences of indebtedness of the government, used as currency, taken from the channels of trade, the greenback circulation was contracted from August, 1865, to July, 1868, $70,736,636.76. The public began to realize, though only partially, the cause of the great change that was going on in the business affairs of the country, and called a halt. Mr. J. A. Stevens, President of the Chamber of Commerce of New York City, in a letter to the New York *Times* in 1873, thus refers to this period: "The country at large had felt the pressure of the screw, but had not been able to discover precisely from what quarter the pinch came, the contraction being confined to those outside forms of Treasury obligations which, though not currency in the strict acceptation of the word, were still used as such in the larger transactions of trade and financial exchange. When, in a time of general pressure, the currency itself became the subject of the pruning knife, the country not only felt the knife, but saw how it was handled, and refused to submit to the 'heroic treatment.' "

Congress was compelled, in January, 1868, by the force of public sentiment, to pass a law declaring "that from and after its passage, the authority of the Secretary of the Treasury to make any reduction of the currency by retiring or cancelling United States notes (greenbacks) shall be and is hereby suspended." But the mischief had already been done. The greenback, however, was saved to the people.

In 1865 and 1866, after the termination of the war, industry, by reason of the abundance of money in circulation, was rife throughout the country, and production went on as it had never done before. During the years 1863, '64, '65 and 66 the failures throughout the country, as reported in Hunt's Magazine, averaged only 545 a year. In 1867 they run up to 2,386, and continued above that number until 1873, when they reached 5,181, with liabilities to the amount of $228,490,000.

In 1865 general prosperity prevailed, and as McCulloch himself has since admitted, the people were individually out of debt. Business then was *done for cash*. But as money grew scarce business men were obliged, as in days before the war, to resort to the banks and borrow bank credit. Business was no longer done on cash principles. As like causes produce like effects, so the use of bank credit, rendered necessary by the scarcity of money, brought the business affairs of the nation back to the same condition in which they had been for sixty years prior to the war. A commercial crash was only a question of time, and accordingly it came in 1873.

AN ACT TO STRENGTHEN THE PUBLIC CREDIT OF THE UNITED STATES.

Every act of Congress relating to the financial measures of the government during the war was passed with a view to depreciating the public credit. So, now, after the war was over, and the money power had obtained possession of all the outstanding obligations of the government, every act that was passed was passed with a view to increasing their value. The 5-20 bonds of the government were payable in lawful money of the United States. It will be remembered that when the first legal tender act was passed, February 25, 1862, the chief bone of contention between the Senate and House was the payment of the *interest* on the bonds in gold. Legal tender notes were made a tender for "all claims and demands against *the United States* of every kind whatsoever, *except for interest upon bonds and notes*, which shall be paid in coin, and shall also be lawful money and a legal tender in payment of all debts, public and private, within the United States, except duties on imports and interest as aforesaid." This language is perfectly plain and explicit and leaves no room for doubt. When the bill was pending in the Senate, Mr. Collamer, of Vermont, offered an amendment depriving the greenback of its legal tender quality so far as the public debt was concerned, and, at the same time, said that if the bill did not mean that bonds were payable in greenbacks, it meant nothing. His amendment was voted down. Senator Wilson, of Massachusetts, declared that greenbacks ought to be a legal tender for the payment of the public debt, and that if they were not he would vote against the bill. The Hon. Thaddeus Stevens subsequently declared, that "when the bill was on its final passage, the question was expressly asked of the chairman of the Committee on Ways and Means, and as expressly answered by him, that *only the interest* was payable in coin. If I knew," he added, "that any party in this country would go for paying in coin that which is payable in money, thus enhancing it one-half; if I knew there was such a platform, and such a determination on the part of any party, I would vote on the other side. I would vote for no such swindle upon the tax payers of this country; I would vote for no such speculation in favor of the large bondholders—the millionaires who took advantage of our folly in granting them coin payment of interest."

The first move made by the bullionists and bondholders was to educate public sentiment, through the press, in regard to the "sacredness of the public faith." The leading newspapers of the principal cities took up the song, and before a great while the gentlemen of the country press, who are quick to learn which way the wind blows, were heard, together with the demagogues of both parties, joining in the chorus. In many of the Western States, whose people are not so completely enslaved by the money power as their brethren of the east, public opinion manifested a disposition to demand that the five-twenty bonds should be paid agreeably to the terms of the acts providing for their issue— in greenbacks. This was not confined to any particular party. Accordingly we find Senator Sherman, in a speech in the Senate, February 27, 1868, uttering the following sentiments. He said: "I say that equity and justice are amply satisfied if we redeem these bonds at the end of five years in the same kind of money, of the same intrinsic value it bore at the time they were issued. Gentlemen may reason about the matter over and over again, and they cannot come to any other conclusion; at least, that has been my conclusion after the most careful deliberation. Senators are sometimes in the habit, in order to defeat the argument of an antagonist, to say that this is repudiation. Why, sir, every citizen of the United States has conformed his business to the legal tender clause. * * Every State in the Union, without exception, has made its contracts, since the legal tender clause, in currency and paid them in currency." And Senator Morton declared that, "we should do foul injustice to the government and the people of the United States, after we have sold these bonds on an average for not more than sixty cents on the dollar, now to propose to make a new contract for the benefit of the bondholder."

The Presidential campaign of 1868 was impending, and it became necessary for the money power to resort to extraordinary efforts to obtain the direction of political affairs. The Rothschilds were in possession of several hundred millions of 5-20 bonds, purchased at about sixty cents on the dollar or less, and were particularly interested. Their agent, August Belmont, who had secured the position of chairman of the Democratic National Committee, was instructed by Baron James Rothschild as early as March 13, 1868, that unless the Democratic party went in for paying the 5-20 bonds in gold, it must be defeated. The first step was to have the national convention held in New York City. It accordingly convened there on the 4th of July, 1868. Belmont and his satellites were unable to control the convention, at least in the matter of the platform. After a stormy session the platform was promulgated on the 7th of July, and contained the following plank: "Resolved, Third: When the obligations of the government do not expressly state upon their face, or the law under which they were issued does not provide that they shall be paid in coin, they ought in right to be paid in the lawful money of the United States." This resolution doomed the party to defeat. At this time Mr. Belmont owned a large interest in the New York *World*, generally regarded as the leading Democratic newspaper in the country. About the first of October this interest is believed to have been transferred to Manton Marble, editor and part proprietor of the paper. On the 15th day of October, a few weeks before the general election, the *World*, to the consternation of the democracy throughout the country, came out in a leading editorial denouncing Horatio Seymour, the candidate of the party for the Presidency, as unfit and unavailable, and advising his withdrawal. This act of treachery has never been equaled in the annals of politics; and, strange to say, the *World*, under the same corrupt influence, continues to occupy the position of a leading Democratic newspaper. The money power was more successful with the leaders of the Republican party. Through its aid Grant was triumphantly elected. President

Grant was duly inaugurated on the 4th of March, 1869, and in pursuance of the programme marked out for him, thus alluded to "the sacredness of the public faith" in his inaugural message. He said: "Let it be understood that no repudiator of one farthing of our public debt will be trusted in public place, and it will go far toward strengthening a credit which ought to be the best in the world, and will ultimately enable us to replace the debt with bonds bearing less interest than we now pay." This was intended as a warning to all those who might desire to stand well with the administration.

On the 12th of March a bill was introduced in the House by Mr. Schenck, of Ohio, entitled "An act to strengthen the public credit of the United States." In due time it passed both branches of Congress, and was approved by the President March 18, 1869. It was the first act of Congress that received his official sanction. This act provides as follows:

"*Be it enacted*, etc., That, in order to remove any doubt as to the purpose of the government to discharge all its obligations to the public creditors, and to settle conflicting questions and interpretations of the law, by virtue of which such obligations have been contracted, it is hereby provided and declared that the faith of the United States is solemnly pledged to the payment in coin, or its equivalent, of all the obligations of the United States not bearing interest, known as United States notes, and of all the interest bearing obligations, except in cases where the law authorizing the issue of any such obligations has expressly provided that the same may be paid in lawful money, or in other currency than gold and silver; but none of the said interest bearing obligations, not already due, shall be redeemed or paid before maturity, unless at such times as United States notes shall be convertible into coin at the option of the holder, or unless at such time bonds of the United States, bearing a lower rate of interest than the bonds to be redeemed, can be sold at par in coin. And the United States also solemnly pledges its faith to make provision at the earliest practicable period for the redemption of the United States notes in coin."

To show conclusively that the 5-20 six per cent. bonds of the United States were not regarded either at home or abroad as payable in coin, Mr. Lawrence, of Ohio, called attention to the fact that, "on the 30th day of November, 1867, (over two years after the war was over) our five-twenty six per cent. bonds sold in London at $70\frac{3}{4}$ cents, while New Brunswick and Cape of Good Hope six per cents sold at 105; Russian five per cents at 85 and Brazilian five per cents at 75."

Congress and the President had done everything in their power to make the 5-20's payable in gold, but the Rothschilds and the money power generally were apprehensive as to the future, inasmuch as the act of Congress of March 18, 1869, was in violation of the terms of the contract under which the bonds had been issued, and might be repealed. No time was lost, therefore, in inducing the Secretary of the Treasury to pay off these bonds in gold. By means best known to themselves, McCulloch had been induced to redeem about $150,000,000 of these bonds, during his administration of the Treasury, and the process was continued under Boutwell and his successors, until the 5-20 bonds, issued under the original act of February 25, 1862, were all redeemed in gold or its equivalent.* This single act of robbery, for it is only one of the many acts of robbery which have been perpetrated by the money power during the past few years under the guise of law, will foot up about as follows:

*See public debt statement, page 231.

Amount of 5-20 six per cent. bonds........$500,000,000 00
Interest in gold at six per cent., compounded
  semi-annually, for ten years............ 403,096,132 71

                    Total..............$903,096,132 71
Cost of $500,000,000 bonds at say sixty cents
  on the dollar........................ 300,000,000 00

    Net profit in ten years, in gold......$603,096,132 71

REFUNDING THE PUBLIC DEBT.

The next move of the money power was to have the public debt refunded, in order to place its payment in coin beyond all question. Accordingly an act entitled "An act to authorize the refunding of the national debt," was passed and approved July 14, 1870. This act provided, "That the Secretary of the Treasury is hereby authorized to issue, in a sum or sums not exceeding in the aggregate $200,000,000, coupon or registered bonds of the United States, in such forms as he may prescribe, and of denominations of fifty dollars, or some multiple of that sum, *redeemable in coin* of the present standard value, at the pleasure of the United States, after ten years from the date of their issue, and bearing interest, payable semi-annually in such coin, at the rate of *five* per cent. per annum." $300,000,000 of like bonds, bearing four and a half per cent. interest, redeemable after fifteen years, and also a sum of bonds bearing four per cent. interest, redeemable after thirty years—in all not to exceed $1,000,000,000, were also authorized. The Secretary of the Treasury was authorized to sell these bonds at par for coin, and with the proceeds to redeem any of the bonds of the United States outstanding, known as five-twenty bonds, "*or he may exchange the same for such five-twenty bonds, par for par.*"

By the act of January 20, 1871, the act last recited was

amended so as to increase the amount of five per cent. gold bonds authorized to be issued to $500,000,000, and to make the interest on the bonds payable, at the discretion of the Secretary, "*quarter yearly.*"

Under these two acts gold bonds to the amount of $465,558,450 were issued up to November, 1875; and a bill, of a like character, introduced by Sherman in the Senate, is now pending in Congress, to complete the job. When it shall have passed Congress, the entire public debt, contracted in lawful money at a time when it was greatly depreciated as compared with gold, will be transformed into a debt payable, principal and interest, in gold.

The following table exhibits the amount and character of the public debt, bearing interest, on the 30th day of November, 1875. It will be observed that the greater part of the debt of the United States, incurred during the war, is now represented by bonds issued since the war:

Loan of 1858, act of June 14, 1858, 5 per cent.	$260,000
Loan of February, 1861, (81's) act of Febru'y 8, 1861, 6 per cent.	18,415,000
Oregon War Debt, act of March 2, '61, 6 per c.	945,000
Loan of July and August, 1861, (81's) act of July 17, and Aug. 5, 1861, 6 per cent.	189,321,350
Loan of 1863, (81's), act of March 3, '63, 6 p. c.	75,000,000
Ten-forties of 1864, act of March 3, '64, 5 p. c.	194,566,300
Five-twenties of June, 1864, act of June 30, 1864, 6 per cent.	46,891,100
Five-twenties of 1865, act of March 3, '65, 6 p.c.	152,534,250
Consols of 1865, act of March 3, 1865, 6 p. c.	202,663,100
Consols of 1867, act of March 3, 1865, 6 p. c.	310,622,750
Consols of 1868, act of March 3, 1865, 6 p. c.	37,474,000
Funded Loan of 1881, acts of July 14, 1870, and January 20, 1871, 5 per cent.	465,558,450
Total	$1,694,251,300

SPECIE RESUMPTION.

It now only remains for the money power to bring about a resumption of specie payments and it will have accomplished all its ends; and the American people will once again be completely under its domination. From the day that the old State banks suspended specie payments until the present time, that object has never been lost sight of for a moment. No system of money has ever been devised that confers such absolute control over the currency, and through it over the property and business affairs of a nation, upon the money power, as banks of issue; and hence the adoption of the National Banking scheme. But the greenback interferes very materially with the workings of the system, and it is important that it should be got out of the way. There is also another great incentive to cause the money power to seek a return to specie payments. By a single stroke the bondholding and creditor class will be enriched to the amount of hundreds of millions of dollars.

In January, 1875, the bullionists found themselves strong enough in Congress to pass a law decreeing specie resumption, January 1, 1879. The composition of the House of Representatives, at this time, is worthy of note, and should open the eyes of the people to the necessity of sending a different class of men to represent them in that body. The Hon. Moses W. Field, of Michigan, in a recent speech gives a detailed statement of the professions and callings of the members of the 43rd House, of which he was a member, as follows: "The forty-third Congress, to which I belonged, was composed of 379 members. In this number there were six lumbermen, thirteen manufacturers, seven doctors, fourteen merchants, thirteen farmers, three millers, one land surveyor, one priest, one professor of latin, one doctor of laws, one barber, one mechanic, ninety-nine lawyers, and one hundred and eighty-nine bankers, which includes stockholders in National Banks." Almost a clear majority of members were either bankers or interested in National Banks. The specie resumption act then passed rests like an incubus upon the industrial interests of the country. Everything, however, is working to the satisfaction of the bullionists and the bondholders. As industry and production languish, property of all kinds depreciates in value, and when resumption takes place, the money power will be enabled to gather it in, to the amount of hundreds of millions more, on its own terms. It seems hard indeed that the farmer, the mechanic, the manufacturer, and the producing classes generally, who bear almost the entire burden of taxation, should thus be oppressed by legislation, and millions of industrious people be deprived of the opportunity of even earning their bread, for no other purpose than to further enrich a single class, which contributes not one iota to the general wealth of the country. But the masses, as long as they sink the duties and privileges of freemen in a blind partisanship, and permit themselves to be manipulated by demagogues through the instrumentality of party machinery, can expect no better fate. The question of resumption is one of such vital importance that it is deserving of more than a passing notice. It will, therefore, receive more particular attention in a separate chapter, (Chapter VIII.)

A BRIEF RETROSPECT.

In 1861, when the Federal Government, unable to borrow money at home or abroad, was obliged to appeal to the masses, who were both able and willing to respond, the great question was as to how the resources of the people were to be rendered available to the government. Taxation was impracticable in the beginning, because the government did not possess the machinery for laying and collecting taxes, and, moreover, there was not a sufficient amount of money in circulation at that time to enable the people to meet the extraordinary demands of the occasion. Products and labor the people possessed in abundance, but they could be rendered available only through the instrumentality of a medium of exchange. Besides it was necessary to establish new forms of production, requiring capital to a large amount in the form of money. The first requisite, therefore, was manifestly a medium of exchange. This could be supplied only by the Federal Government; for all power over the currency of the nation is vested in the Federal Government by the Constitution.

The Federal Government wanted guns, ships, food, clothing, transportation, etc. The farmer could furnish food; the manufacturer, guns, wagons, etc.; and the ship builder, ships. Other classes did not possess such things as the government required, but they did possess property of various kinds and labor, which were wanted by the ship builder, the gun-maker and the farmer. The people collectively desired the gun-maker, the ship builder and the farmer to furnish the Federal Government with such articles as it required and they were able to supply, and were willing in turn to supply the gun-maker, the ship builder and the farmer with such property or labor as they might desire, to whatever amount they might be entitled. But how could this interchange be effected? In no better way than by a medium of exchange representing the property of the nation. The people in their collective capacity, through the government, could issue public notes, representing the entire property of the nation, including gold, silver—everything in a word that could be reached by a tax warrant. The public note, of the value of say one dollar, if paid by the government to the gun-maker, would entitle him to receive one dollar's worth of property, neither more nor less. But suppose that the people, after they had made this arrangement with the gun-maker, the farmer and the ship builder, in their collective capacity, through the agency of the government, should refuse individually to receive this paper dollar, representing the property of the nation on which it is a lien, what then? This would clearly be acting in bad faith with the gun-maker, the farmer and the ship builder, and would be tantamount to the people repudiating individually what they had done collectively. Hence it is nothing more than a matter of equity and fair dealing that the public note should be made a legal tender; in fact in no other way could the farmer, the gun-maker and the ship builder be reimbursed from the property of the rest of the people for the guns, food, etc., furnished to the government. As is generally understood by lawyers, if not by political economists, the legal tender money of a country is the basis of all money contracts among its people and the measure of all values; and necessarily conforms to the unit of value fixed in the minds of the people by usage and education. By making the public note a legal tender, it is clothed with all the functions of money. It possesses value (the value of the property which it represents), and by virtue of its legal tender quality the power to measure and exchange value. A public note, based on sound principles, it will be observed, therefore, is capable of performing a two-fold service. In the first place it enables the government which issues it to draw upon the resources of the people in advance of taxation. The government pays it out for property or services, and receives it again for taxes. In the second place, whilst in circulation, it performs all the functions of money, and in the end furnishes the means for the tax payer to meet his obligations to the government. The amount of greenbacks now in circulation is over $360,000,000. The annual revenues of the government amount to about $300,000,000. It is apparent, therefore, that the greenback circulation could all be redeemed in the revenues of the government in a little over a year. From this it is evident that the clamor of the bullionists for the redemption of greenbacks in gold, or the funding of them in bonds payable in gold, is only for the purpose of enabling them to swindle the government and people to the extent of the premium which the government would be obliged to pay to obtain gold for that purpose.

It is clear, then, that the first step for the government to take at the breaking out of the rebellion, to enable it to draw upon the resources of the people, was to issue a legal tender public, or Treasury note. But no more money can be used by a people than is required by the legitimate operations of trade. Professor Bonamy Price, whom we are glad to find right occasionally, illustrates the point in this way: "Carts and money are both tools—instruments of conveyance, endowed with the same nature and subject to the same general laws. The question for each is the same—how many are wanted for the work which they were invented to do. In the case of money, how much gold (or legal tender paper money) can a nation use? How much can it find employment for? The answer, as with carts, must be sought from the special work money has to perform—that is, from the amount of exchanging which calls for the agency of this tool, the quantity of property of which the ownership has to be transferred by this instrument. A cart transfers weight; money, ownership; and all the world knows that the cartage to be done determines the number of carts. In the same way, the ownership of property which requires to be transferred by the actual employment of money itself, determines how much money there ought to be in a nation. No other answer is possible, unless it is denied that money is only a tool; if so, another explanation of the nature of money must be produced." For the government to issue legal tender notes in return for property to an indefinite amount after the channels of circulation had been supplied, would be contrary to all sound principles of finance, as well as political economy. The next step for the government to have pursued was to draw upon the resources of the people by taxation. But as it was manifest at the time that the extraordinary expenses of the war could not be wholly defrayed by taxation—in other words, that the government could not, under the circumstances, act upon the principle—"pay as you go"—without causing oppression and interfering materially with the producing ability of the nation, the third and last step was to issue a bond bearing interest, in order that the governmernt might avail itself of the surplus capital of individuals.

No more perfect system of money or finance than this has ever been devised. It is, moreover, simple and easily understood by the people. This system was embodied in the original legal tender act, as framed by the Hon. E. G. Spaulding, an able financier and statesman. It was ardently supported by the Hon. Thaddeus Stevens, who had thoroughly acquainted himself with all the systems of money and finance of ancient and modern times, with all his powerful ability. It met with the hearty endorsement of the Boards of Trade and Chambers of Commerce of all the principal cities of the North and West. Its adoption by the House of Representatives was hailed with marks of approbation and satisfaction by the intelligent classes everywhere throughout the country. That it would have worked admirably in practice is abundantly demonstrated by the performances of the greenback in the most trying period of the nation's history, and by the manner in which the people took the loan of $500,000,000 of five-twenty bonds.

But through the machinations of the money power, and the weakness and venality of the United States Senate, a full legal tender money system was rejected, and in its stead was adopted a policy, which would have bankrupted, in a short time, any nation not possessing the boundless resources of the United States.

During the war every act and measure relating to finances was calculated to depreciate the public credit; but as soon as the war was over an entire change of policy ensued, calculated to render the burdens of the people doubly oppressive. That this may be seen at a glance, we give below a recapitulation of the leading incidents and measures which marked the two periods—during and after the war, as follows:

FIRST PERIOD—DURING THE WAR.

1. The banks of New York, Boston and Philadelphia procured the suspension of the Sub-Treasury act, Aug. 5, 1861.
2. The banks of New York, Boston and Philadelphia combined to prevent the passage of the legal tender act, and sent delegates to Washington City for that purpose, January, 1862.
3. The representatives of the banks of New York, Boston and Philadelphia effected an arrangement with the Secretary of the Treasury and leading members of the Senate to oppose a full legal tender bill, and to urge the passage of a National Banking law.
4. The legal tender act passed in a mutilated form—interest on bonds and duties on imports made payable in gold, February 25, 1862.
5. Paper emissions authorized by Congress and issued by the Secretary of the Treasury, to an enormous amount, in fifteen different forms.

6. The $500,000,000 of 5-20 six per cent. bonds held by the Secretary of the Treasury for over a year, until the country was flooded with paper emissions of all kinds, and then put out as a popular loan at par amongst the people, to be bought in by the bullionists at fifty cents or less on the dollar.
7. Legal tender Treasury notes (greenbacks) further mutilated (March 3, 1863) by repealing the clause in the original act which made them interchangeable with 5-20 bonds.
8. Immense sums of Treasury notes, bearing interest, payable in one, two and three years, issued, when it was well known that the Treasury Department was unable to make any provision for their payment at maturity.
9. A bill passed (Feb'ry 25, 1863,) authorizing the establishment of National Banks, which could render no aid to the government, and whose currency tended to swell the volume of paper in circulation.
10. The $500,000,000 loan of six per cent. bonds no sooner taken than the Secretary attempted to put out a new loan bearing only five per cent. interest.
11. The failure to float the five per cent. bonds made an excuse for emitting additional sums of Treasury notes, bearing interest, and other forms of paper suitable for a circulating medium.
12. The emission at the close of the war of immense sums of 7-30 Treasury notes, payable in three years, and convertible at the option of the holder into long bonds bearing gold interest.

SECOND PERIOD—AFTER THE WAR.

1. "All bonds, Treasury notes and other obligations of the government shall be exempt from taxation by or under State or municipal authority." (Act of June 30, 1864.

Although passed before the termination of the war, this act belongs to this period. Like the National Banking law, it simply anticipated events.)

2. McCulloch issued his Fort Wayne decree, announcing his determination to contract the currency.
3. McCulloch submitted his annual report, December, 1865, in which he recommended contraction.
4. Congress passed a resolution, December 18, 1865, concurring in the views of the Secretary of the Treasury in relation to the necessity of contracting the currency.
5. Congress passed an act, April 12, 1866, authorizing a contraction of the currency.
6. McCulloch began to pay off the 5-20 bonds in gold or its equivalent.
7. McCulloch substituted long bonds bearing gold interest for Treasury notes, etc., to the amount of about $1,200,000,000, which operated as a contraction of the medium of exchange of the country to that amount, occasioning great financial derangement. Also retired over $70,000,000 of greenbacks between August, 1865, and July, 1868.
8. Congress, compelled by public sentiment, repealed (January, 1868) so much of the act of April 12, 1866, as provided for the retirement of greenbacks, but took no note of the contraction in other forms of the currency.
9. The people of both political parties began to protest against the payment of the 5-20 bonds in gold, as a violation of the spirit and letter of the act under which they were issued.
10. The money power selected a President of the United States (1868.)
11. The President of the United States, in his inaugural message, March 4, 1869, notified the public that he would regard all who did not favor the payment of 5-20 bonds

in gold as repudiators, who need expect no favors from his administration.

12. Congress passed a credit strengthening act, March 18, 1869, the first act which received President Grant's official sanction.
13. The original loan of 5-20 bonds paid off in full in gold or its equivalent.
14. Congress passed a law, July 14, 1870, authorizing the Secretary of the Treasury to refund $500,000,000 of the public debt in bonds payable, principal and interest, in gold.
15. McCulloch's contraction policy bore its legitimate fruits, and the country was visited by an old fashioned commercial crash and money panic, September, 1873.
16. The people demanded relief, and Congress, at its next session, passed a bill authorizing the reissue of the greenbacks which had been retired (44,000,000), and fixing the amount of the greenback circulation at $400,000,000. This bill was denounced by the money power as an "inflation" measure, and accordingly was vetoed by President Grant, April 22, 1874.
17. The people rebuked the action of the President by electing, at the next general election, in the fall of 1874, a Democratic House of Representatives.
18. At its next session, Congress (the old Congress), under the pretense of affording relief to the oppressed industries of the country, made National Banking free to bondholders, by act of January 14, 1875.
19. And at the same time decreed specie resumption, to take place January 1, 1879.
20. An act to complete the refunding of the public debt in gold bonds is now pending before Congress.
21. Bonds of the United States, which during the war were bought and sold at as low as thirty-five cents on the dollar

in gold, now sell for over $1.18, or at a premium of over five per cent. in gold.

In 1865, when the Rebellion terminated, the producing forces of the Northern and Western States, the workingmen, the land, the machinery, the mines, the water power, etc., were developing wealth in every possible direction, and the people, individually free from debt, were in the enjoyment of unparalleled prosperity. The wealth of the nation, in spite of the ravages of war, had increased as it had never done before. The assessed valuation of the property of the nation in 1870, notwithstanding the ruined condition of the South, was over $30,000,000,000, as against $16,000,000,000 in 1860. Out of the abundance of their productions the people were enabled to meet all the demands of the government with ease. The Federal Government, indeed, began to pay off the public debt rapidly. But in carrying out the policy of the money power, it first paid off, by substituting bonds, all those forms of indebtedness of the government which served the purposes of money, thus depriving the producing forces of the nation of their most important tool.

At this time the South, with all her magnificent resources, had been restored to the Union. Money was necessary to set the producing forces of that section at work. Instead of wisely taking this fact into consideration, and making some provision that would enable the people of that section to recover from the disasters of the war, and contribute their share towards bearing the burdens of government, an entirely opposite policy was pursued. The production of cotton, the chief staple of the South, in 1870 amounted to only 3,011,996 bales, or a little over 50 per cent. of the amount raised in 1860.

Now the American people are poor and in debt. Nearly all forms of productive industry are paralyzed, and the channels of trade are stagnant or sluggish. Real estate is rapidly depreciating in value, which will inevitably result in a general foreclosure of mortgages and transfer of property from the debtor to the creditor class throughout the country. Instead of a million of non-producers carrying muskets, as was the case during the war, there are now several millions of people, who would gladly work for a mere subsistence, in a state of enforced idleness, living on the bitter bread of public or private charity. In a country possessing boundless natural wealth, tramps and paupers have become common. The nation is scarcely producing more now than the necessities of life. And yet the people are told that the present condition of affairs is due to over production and like causes. The only over production troubling the nation just now is an over production of fools and rascals—rascals who teach such nonsense, to divert the public mind from the true source of the trouble, and fools who believe it. Since the attempt to re-establish a false monetary system by means of contraction has worked such wide spread ruin, it would seem to be but the part of common wisdom, on the part of the people, to demand a different policy, if not from conviction, at least as an experiment. It certainly could not make matters worse.

CHAPTER VII.

THE NATIONAL BANKING SYSTEM.

SECRETARY CHASE, soon after he entered upon the discharge of the duties of Secretary of the Treasury, became enlisted in a scheme to destroy the old State banks and erect in their stead a system of National Banks whose circulation would be uniform throughout the country. In his first report to Congress, in December, 1861, he recommended the passage of a law to accomplish this end. A bill was immediately prepared by the Hon. E. G. Spaulding, chairman of the Sub-Committee of Ways and Means, but it became manifest that the machinery of such a system could not be put into operation in time to meet the demands upon the government, and Congress was obliged to pass a law authorizing the Secretary of the Treasury to issue Treasury notes (greenbacks.)

The admirable manner in which the greenback performed the uses of a medium of exchange and its great popularity rendered it tolerably certain that the people would never willingly abandon it to return to the use of State bank currency. The money power was quick to perceive this, and also that in no other way than through the instrumentality of such a scheme as that proposed by Secretary Chase and his advisers could it hope to again obtain its former control over the currency of the country. The National Banking scheme, therefore, which at first excited some opposition on the part of the old State banks, soon came to be regarded by the majority of them as of the highest importance. In December, 1862, Secretary Chase, in his second annual report, again urged the passage of a National Banking law, for the purpose of establishing "one sound, uniform circulation of equal value throughout the country, upon the foundation of national credit, combined with private capital." There was no expectation or even pretense that the system could aid the government in any way in the war then pending.

On the 2d of February, 1863, Senator Sherman reported a National Currency Bank bill from the Finance Committee to the Senate. It was taken up in the Senate on the 9th, and passed on the 12th by a vote of 22 to 21. On the 13th it was sent to the House, but was not referred to the Committee on Ways and Means. On the 19th it was taken up for consideration in the House, and was passed on the 20th by a vote of 78 to 64. It was approved by the President and became a law February 25, 1863.

The brief time given to the consideration of this important act, establishing a consolidation in the interest of the money power, compared with which the monster that Jackson slew (the United States Bank) was a mere pigmy, cannot escape notice. The people were absorbed in the war, and the money power had full sway in Congress. The Hon. W. P. Noble, one of the few members who protested against the passage of the act, alluded to this fact in the opening of his speech against the bill in these terms: "Mr. Speaker, it is not because I expect, by anything I can say, to change a single vote upon this bill, that I now claim the attention of the House. On the contrary I am satisfied, from the great and untiring efforts that are being made by the Secretary of the Treasury in its favor, that the passage of this bill is a foregone conclusion; not because it, or anything like it, is demanded by the people, but simply because it is a pet measure of the present head of that department."

THE NATIONAL BANKING LAW.

The National Banking law provides: First: That any number of persons not less than five may form an association for carrying on the business of banking.

Second: That any such association shall have corporate power, to have succession for the period of twenty years, to make contracts, to sue and be sued, etc.

Third: The capital of such associations shall be not less than $50,000 in places whose population does not exceed six thousand; not less than $100,000 in places whose population exceeds six thousand; and not less than $200,000 in places whose population exceeds fifty thousand.

Fourth:* The aggregate amount of circulation is fixed at $354,000,000, to be apportioned as follows: $150,000,000 among the several States and territories according to representative population; $150,000,000 to be distributed by the Secretary of the Treasury according to his discretion; and the remaining $54,000,000† to such States and territories, having less than their share, as may make application prior to July 12, 1871.

Fifth: No association is authorized to commence business until it shall have deposited United States bonds to the amount of $30,000 with the Treasurer of the United States.

Sixth: Every such association is entitled to receive from the Comptroller of the Currency circulating notes to the amount of ninety per cent. of the capital stock, if it does not exceed $500,000; eighty per cent. if it exceeds $500,000, but does not exceed $1,000,000; seventy-five per cent. if it exceeds $1,000,000, but does not exceed $3,000,000; and sixty per cent. if it exceeds $3,000,000.

*By the act of January 14, 1875, this section was repealed.
†$54,000,000 additional bank notes were authorized by the act of July, 1870.

No National Bank currency was issued until about the beginning of 1864. It will be remembered that the $500,-000,000 of 5-20 bonds were not sold until the latter part of 1863; consequently matters were not yet ripe for the bullionists and bankers. In 1864, however, their plans were sufficiently matured to enable them to run gold up to an enormous premium, in what Mr. Fessenden, who was then Secretary of the Treasury, considered a very "unpatriotic" manner. For more than a year gold fluctuated between about 1.50 and 2.50, according to the success which attended the efforts of the gold operators in controlling the market. Bonds of the government were bought during this period at as low a price as thirty-five cents on the dollar in gold. This gave the bullionists and bankers an excellent opportunity to lay in, at low figures, all the bonds that were needed to establish National Banks.

The amount of National Bank notes in circulation on January 1, 1864, was $280,000; on July 1, 1864, it was $31,234,420; and on July 1, 1865, it was $146,336,030. Shortly after this the whole amount authorized by law was taken, and National Bank stock began to command a premium. Thus was the National Banking system foisted upon the country at a time when it was neither needed nor desired, solely for the purpose of enabling the money power to again usurp the right of supplying the nation with a medium of exchange. It only remains now to retire the greenback and resume specie payments, and the money power of the United States will be clothed with a more absolute control over the monetary affairs of the country than it ever had before.

OF THE ORGANIZATION OF NATIONAL BANKS.

National Banks are established on the theory of combining private capital with public credit. It will be found on examination, however, that this is purely a delusion. Private capital is not an essential element in the establishment of a National Bank; private credit will do as well. This may be illustrated in various ways. Suppose A. owns $100,000 in 6 per cent. United States bonds. B., C., D., E. and F., five persons, jointly borrow these bonds from A., agreeing to pay him the interest regularly as it matures, and return the same or like bonds at some specified time, say in five or ten years. B., C., D., E. and F. organize a National Bank, deposit the bonds with the Treasurer of the United States, and obtain $90,000 of National Bank currency from the Comptroller. So far as the bank or its currency is concerned, there is no element of private capital involved in the matter. Its corporators or stockholders have not paid in a dollar for the capital stock of the concern. A.'s bonds are not capital, because the people have already borrowed A.'s capital and are paying him six per cent. interest in gold for it. Upon what capital then is the bank established? Upon no other capital clearly than the public credit represented by the $90,000 of bank currency lent to B., C., D., E. and F., without interest, on the strength of what the government owes A.

There are of course innumerable ways in which individuals can utilize their capital or credit in the establishment of National Banks. The Hon. S. S. Marshall, of Illinois, in a speech on the floor of Congress, July 21, 1868, mentioned the following instance: "An association of gentlemen (in an Eastern State) raised $300,000 in currency. They went to the office of the Register of the Treasury and exchanged their currency for $300,000 in six per cent. gold bearing bonds. They then went to the office of the Comptroller of the Currency, in the same building, organized a National

Bank, deposited their $300,000 in bonds and received for their bank $270,000 in national currency. They had let the government have $30,000 in currency more than they received for banking purposes, and had on deposit $300,000, on which they received as interest from the government $18,000 a year in gold (and exempt from taxation.) This was pretty good financiering for these bankers to receive $18,000 a year in gold on the $30,000 in currency which they had thus loaned to the government. But this is not the whole story. They had their bank made a public depository. They soon discovered that there was scarcely ever less than $1,000,000 of government money deposited within their vaults. They did not like to see this vast sum lie idle. They, therefore, took $1,000,000 of this government money and bought $1,000,000 of five-twenty bonds with it. In other words they loaned $1,000,000 of the government's own money to the government, and deposited the bonds received in the vaults of their bank, on which they received from the same government $60,000 a year in gold as interest. Thus for the $30,000 in currency, which they originally loaned the government, they received annually in all $78,000 in gold." But this was by no means the limit to the legalized robbery which these gentlemen were capable of perpetrating under the National Banking law. Since they had no scruples about investing the government deposit of $1,000,000 in 5-20 bonds and appropriating the interest to their own use, it is not at all likely that they would stop there, when, by simply depositing the $1,000,000 in 5-20 bonds with the Comptroller of the Currency, instead of in their bank vaults, they could draw eighty per cent. more currency, or by starting two new banks of $500,000 each, they could draw ninety per cent. more currency, to substitute for that amount of the original deposit of the government used by them.

The following table exhibits the number, nominal capital, etc., of the National Banks in existence September 1, 1873, together with the amount of their earnings, from March, 1873, to September, 1873:

	No. Banks.	Capital.	Surplus.	Net Earnings.
New England States,	496	$157,014,832	$38,303,887	$10,103,736
Middle States,	591	192,234,009	53,431,089	12,565,331
Southern States,	161	33,259,530	3,600,607	2,246,024
Western States,	707	105,592,580	22,778,265	8,206,909
Totals,	1955	$488,100,951	$118,113,848	$33,122,000

At this time, September, 1873, the National Bank circulation was as follows:

	Amount of Circulation.	Circulation per capita.
New England States	$110,489,996	$31.68
Middle States	124,608,139	12.82
Southern States	38,160,308	2.91
Western States	78,785,148	7.09
Pacific States and Territories	1,924,688	1.82
Total for States and Territories	$353,968,279	$9.18

The profits of the National Banks, according to their own reports, as set forth in the foregoing tables, are enormous. This will appear from the following:

Nominal capital of National Banks in 1873...$488,100,951
Bank note circulation furnished by the government, without interest.................... 353,968,279

Real capital.......................$134,132,672
Surplus earnings................... 118,113,848

Total real capital and surplus earnings........$252,246,520

Net earnings from March to September, 1873, (six months) $33,122,000. The net earnings consequently amounted to 25½ per cent., or 51 per cent. a year on the real capital ($134,132,672); or 13 per cent., or 26 per cent. a year on the real capital and surplus earnings added together ($252,246,-520.)

These enormous profits operate as a tax on the medium

of exchange of the nation, and enter into the price of all commodities. They also enable the banks to control the circulating medium of the country, and explain why it is that periodically money leaves the channels of trade and becomes concentrated in the vaults of the banks.

THE PANIC OF 1873.

The enormous contraction of the circulating medium of exchange and evidences of indebtedness of the government, which were used as such, inaugurated and carried on by McCulloch, together with the operations of the National Banking system, began to affect the industries of the country injuriously as early as 1867. Mr. Spaulding estimated the amount of paper issues which served the purposes of currency, on the 30th of January, 1864, at $1,125,877,034, and to this amount is to be added several hundred millions of 7-30 Treasury notes issued in 1864 and 1865. The greater part of this vast sum was called in by the government prior to 1868, and its place supplied in part by bank note currency and bank credit. Business could no longer be done for cash, as was the case when the channels of trade were fully supplied with a medium of exchange, and business men were compelled, by reason of the growing scarcity of money, to resort, as in days before the war, to the banks and borrow bank credit. During the year 1866 the banks increased their loans (inflated their credit) $107,600,000. As contraction went on, bank loans increased, and it was only a question of time as to when the bubble of inflated bank credit would burst.*

That McCulloch and the bankers generally anticipated financial distress amongst the people, and probably a commercial crash and money panic, is clear from the correspondence between Mr. Spaulding and Secretary McCulloch,

*See page 20.

in December, 1866, from which we take the following extracts: Mr. Spaulding, in a letter dated at his banking house in Buffalo, December 4, 1866, to McCulloch, says: "You have no doubt now, to a large extent, control of the finances of the country (by virtue of the contraction act of April 12, 1866), and I think that you will, of necessity, contract moderately, so as to preserve a tolerably easy money market, in order to be able to fund the compound 6's and 7-30's into long gold bearing bonds between this and the 15th of July, 1868. There may be occasional spasms and tightness for money with the speculators, but generally I shall look for plenty of money for legitimate business *for at least a year to come.*" To this McCulloch replied, December 7, 1866: "What we need is an increase of labor. If we could have the productive industry of the country in full exercise, we could return to specie payments without any very large curtailment of United States notes. My object has been to keep the market steady, and to work back to specie payments *without a financial collapse.*" Whilst thus prating about "having the productive industry of the country in full exercise," McCulloch was straining his authority as Secretary of the Treasury to deprive the productive industry of the country of its most essential tool, a medium of exchange, and give to the banks the entire control of its monetary affairs. That a financial collapse or commercial crash did not immediately follow the sudden and complete retirement of the various forms of indebtedness of the government used as a currency, was due, first, to the productive strength of the country which had been enormously developed during and after the war, by reason of the abundance of money in circulation; second, to the large increase of bank note circulation, and the great inflation of bank credit which followed; and, third, to the large volume of greenback money in the hands of the people, which, not being burdened with interest, was as yet beyond the control of the banks.

In 1866 the best 60 day paper ruled in New York City at 5 to 7 per cent. In January, 1867, the same paper rated at 8 to 10 per cent., and during the following summer a great many failures occurred. The effects of McCulloch's policy of contraction began to be seriously felt throughout the country. In obedience to public sentiment, Congress was compelled, in January, 1868, to suspend the law authorizing the retirement of the legal tender notes (greenbacks.) The amount of greenbacks outstanding at this time was $356,000,000. Congress, however, took no action in reference to the enormous contraction of paper emissions in other forms. The amount of paper emissions of the government which were actively employed as a tool of industry in the production and distribution of wealth in 1865 and 1866 was about $1,800,000,000. When McCulloch, under the flimsy pretense of bringing the country back to "honest money," set out to retire this vast volume of currency, *what provision had been made by the government to supply its place? None whatever, except the establishment of National Banks*, authorized to issue bank currency to the amount of $300,000,000. The practical effect of McCulloch's policy, therefore, was simply to deprive the nation of any other circulating medium than bank currency. In view of these circumstances it is impossible to arrive at any other conclusion than that McCulloch had deliberately conspired with the money power to enrich the bondholders and **to give the National Banks control of the monetary affairs of the nation**. The history of the world furnishes no parallel to this gigantic scheme, having for its **object the robbery of a nation** under cover of law, so **successfully carried out by McCulloch** and his associates.

The policy of contraction and the National Banking system together soon wrought a complete revolution in the business affairs of the country. In 1865-66 the producing forces of the nation were in active operation, producing wealth as it had never been produced before. "The American people waked up each new morning to feel that there were great duties before them." Labor was fully employed at the very time that McCulloch was hypocritically prating about "the need of an increase of labor" and the necessity of having "the productive industry of the country in full exercise." Business was everywhere done cheaply, because it was done for cash, and, as McCulloch himself has since admitted, the people, "individually, were free from debt." The enormous productive strength of the country was in full exercise, and the immense burden of taxation imposed by the war was scarcely felt. Indeed, the revenues of the government were so large during this period that the public debt was extinguished to the amount of about $500,000,000.

We now turn to what followed. All evidences of indebtedness of the government used as a currency, except the greenback, had been retired—paid off or converted into long bonds bearing gold interest. The National Banking system was in the full tide of successful operation. By the act of July, 1870, an additional issue of bank notes, to the amount of $54,000,000, was authorized, making in all $354,000,000. The entire issue authorized by law was in active employment, and bank stock commanded a high premium. The circulating medium of the country in 1869 consisted of lawful money and bank currency as follows:

Legal tender notes..............................	$356,000,000
National Bank Currency.....................	300,000,000
Fractional Currency about.................	37,000,000
	$693,000,000
To this add amount of National Bank currency authorized by act of July, 1870.........	54,000,000
	$747,000,000

The National Banks of the principal cities were required by law to keep on hand in lawful money of the United States an amount equal to at least twenty-five per cent. of the aggregate amount of their notes in circulation and their deposits; and other associations fifteen per cent. As bank deposits and loans increased, requiring a proportionate increase of the reserve of lawful money, it is manifest that a further contraction of the circulating medium followed. The following table exhibits the inflation of bank credit that took place from 1866 to 1873:

DATE.	CIRCULATION.	DEPOSITS.	LOANS.
Jan. 1, 1866	$213,100,000	$513,600,000	$498,800,000
" 1867	291,000,000	555,100,000	608,400,000
" 1868	294,300,000	531,800,000	616,600,000
July 1, 1868	294,900,000	575,800,000	655,700,000
Jan. 1, 1869	294,400,000	568,500,000	644,900,000
July 1, 1869	292,700,000	574,300,000	656,300,000
Jan. 1, 1870	292,800,000	546,200,000	688,800,000
July 1, 1870	291,100,000	542,100,000	719,300,000
Jan. 1, 1871	302,200,000	561,900,000	768,300,000
July 1, 1871	307,700,000	602,100,000	789,400,000
Oct. 1, 1872	333,400,000	625,700,000	872,500,000
Sep. 12, 1873	339,000,000	622,600,000	940,200,000

Instead of $1,800,000,000 of paper currency, a large portion of which bore interest in the hands of the holders, filling the channels of trade, the business of the country was now carried on with bank currency and bank credit (about $1,000,000,000), involving the payment of an enormous tribute to the National Banks for its use. The business of the country was no longer done for cash. Money became scarce and commanded a high price, and the price of property fell in a corresponding ratio. New business enterprises were no longer thought of. Those already established, yielding small profits and requiring ready money for their successful operation, were obliged to succumb. The ability of the nation to produce wealth was enormously diminished. Taxes, which before were scarcely felt, now became a great burden. Merchants and manufacturers who were obliged to pay interest for money and bank credit added the amount to the cost of their goods. The retail dealer was obliged to do the same, and the cost of bank currency and bank credit, several times multiplied, had to be paid in the end by the consumer, whose ability to pay had, for the same reasons, been greatly diminished. Such is the natural course of affairs under a system of currency furnished and controlled by banks of issue. The same system had been tried for over sixty years prior to the war and had proved utterly unsound. It had inflicted upon the country a commercial crash on an average every six years. And the marvelous thing is, that notwithstanding all their bitter experience, the people of the United States should suffer such a system to be re-established in a more powerful and dangerous form than ever. During this period the industries of the country were sustained and buoyed up in a manner that is worthy of special mention. Congress had granted a large number of subsidies in the shape of lands to aid in the construction of railroads. Bonds secured by mortgages on the lands granted by Congress had been negotiated, mostly abroad, to the amount of many hundreds of millions of dollars. The funds thus acquired contributed largely to the support of many industries, which otherwise would have been obliged to succumb to McCulloch's policy. Among other corporations thus subsidized was the Northern Pacific Railroad Company, owned and controlled by the banking house of Jay Cooke and Company. It was confidently expected by Jay Cooke and Company that the bonds of the Northern Pacific Railroad Company could be negotiated abroad. The Austrian and German bankers, to whom they were offered, however, sent over two experts to examine the road and the country through which it extended. They reported adversely to taking the bonds. Jay Cooke and Company then attempted to dispose of their bonds to the American public, through the aid of the religious press and the clergy of the country. Their plan was only partially successful. The times had become too stringent, and on the 18th of September, 1873, the banking house of Jay Cooke and Company failed. The country had been ripe for a commercial crash for some time, and this brought matters to a crisis. The failure of Jay Cooke and Company was immediately followed by the failure of a number of leading banks in New York City. The Stock Exchange of that city also closed its doors for a period of ten days. The premium on gold began to decline, and fell during the month to $7\frac{3}{8}$ per cent. Greenbacks commanded a premium over certified checks of from $\frac{1}{4}$ to 3 per cent. The suspension of payments by the banks of New York soon extended to all the principal cities and towns throughout the country. Exchange on New York, which usually commanded a premium, was at a discount, if not entirely unavailable. The suspension lasted about forty days, and the industrial interests of the country received a shock from which they have not yet recovered.

To the great mass of the people, who judge of the prosperity of the country by the activity observable in its business affairs, the panic of 1873 was wholly unexpected and came like a clap of thunder from a cloudless sky. The harvest of the year was about over, and the crops were good. The mining and manufacturing interests seemed to be flourishing, and to all external appearances there was abundant evidence of general prosperity. But, beneath the surface, matters presented a very different appearance. The industries of the country had been laboring from year to year since 1866 under an increasing burden imposed by the banks. Business had ceased to be done for cash, and business men everywhere were carrying a load, more or less, of credit—struggling on from year to year in the hope that the coming spring or the coming fall would in some way bring a change that would afford relief. A temporary spurt in business might relieve an individual here and there; but under such a system of money there could be no general relief. A commercial crash was inevitable. The reason of this is easily explained. The average growth of national wealth is about three and one-half per cent. per annum. Individual wealth cannot increase more rapidly than that. The higher gains of some are counterbalanced by the lower gains or absolute losses of others. As money is an essential tool in the production and distribution of wealth, it is important that it should be abundant and rule at low rates of interest. But under a system of banks of issue money scarcely circulates at all. It is locked up in bank vaults, and in its stead the public is obliged to use bank currency. Bank currency can only be obtained by the payment of a high rate of interest. It is, therefore, far more expensive than even gold and silver. These metals simply cost their equivalent in labor or products. When once obtained they will circulate in the channels of trade, whilst they remain in the country, unburdened with interest. Individuals may acquire a surplus and lend it to others, but this is an individual transaction. The gold or silver thus lent is put to use by the borrowers and passes into the channels of circulation free of interest. The same is true of legal tender paper money issued by the government. It costs its face value in labor or products to obtain it from the government. It enters into circulation unencumbered by interest. Individuals may acquire a surplus of legal tender paper money and lend it to others. As in the case of gold or silver, this is purely an individual transaction. Neither gold nor legal tender paper money can accumulate value except when employed. But bank currency constitutes a peculiar medium of exchange very different in its nature from gold money or legal tender paper money. Bank currency is not money. Bank notes are simply evidences of indebtedness of the banks which issue them—promises to pay money. They enter into circulation encumbered with interest, and continue to accumulate value for the bank which issues them, whether they are performing the uses of money or not. For the sake of illustration, say that A., a manufacturer, borrows a $100 bank note from a National Bank for sixty days at six per cent. interest. He uses this note in the prosecution of his business, and adds the interest which he is obliged to pay to the bank to the cost of the article manufactured by him. At the expiration of sixty days, A., unable to return the identical note borrowed by him, pays the bank with a $100 greenback. This in turn is lent by the bank to B., and so on indefinitely. The bank is thus enabled to realize compound interest indefinitely on the original note lent to A., which was not money but simply credit—no matter what becomes of it, whether it is occupying the channels of circulation or rotting at the bottom of the ocean. It is apparent, therefore, that when the nation uses a medium of exchange consisting of bank currency it is obliged to pay compound interest for its use. As must be manifest this is a great burden upon the industries of the nation. The more this kind of currency is inflated the heavier will be the burden imposed upon the industries of the country. A great deal is said by the money power and their organs in regard to the evils of inflation, whenever it is proposed to increase the issue of legal tender paper money, but nothing is ever said about the real danger, which invariably attends the inflation of bank currency and bank credit. By reference to the table given on page 255, showing the deposits and loans of the banks from 1866 to 1873, it will be seen that the banks inflated their credit from $498,800,000 in 1866 to $940,200,000 in 1873. This immense sum of inflated credit, bearing compound interest, entered into and ramified all the industries of the country, and added immensely to the cost of production.

The following table exhibits the discounts on six months' notes for a term of sixty years. We copy it, along with the following explanatory remarks, from Kellogg "A thousand dollars in money are taken, and with this sum a note payable at six months is discounted. When the first note is paid, a second note having six months to run is discounted with its proceeds, and a third note with the proceeds of the second. This calculation is continued on six months' notes for sixty years. The table shows the accumulation on $1,000 for sixty years, at the various rates of 1, 2, 3, 4, 5, 6, 7, 8, 12, 18, 24 and 30 per cent. per annum, taking off the discount, as is always done by banks and brokers.

1 PER CENT.	5 PER CENT.	12 PER CENT.
10 years...... $1,105 45	10 years...... $1,659 24	10 years.... $3,447 13
20 " 1,222 02	20 " 2,753 06	20 " 11,881 90
30 " 1,350 87	30 " 4,567 97	30 " 40,957 07
40 " 1,493 33	40 " 7,579 33	40 " 141,177 95
50 " 1,650 78	50 " 12,575 87	50 " 486,644 91
60 " 1,824 87	60 " 20,866 35	60 " 1,677,481 45

2 PER CENT.	6 PER CENT.	18 PER CENT.
10 years...... $1,222 64	10 years...... $1,838 93	10 years ... $6,594 35
20 " 1,494 83	20 " 3,381 66	20 " 43,485 48
30 " 1,827 63	30 " 6,218 65	30 " 286,758 62
40 " 2,234 52	40 " 11,435 67	40 " ...1,890,988 71
50 " 2,732 00	50 " 21,029 39	50 " ...12,469,831 63
60 " 3,340 23	60 " 38,671 58	60 " ...82,230,496 79

3 PER CENT.	7 PER CENT.	24 PER CENT.
10 years...... $1,352 93	10 years...... $2,039 17	10 years.... $12,892 78
20 " 1,830 46	20 " 4,158 22	20 " 166,223 76
30 " 2,476 43	30 " 8,479 32	30 " ...2,143,086 39
40 " 3,350 44	40 " 17,290 79	40 " ...27,630,338 24
50 " 4,532 91	50 " 35,258 90	50 " ..356,231,914 13
60 " 6,132 73	60 " 71,898 92	60 " 4,592,819,317 86

4 PER CENT.	8 PER CENT.	30 PER CENT.
10 years...... $1,497 89	10 years...... $2,262 43	10 years, $25,800 11
20 " 2,243 66	20 " 5,118 59	20 " 665,645 68
30 " 3,360 75	30 " 11,580 46	30 " 17,173,731 66
40 " 5,034 01	40 " 26,199 97	40 " 443,084,165 99
50 " 7,540 36	50 " 59,275 70	50 " 11,431,620,222 06
60 " 11,294 60	60 " 134,107 05	60 " 294,936,059,207 37

"The highest rate calculated is thirty per cent. per annum, or two and a half per month, a rate not nearly so high as is often paid in Wall street.

"In the foregoing table it appears that interest at one per cent. would transfer $824 worth of the products of labor to the capitalists to pay for the use of $1,000 for the sixty years; at six per cent., $37,671.58; at seven per cent., $70,898.92; and at thirty per cent., $294,956,058,207.37. In any community the rise of the rate of interest on all the money used, whether for a longer or a shorter period, transfers from producers to capitalists a sum proportioned to the increase of the rate per cent., as demonstrated in this table."

The power of money at interest to accumulate value is not fully understood or appreciated by the public. The following extract, which will further serve to illustrate this point, is taken from an able lecture delivered by Wallace P. Groom, Esq., editor and publisher of the New York Mercantile Journal, on the subject of the "Currency Needs of Commerce:"

"Many carelessly infer that the increase of money at six per cent. is just twice as rapid as at three per cent.; but in reality the increase is vastly more rapid than this. In one hundred years, at six per cent., the increase on any given sum is about eighteen times as much as at three per cent.

"If one dollar be invested and the interest added to the principal annually, at the rates named, we shall have the following result as the accumulation of one hundred years:

One dollar, 100 years, at				One dollar, 100 y'rs, at 7 per cent.,		$ 868
"	"	2	"	7¼	"	2,903
"	"	2½	"	11¾	"	5,543
"	"	3	"	19¼	"	13,809
"	"	3½	"	31¼	"	84,676
"	"	4	"	50½	"	1,174,405
"	"	4½	"	81½	"	13,145,007
"	"	5	"	131¾	"	2,551,799,404
"	"	6	"	340		

"There are probably few, however familiar with the subject of the rapid increase of capital put out at interest, who would not be startled at the statement that the cost of the outfit of Cristopher Columbus in his first voyage of discovery, put at interest at six per cent., would by this time have amounted to more than the entire money value of this continent, together with the accumulations from the industry of those who have lived on it. If any doubt this, let them reckon the amount, estimating the entire outfit to have cost only the small sum of five thousand dollars, and remembering that money doubles, at six per cent., in a little less than twelve years—or accurately in eleven years, ten months and twenty-one days. Allowing it to double every twelve years, this five thousand dollars at interest at six per cent-, since 1492, it will be found, will have amounted to $17,895,700,000,000; which, estimating the population of the entire continent of America (North and South) to be eighty-five millions, or seventeen million families (averaging five members each), would give more than a million dollars as the possession of every one of these. The interest upon a million of dollars at six per cent. is sixty thousand dollars, which would now be the princely annual income of each of these seventeen million families from the accumulations up to this time upon so small a sum as that named for the outfit of the discoverer."

But it must not be forgotten that banks of issue do not lend capital or money, but simply credit; and in this consists the great injustice of the system. A single class is clothed with authority to emit bills of credit, and compel all other classes to use them as a circulating medium and pay compound interest for their use. The fact that the government issues the National Bank notes to the banks does not change their nature. It is simply equivalent to the government guaranteeing their payment. The notes themselves represent the credit of the institutions which issue them. There is no sound reason why the government should confer this privilege upon the bondholder and the banker, and not upon the farmer, the merchant or the manufacturer. On the other hand it is in violation of the plainest principles of equity, as well as public policy, for the government to bestow such a privilege upon any class.

How long it takes the money power, through the machinery of banks of issue, to rob the people of their annual increase of wealth ($3\frac{1}{2}$ per cent.) is not a matter of speculation. The experience of sixty years demonstrates that the system will bring about a commercial crash on an average every six years. A commercial crash is simply a general settlement and a re-distribution of property rendered necessary by the natural operations of the system—by the manner in which the people are obliged to conduct their affairs.

The enormous cost of a medium of exchange, consisting of bank currency and bank credit, may be arrived at approximately in several ways. On the 1st of September, 1875, there were in operation 2,087 National Banks. The net earnings of the banks for the previous six months amounted to about $30,000,000, or $60,000,000 for the year. The officers of the banks, including presidents cashiers, tellers, bookkeepers, clerks, attorneys, notaries, etc., constitute an army of non-producers. Averaging the number at ten for each bank would give 20,000 persons. The chief officers of a bank are usually large stockholders, and the subordinate positions are mostly filled by their relatives, and in no other business, perhaps, do salaries rate so high. Averaging the salaries at $2,000 per year each for 20,000 persons will give a total of $40,000,000, which, added to the net earnings, gives a grand total of $100,000,000 a year. Or, again, the aggregate loans and discounts of the National Banks on the first day of October, 1875, amounted to $980,222,951. At ten per cent. interest the amount paid for this sum would be over $98,000.000. To this add the interest paid by the people on the bonds deposited with the Treasurer of the United States—about $390,000,000—at six per cent. in gold—about $27,000,000, and it will give a grand total of $127,000,000. From this it appears that the people are paying annually to the banks the enormous sum of about $127,000,000, a sum greater than the interest on the public debt, for the use of some $350,000,000 of bank currency. This burden is entirely unnecessary. A medium of exchange could and ought to be furnished by the government; or, in the language of Jefferson, "bank currency should be suppressed and the circulation restored to the nation to whom it belongs." The people would then have a medium of exchange unencumbered with interest, and, what is vastly more important, one that would occupy the channels of circulation, subject only to the natural laws of trade.

THE PROSTRATION OF INDUSTRY.

The prostration of all forms of industry which followed the panic of 1873 still continues. Indeed, matters are growing worse. The following table exhibits the number of failures, with the aggregate amount of liabilities, which have taken place since 1863:

IN THE NORTHERN STATES.

Year.	Number of Failures.	Aggregate Liabilities.
1863	495	$7,899,000
1864	520	8,579,000
1865	530	17,625,000
1866	632	47,333,000
1867	2,386	86,218,000
1868	2,197	57,275,000
1869	2,411	65,246,000

IN THE WHOLE COUNTRY.

1870	3,551	88,242,000
1871	2,915	85,252,000
1872	4,069	121,056,000
1873	5,181	228,490,000
1874	5,695	151,689,000
1875	7,404	195,289,000
1876 (first quarter)	2,806	64,644,000

The failures during 1875, it will be seen, numbered 7,404. The failures for the first quarter of 1875 numbered 1,733; and for the first quarter of 1876, 2,806, or an increase of over 60 per cent. over the corresponding quarter of last year. At the same rate the failures this year will reach about 12,000.

In times prior to the war, when bank currency was nominally redeemable in specie, the banks did not hesitate to expand their circulation as soon as a general settlement had been effected and "confidence had been restored" through the instrumentality of the Sheriff, which usually took about one year. Business then began to improve, and the banks and the people together soon started on another era of inflation and speculation, only to wind up in a few years in another crash. But now a different condition of affairs exists. Gold bears a premium over the lawful money of the country, because it is a full legal tender, whilst lawful money (greenbacks) is only a partial tender. It is true in ante-war times bank currency was at a discount as compared with gold, but then it was issued at par and the loss fell upon the people. Now, however, specie payments have been decreed to take place January 1, 1879, and the banks do not intend to redeem their notes in specie until the government has first furnished them with the specie. Consequently they are calling in their circulation. This contributes largely to the general depression All transactions, since the passage of the law decreeing forced specie resumption, except of the most limited character, both in respect to time and amount, have naturally ceased. Money is appreciating in value by operation of law, and property of all kinds is depreciating in a corresponding ratio. No one, with forced specie resumption in view, will invest either in property or business. Money is borrowed only in cases of great urgency, or for a short period for purposes of speculation. As production diminishes the people grow poorer and failures multiply. The producing forces of the nation are paralyzed for the want of a healthy circulation of money, and general bankruptcy and ruin are inevitable. As for the money power, it awaits the final convulsion with serene composure. The fall in the price of all commodities renders living cheap to all who have an income. As their investments are mostly exempt from taxation, they are not concerned about the burdens of government. The appreciation in the value of money and bonds, as compared with property of all kinds, which is silently going on, is adding enormously to their wealth, and when the crisis arrives they will be enabled to reap where they have not sown and gather in a rich harvest.

EXTRAVAGANCE.

When the panic of 1873 occurred the bullionists and the money power generally raised the old cry of extravagance and over production. The same cry has been used to account for every crash that has occurred during the present century. The charge of extravagance scarcely requires refutation. The producing classes as a rule are anything but extravagant. The farmers, with the help of their wives, sons and daughters, as is well known, are enabled only by hard labor and strict economy to come out ahead at the end of each year. The same is true of the mechanics, the trades people, the laborers, and the toiling masses generally. The only extravagance that has developed itself to any extent in the United States is among those who, by means of corrupt legislation and a false monetary system, are enabled to riot in wealth stolen from the people.

OVER PRODUCTION.

The cry of over production is equally groundless. Human ingenuity is being constantly taxed to increase and cheapen production, in order that the good things of life may be within the reach of all. The production of commodities is governed entirely by the laws of supply and demand. When it happens, as at the present time, that productive industry in many forms becomes paralyzed, on account of the want of a healthy circulation of money in the channels of trade, large classes are deprived of the means of supplying their wants, and the markets become suddenly gorged with certain commodities. For the sake of illustration we give the following table exhibiting the comparative production of five staple articles in 1860 and 1870, five years after the termination of the war:

	1860.	1870.	Decrease.
Cotton,	2,200,000,000 lbs.	1,200,000,000 lbs.	49 per cent.
Hemp,	149,000,000 "	25,000,000 "	83 "
Rice,	187,000,000 "	73,000,000 "	60 "
Silk,	12,000 "	4,000 "	66 "
Tobacco,	434,000,000 "	262,000,000 "	40 "
Total,	2,970,012,000	1,560,004,000	52

During this period the manufacturing establishments of the country increased in number from 140,433 to 252,148, and their products from $1,885,861,676 to $4,232,325,442; and the population of the country increased from 31,443,321 to 38,558,371.

That over production can produce a commercial crash is now acknowledged by all political economists, whose opinions are entitled to any weight, to be an exploded fallacy. John Stuart Mill, in his work on political economy, says:

"A general over-supply or excess of all commodities above the demand, so far as demand consists in means of payment, is thus shown to be an impossibility. I have already described the state of the markets for commodities which accompanies what is termed a commercial crisis. At such times there is really an excess of all commodities above the money demand—in other words, there is an under-supply of money. But it is a great error to suppose that a commercial crisis is the result of a general excess of production."

And E. Peshine Smith, a distinguished American political economist, disposes of the question as follows:

"In treating of supply and demand, no reference has been made to the notion, by which some writers have been bewildered, of a general over production in commodities. The proposition that any good thing has ever been produced in excess of the wants of humanity will not bear a moment's examination; nor is there the slightest reason to apprehend that such an event is likely to occur. The truth of the matter may be quite as correctly rendered by the statement that the supply of other commodities is deficient, as that any particular one is redundant. Where has it been, in any community, sufficiently numerous to permit the application of the general considerations in which political economy deals, that any product of industry has been offered in such a quantity as to surpass what the comfort of all its members would require? The trouble is, that many of those who would gladly be consumers have not produced enough to enable them to be. The true remedy for what is called over production in any article is an increased production of other things."

When Congress convened in December, 1873, there was a strong public sentiment in favor of increasing the amount of legal tender paper money. The people as a body have never failed, when an opportunity offered, to signify their preference for legal tender Treasury notes. This is undoubtedly to be attributed to "the instinctive sagacity of the people," to use Benton's language, "which is an overmatch for book-learning; and which being the result of common sense, is usually right; and being disinterested, is always honest." In obedience to this sentiment Congress passed a bill authorizing the Secretary of the Treasury to reissue $44,000,000 of legal tender Treasury notes which had been retired under the policy of contraction. This step would undoubtedly have afforded great relief to the oppressed industries of the country, but it would have been only temporary. In a short time the whole amount would have been absorbed by the banks. Individuals here and there would have been benefited, but in the end the nation would have been as poorly off as ever. The money power, however, was unwilling to have its plans interfered with to even this extent; a howl was at once set up by their organs against inflation, and a large delegation of bankers, requiring a special train of cars, at once proceeded to Washington to induce the President to interpose his veto. They succeeded as usual, and on the 22d of April, 1874, the bill was returned to Congress with the President's veto. Five months prior to this President Grant, in his annual message, argued that the panic was due to the great contraction of the currency that had taken place, and referred to the greenback in the following eulogistic terms. He said: "The experience of the present panic has proved that the currency of the country, based as it is upon the credit of the country, is the best that has ever been devised. Usually in times of such trials, currency has become worthless, or so much depreciated in value as to inflate the values of all the necessaries of life as compared with the currency. Every one holding it has been anxious to dispose of it on any terms. Now we witness the reverse. Holders of currency hoard it as they did gold in former experiences of a like nature."

Public indignation at this betrayal of the interests of the people by the President found vent at the polls at the next general election, and a Democratic House of Representatives was elected by an overwhelming majority.

When Congress met in December, 1874, it was apparent that some measure, looking to the relief of the oppressed industries of the country, must be adopted. The result of the election also occasioned great consternation among the bullionists and bondholders. Their plans had not been fully carried out. Specie resumption had not yet been attained. They could manage Congress as it was then constituted, but their influence with a new Congress was not so well assured. An act to force specie resumption was at once prepared and entrusted to that subservient tool of the money power, Senator Sherman. It was introduced in the Senate at an early period in the session, was passed by both houses and was signed by the President on the 14th of January, 1875. In order to deceive the public, banking was made free, a measure that had been contemplated from the beginning, and which, as has since been fully demonstrated, could contribute nothing to the relief of the public. The banks at the time had abundance of currency, and there were several millions of bank note circulation assigned to States having less than their quota, not yet taken. It is now possible for the bondholders to inflate the bank currency of the country to the full amount of the bonded indebtedness of the Federal Government, about $1,700,000,000. That advantage is not taken of this act to increase the bank note circulation is due entirely to the specie resumption act. Banks, on the contrary, are withdrawing their circulation and going out of business. Two hundred National Banks have already withdrawn their circulation, as is disclosed by the records of the office of the Comptroller of the Currency, and four hundred more are engaged in doing the same. The amount of National Bank note circulation withdrawn during the past year is $13,482,546, and the legal tender notes held on deposit for the redemption of National Bank notes in process of retirement amount to $27,098,429, making in all a contraction of $40,580,975. During the same period the greenback circulation has been contracted $11,244,752, and the fractional currency $2,758,278.

AN EXTRAORDINARY ACT.

The specie resumption act, passed in January, 1875, provided for the retirement of the fractional currency issued by the government. Long before specie payments are resumed the nation will be deprived of a circulating medium of any kind. Under the specie basis system of banking, as it existed before the war, the people were frequently driven, in times of great stringency, to use the notes of individuals, firms and corporations, which circulated under the name of shinplasters, and cities, towns and boroughs were obliged to issue promises to pay, which were commonly known as scrip. To prevent the people, in the approaching stringency, from availing themselves of even this method of relief and to give the National Banks absolute control over the circulating medium of the country, an act, approved February 8, 1875, was passed by Congress, which imposes a penalty of ten per cent. on any individual, firm, association, city, town or municipal corporation, except National Banks, that shall issue or use such notes. This bill was smuggled through Congress under the title of an act "To amend existing customs and internal revenue laws and for other purposes," and reads as follows: "Section 19. That every person, firm, association other than National Bank associations, and every corporation, State bank, or State banking association, shall pay a tax of ten per centum on the amount of their own notes used for circulation and paid out by them."

"Section 20. That every such person, firm, association,

corporation, State bank, or State banking association, and also every National Banking association, shall pay a like tax of ten per centum on the amount of notes of any person, firm, association other than a National Banking association, or of any corporation, State bank, or State banking association, or of any town, city, or municipal corporation, used for circulation and paid out by them." The National Banks evidently expect, in due time, to furnish the entire circulation of the nation, including fractional currency.

When specie resumption takes place it will be found that the greenbacks will all be in the possession of the banks. The reserve held by the National Banks, on the first day of October, 1875, amounted to $235,000,000. They have still over two years to gather in the greenbacks that are still outstanding. On the 1st of January, 1879, the government will be called upon to pay the sum of $300,000,000 in specie to redeem the greenbacks. The banks will then be in possession of abundant specie, furnished at the expense of the people, to enable them to begin banking on a genuine specie basis, in the manner in which banking was conducted prior to the war. In the meantime the nation will be entirely stripped of a medium of exchange, involving an almost entire cessation of production, attended by general ruin and bankruptcy. The suffering, want and misery, which the people of the United States will be called upon to endure, during the next few years, on account of the machinations of the money power, will be terrible beyond that experienced by any nation in modern times, not even excepting the experience of the people of Great Britain, under like circumstances, in 1819-25. (See next chapter.) Beyond that it is idle to speculate, for then there will probably be no National Banks, unless the liberties of the American people shall, in the meantime, have been entirely subverted.

CHAPTER VIII.

THE RESUMPTION OF SPECIE PAYMENTS.

A PREMIUM was placed on gold by the first legal tender act, passed February 25, 1862, which declared that interest on United States bonds and duties on imports should be paid in coin. This was not only unnecessary, but was in violation of the plainest principles of public policy. The people were obliged to respond to the requirements of the government, and a medium of exchange was absolutely necessary to enable them to render their resources available to the government. It was manifest that this medium of exchange had to be supplied by the government, and it could be done only by issuing public notes, made a full legal tender. In no other way than by making the public note a full legal tender was it possible to place the people all on the same platform with respect to the government and to each other, and compel each individual in the nation to bear his proportionate share of the public burden. These principles were fully embodied in the original legal tender act as it passed the House of Representatives, but the sharks of Wall street and the money power generally perceived that if it became a law they would be deprived of all power to shave either the government or the people. The passage of the bill, therefore, met with a desperate opposition in the Senate. In the conference between the committees of the Senate and the House which followed, the Senate committee was stubborn and the House committee was obliged to yield. The Hon Thaddeus Stevens declared, whilst shedding bitter tears over the result, that the House committee did not yield until it found that either the banks must be gratified or the country be lost.*

The only plea or justification offered for making the interest on the bonds payable in gold was that it would induce capitalists to invest in them. Subsequent events have wholly disproved the necessity of any such step. As a matter of fact the war was carried on for over a year with partial legal tender paper money (greenbacks), and the $500,000,000 of bonds authorized by Congress were in the end taken at par by the people (not capitalists or bankers) out of a spirit of patriotism. If further proof is required it is to be found in the fact that the currency bonds of the government to-day command a higher premium than the gold bonds, simply because they have a longer time to run. Having made the interest on the bonds payable in gold, duties on imports were made payable in gold in order to obtain the gold to pay the interest on the bonds. This was also entirely unnecessary. No bonds, as we have mentioned, were issued for over a year, and as the interest would not fall due until six months after they were issued, the government would then have had ample time to devise a way to obtain the necessary gold.

The effect of making the interest on government bonds and duties on imports payable in gold was to impose a tax on all foreign commodities for the benefit of the bankers, bullionists and bondholders, and to greatly disarrange the monetary affairs of the country. A great many people are partially reconciled to the payment of this tax under the mistaken belief that it inures in some way to the advantage of the government. Such is not the fact. Commodities are purchased abroad with American products; and the price of American products abroad is regulated solely by the laws of

*See page 200.

supply and demand. The total imports and exports of the United States for the years 1873 and 1874 were as follows:

Imports in 1873.............	$642,136,210
Exports "	575,227,017

Balance against United States..	$66,909,193

Exports in 1874.............	$633,339,368
Imports "	567,406,342

Balance in favor of United States	$65,933,026

Balance against the United States in two years,	$976,167

It appears, therefore, that the imports and exports of the United States during the two years (1873 and 1874) balanced each other to within less than one million of dollars. The exchange of commodities between different nations is effected principally by means of bills of exchange. The manner in which this is done is thus referred to by Colwell: "If the United States and Great Britain have mutually exported to each other commodities to the value of $100,000,000, the amount is adjusted by the familiar process of bills of exchange. He who has exported commodities to the value of $10,000 is paid when he sells a bill for the amount. The adjustment proceeds afterwards without any further trouble on his part. The bills are concentrated in a few hands in each country. If a house in London purchases in each week a million of dollars of American paper, and a house in New York with which it is in business relations purchases a million of dollars each week in bills on London, it is easy to see that it requires no money to pay to each other the two millions. As business is generally conducted, the bills are forwarded from this country, and the respective claims are balanced and extinguished on the books of the London house." After an adjustment is thus effected the balance is paid in bullion. As this process is going on constantly, bullion (gold and silver) will flow into the country when the exports exceed the imports, and out of the country when the imports exceed the exports. In order to cause gold to flow into and remain in the country, it is manifest, therefore, that the thing to do is to develop the producing forces of the country to such an extent as will enable it to export more than it imports. This fact was fully recognized and endorsed by President Grant in his annual message in 1873. He said: "My own judgment is * * that a specie basis cannot be reached and maintained until our exports, exclusive of gold, pay for our imports, interest due abroad, and other specie obligations, or so nearly so as to leave an appreciable accumulation of the precious metals in the country from the products of our mines."

When foreign commodities are received in the United States the merchant to whom they are consigned is obliged to pay the custom duties, established by law, in gold. Bankers and brokers deal in gold, and sell it at the highest price that they can get. During the war it will be remembered that the bullionists succeeded in running up the premium on gold to as high as $1.85½ over the lawful money of the country, while the volume of the currency and the price of domestic products remained unchanged. This of course added greatly to the cost of all imported articles. The premium on gold, which was paid by the merchant in the first place and by the people in the end, was a clear profit to the bullionists. Until 1864 no gold was required by the government to pay interest on bonds, consequently the burden thus imposed on the people was entirely unnecessary, and inured to the advantage of no one except the dealers in gold. If the war had terminated in the early part of 1863, there would have been no necessity for issuing any gold interest bonds at all. The total funded and unfunded debt of the government then was only $783,804,252, consisting chiefly of legal tender notes, 7-30 Treasury notes and certificates of indebtedness, all of which could have been called in, or provided for, by taxation in two years, if desired. But the bullionists had their plans well laid. The Treasury notes bearing interest were purposely made payable in one, two and three years, in order that, as soon as the gold interest bonds were issued, they could be advantageously converted into money and the proceeds invested in bonds. With the gold of the country and the bonds both in their possession, the business of selling gold was wonderfully simplified. The bankers and bullionists sold their gold to the merchant to pay the government, and the government immediately returned it in the shape of interest on bonds to the banker and bullionist. Under this arrangement it was not even necessary to transfer the gold from the vaults of the banks. The whole matter could be adjusted by means of gold certificates and checks.

The amount of gold held by the National Banks, at any one time during the past ten years, would scarcely have sufficed to pay the duties on imports at New York City alone for two weeks. On the 1st of October, 1875, the gold held by the National Banks of New York City was $4,955,624, of which sum $4,201,720 was in U. S. gold certificates and only $753,904 in coin. The amount received by the government for duties on imports during the past ten years has averaged $180,000,000 a year, or in all $1,800,000,000; the interest on the public debt for the same period has been about $100,000,000 a year, or in all $1,000,000,000. It is manifest, therefore, that if the payment of duties on imports and interest on bonds in gold was not a pure fiction, the government could have accumulated $800,000,000 of gold in the past ten years.

Since specie resumption became desirable to the bullionists and bankers, it is common to hear it asserted that the difference between paper money and gold compels the people of the United States to trade with the rest of the world at a disadvantage. This would imply that foreigners are enabled to reap some advantage on account of the premium on gold in the United States. A moment's consideration will satisfy any one that this is not true. . Foreign commodities, as we have seen, are purchased with American products. The premium paid by Americans on gold and for bills of exchange is not an essential part of the transaction. The products of America are sold in foreign markets at the ruling price there, and with the proceeds commodities are purchased in turn. To say that American products sell for any more or less in foreign markets because of the premium on gold in the United States is simply absurd. As has already been suggested, not even the interest on the bonds held abroad is paid in gold. It is paid in products, against which bills of exchange are drawn. When the exports of the United States fall short the balance is paid in bullion, the product of our mines; and this would be done just the same whether there were any bonds held abroad or not. The same is true of the bonds held at home. Interest on them is paid in current money at gold rates. The conclusion, then, is unavoidable that the only persons who are benefited by the premium on gold, established by the legal tender act, are the bullionists and bondholders of the United States.

The bankers and bullionists having secured possession of the bonds, their convertibility with greenbacks was then taken away, and they were also exempted from taxation. The original loan of $500,000,000 of 5-20 bonds has been retired or converted into gold bonds. By the act of March 18, 1869, the Secretary of the Treasury is forbidden to redeem any of the 5-20 bonds, payable in lawful money, still outstanding (some several hundred millions) until greenbacks are on a par with gold. The bonds of the United States now command a high premium. The following is a list of the quotations of United States bonds on the 26th of April, 1876:

U. S. 6 per cent. bonds of 1881..................... 122
U. S. 5-20 bonds of 1865, Nov..................... 118
U. S. 5-20 bonds of 1865, July..................... 119
U. S. 5-20 bonds of 1867, July..................... $121\frac{1}{4}$
U. S. 5-20 bonds of 1868, July..................... $122\frac{1}{2}$
U. S. 5 per cent. 10-40 bonds...................... $118\frac{3}{4}$
U. S. 5 per cent. funded loan bonds................ $117\frac{1}{2}$
U. S. 6 per cent. currency bonds................... $126\frac{1}{8}$

The money power having thus succeeded in robbing the people to the utmost extent in this direction, it is now proposed to continue the process by means of specie resumption. The action of the bullionists and bankers, in this particular, was hastened, as we have seen, by the result of the elections in 1874.

SPECIE RESUMPTION.

Soon after Congress convened in December, 1874, a specie resumption act was hurried through that body and was approved by the President, January 14, 1875. The act provides as follows:

The first section requires the Secretary of the Treasury, as rapidly as practicable, to cause to be coined, silver coins of the denominations of ten, twenty-five and fifty cents, of standard value, and to issue them in redemption of an equal number and amount of fractional currency, until the whole amount of such fractional currency outstanding shall be redeemed.

The second section repeals the authority to charge a per centage for coining bullion.

The third section repeals so much of the National Banking law as limits the aggregate circulation of the banks to $354,000,000, and makes banking free to bondholders. It also provides that "on and after the 1st day of January, 1879, the Secretary of the Treasury shall redeem in coin the United States legal tender notes then outstanding, on their presentation for redemption in sums of not less than fifty dollars."

The greenback, although issued in a mutilated form, (not payable for interest on bonds and duties on imports) was made a legal tender for private debts. It was not, therefore, simply an evidence of indebtedness of the government—a mere promise to pay money; it was something more than that. It became the measure of all values, the basis of all money contracts, and the standard of all payments among the people. For fourteen years it has constituted the lawful money of the country. All exchanges of property, during this period, have been made and all existing debts have been contracted on the basis of greenback money. If the standard of payment is changed, all existing indebtedness will change with it. For example if A. owes B. $10,000 and he is compelled to pay the amount in gold, which rules at say $1.12, he is obliged to pay $11,200 instead of $10,000. When the entire indebtedness of the country, individual, corporate and municipal, is taken into consideration, it will be seen that the amount thus added by changing the standard of payment is enormous. Estimating the aggregate indebtedness of the country, of individuals, towns, cities, townships, counties, states, railroads and other corporations, at $10,000,000,000, the amount would be increased $1,200,000,000.

The alteration of the coinage of a nation is universally regarded as a matter of the greatest delicacy, only to be attempted when absolutely required by the highest considerations of public policy. When the legal tender act was pending the only plausible argument offered by the money power against its passage, was that it would work injustice to the creditor class, by enabling debtors to pay their debts in a depreciated money. The specie resumption law, however, compels the debtor class to pay one-eighth more than it contracted to pay, and the debtor class, owing to the workings of contraction and the National Banking system, now embraces all the industrial classes of the country. No alteration of the coinage was ever attempted by any nation that would at all compare with this.

(The bondholders have provided against any alteration of the coinage so far as they are concerned. The act of Congress of July 14, 1870, for refunding the public debt provides that the bonds shall be redeemed "in coin of the *present standard value*.")

Th amount of gold in the ountry, in view of the resumption of specie payments, has become a matter of serious importance, because the circulation of the country, whether the gold is actually used as a medium of exchange, or made the basis of a bank note currency, as in times prior to the war will necessarily be limited by the amount of gold on hand. On the 27th of February, 1876, the Secretary of the Treasury, in response to a resolution passed by the House of Representatives calling for a statement of the gold coin in the possession of the government, submitted the following report:

Coin coupons.........................	$1,547,402 06
Coin certificates......................	1,427,200 00
Sinking fund and interest...............	1,873,825 00
Bonds redeemed and interest............	13,832,553 65
Interest due and unpaid.................	9,254,634 50
Outstanding bonds called for sinking fund.	2,548,000 00
Outstanding coin certificates.............	33,968,300 00
Silver coin and bullion..................	14,193,618 70
	$78,645,533 91
Actual gold coin available...............	13,341,423 76
Total.......................	$91,986,957 67

By the terms of the specie resumption act the government will be required to redeem the legal tender notes outstanding on the first of January, 1879, ($300,000,000) in coin. This will take nearly $290,000,000 more coin than there is available gold in the Treasury. Where and how is this immense amount of gold to be obtained? The estimated product of the mines of the United States for the past three years has been about $50,000,000 a year. The annual interest on the public debt, one-half of which, it is estimated, is held abroad, is about $100,000,000. As long as the imports of the country exceed the exports, the difference will have to be made up in specie. The imports of the United States as a rule have exceeded the exports for many years past, and to such an extent, that notwithstanding the enormous yield of American mines, there is not at the present time $100,000,000 of specie in the country. And now that the productive ability of the nation has been greatly diminished, and is still diminishing under the operations of contraction and of the National Banking system, the excess of imports over exports must naturally increase, and thus augment the necessity for sending the product of American mines to foreign countries. It is clear, therefore, that until the producing forces of the nation are sufficiently developed to enable it to export more than it imports, there can be no accumulation of gold obtained from the mines of the country. The amount required to resume specie payments then, if obtained at all, must come from other nations. The demand for gold at the present time abroad is unusually great on account of the demonetization of silver in Germany and other countries. The government of the United States has already had some experience in trying to obtain gold in Europe. When the gold bonds of the United States were put on the market in Europe, $21,000,000, resulting from their sale, accumulated in the Bank of England. The Bank of England objected to the transfer of this sum to the United States, and the government was forced to turn round and invest it in other bonds, which had been purchased probably at less than 60 cents on the dollar. Senator Boutwell detailed the facts in this case, in a speech in the United States Senate, January 22, 1874, as follows: "When the negotiations were going on in London for the sale of the largest amount of United States bonds that have ever been sold there at one time, it was foreseen by the Bank of England that a quantity of coin would accumulate as the proceeds of these bonds to the credit of the government of the United States. As a matter of fact, there was an accumulation of about $21,000,-000. The Bank of England, foreseeing that there would be an accumulation of coin to the credit of the United States which might be taken away bodily in specie, gave notice to the officers of the Treasury Department of the United States that the power of that institution would be arrayed against the whole proceeding unless we gave a pledge that the coin should not be removed, and that we would reinvest it in the bonds of the United States as they were offered in the markets of London. We were compelled to do it." Mr. Boutwell also mentioned another case in point, which is equally significant, as follows: "There is another fact, known to all. We recovered at Geneva an award against Great Britain of $15,500,000. When this claim was maturing, the banking and commercial classes of Great Britain induced the government to interpose, and by diplomatic arrangements through the State Department here, operating upon the Treasury Department, secured the transfer of securities and thus avoided the transfer of coin. In the presence of these facts, is it to be assumed for a moment that we can go into the markets of the world and purchase coin with which we can redeem one, two, three or four hundred millions of outstanding legal tender notes."

If any further argument is required to show that it is not only utterly impossible for the government of the United States to obtain the requisite amount of gold to resume specie payment at a fixed time, but that it is also undesirable, even if it were possible, because it would disturb all the industrial and social relations of the world, it will be found in the following extract from an able speech delivered on the 26th of April, 1876, by Senator Jones in the Senate of the United States, in favor of placing silver on an equality with gold as a medium of exchange. He said:

"The world's stock of coin is $5,700,000,000, of which nearly one-half is silver. Of this sum Europe, America, and the rest of the Occidental world employ about $3,600,000,000. Previous to the late demonetizations of silver in the Latin union, and in Germany and the United States, these $3,600,000,000 consisted of, let us say, $2,000,000,000 of gold and $1,600,000,000 of silver. They now consist of about $2,600,000,000 gold and $1,000,000,000 silver. By continuing to exclude silver from equal participation with gold in the currency of the United States and attempting to resume specie payments, we occasion a demand for say $350,000,000 of gold wherewith to pay off the greenbacks and furnish bank reserves, and $50,000,000 of silver in lieu of the fractional notes. If we could obtain these $400,000,000 of metal without drawing it from other countries in Europe or America, they would add so much to the stock of coin in the Occidental world, which would then be $2,950,000,000 of gold and $1,050,000,000 of silver. This is the answer to the question so far as the Occidental world is concerned. The quantity of the precious metals needed for money and the basis of credit in the Occidental world—that is to say, the quantity needed to maintain prices at their present level —is at least $4,000,000,000. Of this sum the United States, if it succeeds in resuming specie payments, will hold about $400,000,000, of which $350,000,000 must be in gold. Where is it to come from?

"Anticipating the argument that no such sum is necessary to specie resumption, because prior to suspension in 1862 our entire stock of coin included not more than $225,000,000 of gold, he reminded the Senate that population since then had increased per 50 cent., and that in 1861 our whole circulating medium consisted of $300,000,000 in coin and $200,-000,000 in bank notes, which circulated within limited areas at nearly par; whereas now it consists of not more than $100,000,000 of coin and some $850,000,000 of government and bank paper, the latter circulating (throughout nearly the whole country) at about 87½ cents on the dollar; say total circulation at par equal to $850,000,000. This is 70 per cent. more than the par circulation of 1861, an incontestible proof that the exchanges have increased in volume at least 70 per cent. It cannot be doubted that the bulk of to-day's exchanges in this country is at least double that of a corresponding day in 1862. Put it at only 70 per cent. higher; then, in order to resume specie payments upon at least as firm a footing as specie payments in 1861, we shall require at least 70 per cent. more specie than we employed in 1861. Add 70 per cent. to $300,000,000 and you have $510,000,000. Allow $100,000,0C0 for specie already in the country, in the banks, in private hands, and in the vaults of the Treasury, and you will need $410,000,000 in order to resume, say, for round figures, $400,000,000 of specie, of which, under the operation of the act of 1873, about $350,000,000 must be gold.

"I warn gentlemen to beware of making a mistake in

respect to this matter, for a mistake will set us back many years. The British government tried to resume in 1817, after a suspension of 20 years, but it failed, and suspension was deferred until 1823. If we try to resume in 1879 with $100,000,000 and fail, we may be set back a quarter of a century. Moreover, if we fail, some clique of stock gamblers will make 15 or 20 per cent. out of the operation. Knowing that $100,000,000 was the limit of the government's ability to pay, they could easily make arrangements with the banks and depositories throughout the country to withdraw $100,000,000 of greenbacks on the eve of the day of resumption, and present them for payment at the Treasury After having drawn the last dollar of specie out of the latter, they could, by presenting an additional note, compel it to suspend again. Then gold would go up once more, perhaps to the full extent of the figure from which it would have fallen, and the clique could sell their specie in the market and realize their profit. We cannot resume with $100,000,000 nor with $200,000,000. We have had $200,000,000 in specie in the Treasury on several occasions during the past ten years. If it is practicable to resume now with $100,000,000, why was it not practicable on those occasions with $200,000,000? It was certainly not for lack of desire on the part of the Secretary of the Treasury, but simply that both the Secretary and Congress saw that the thing could not be done. Where are the needed $350,000,000 in gold to come from? The annual gold product of the world is $97,000,000. More than half of this is needed in the arts. One and a half per cent. on $2,600,000,000, the present Occidental stock, is needed for the maintenance of money to replace abrasion and loss. This is $39,000,000. Deduct these sums and there remains a surplus of $10,000,000 a year, out of which our needed $350,000,000 must come, unless it comes out of the existing stock in other countries. It would take 35 years to accomplish the result upon the most favorable hypothesis.

"But the increased population of the Occidental world will make increased demand for gold exchanges and for its use in arts equal to at least $6,000,000 annually, and the annual product of gold is diminishing instead of increasing. When these elements of the circulation are all moderately provided for, there will remain perhaps $500,000 per annum of surplus, taking 700 years to get our $350,000,000. And even this cannot be done unless Austria, Italy and Russia shall leave us to monopolize all the gold we need before they reform their own debased currency. I tell you, gentlemen, the thing cannot be done. Redemption in gold is out of the question. It is not practical financially, metallurgically, internationally, or politically; in short, it is not practical at all.

"The stock of coin which forms the substratum of the world's prices is the accumulation of 50 centuries, and bargains are being made every day which cover long periods of time. To disturb these prices and contracts by forcing the exchanges of the country to be measured by a sum of specie so vastly less than its usual measure, as $100,000,000, or even $200,000,000, would be tantamount to the violent destruction of vast interests and a wrenching of all the relations of industrial and social life.

"The Senator proceeded to argue that we cannot get the gold from Europe, with which to resume, because its whole supply is only $2,600,000,000, and on every one of these dollars stands a vast and almost toppling superstructure of credit in every conceivable form. Try to buy one sixth or seventh of that amount, and the rate of interest would go up in Europe in order to check the outflow of gold; and so the price of gold would rise until, in order to secure the amount required, we would be obliged to sell all our movables at prices that would bankrupt every interest in the country. We might get $50,000,000 or $100,000,000 possibly, but it would be at the expense of a tremendous financial convulsion abroad, reacting with equally alarming disaster to ourselves. Recollect that the problem is that of taking $350,000,000 in gold out of a fully occupied and heavily overtopped basis of only $2,600,000,000 in the Occidental world. It is not the whole stock of metal, both in silver and gold, that we can now call upon. Silver has been demonetized in several countries in Europe, and here we have so thoughtlessly worded our laws that, until we alter them, we can only pay in gold."

By the act of April 12, 1873, the silver coins of the United States were declared to be a legal tender at their nominal value for any amount not exceeding five dollars in any one payment. Silver as a commodity fluctuates in value agreeably to the laws of supply and demand. The effect of the law above mentioned was to partially demonetize silver, and hence silver coins are now (May, 1876) quoted at about 3 per cent. less than legal tender Treasury notes.

There is no good end to be attained by specie resumption that could not be attained by simply making the greenback a full legal tender, as should have been done in the first instance. By making the greenback a full legal tender, the products of the country would be placed upon the same footing with foreign commodities, and that is all that is proposed to be accomplished by specie resumption. The public would then be relieved of the onerous tax imposed on gold to pay duties on imports, which redounds solely to the advantage of the bullionists and bondholders of the United States. If this method were adopted, no disturbance of the industrial or social relations of the country could possibly occur. Forced specie resumption can be accomplished only through a complete revolution of all the business and social relations of the country. This will appear from a brief consideration of the steps that will necessarily precede resumption. The circulation of the country on the 1st of April, 1876, was as follows:

Legal tender Treasury notes	$370,755,248
Fractional currency	42,604,893
National Bank notes	330,378,904
Total	$743,739,045

The lawful money reserve of the National Banks on the 1st day of October, 1875, was as follows:

Legal tender Treasury notes	$76,366,921
United States certificates of deposit	48,810,000
Due from reserve agents	85,644,964
Redemption fund with Treasurer	16,233,193
	$227,055,078
Specie	8,050,328
Total	$235,105,406

It will be seen that the lawful money reserve of the National Banks, exclusive of specie, now amounts to over two-thirds of the entire greenback circulation. The banks have still two years and a half to gather in the remainder of the outstanding greenbacks—all that are not locked up in private hoards. To call in their own circulation is an easy matter. If the banks cease discounting paper for six months there will scarcely be a bank note left in circulation. That they will do so is not to be doubted. The notes of the banks are simply evidences of their own indebtedness, and it is not to be supposed that they will voluntarily add twelve per cent. or more to their own indebtedness when they can easily avoid it. Long before the first day of January, 1879, the banks will have possession of the entire circulation of the country, both greenbacks and bank notes, and the nation will be completely stripped of a medium of exchange. The public will be helpless. The people will not possess even the poor privilege of issuing and using shinplasters and scrip, because it will be impossible to raise money enough to pay the ten per cent. tax imposed upon all notes not issued by National Banks. Forced resumption, therefore, means something more than adding 12 per cent. to the amount of every debt owed in the United States. Without a medium of exchange people will be unable to pay their debts at all; industry and trade will be completely paralyzed; and bankruptcy, distress, starvation and riot will ensue.

SPECIE RESUMPTION IN ENGLAND.

The experience of the people of Great Britain from 1819 to 1825, under similar circumstances, is full of instruction to the people of the United States. In 1797 the Bank of England was obliged to suspend specie payments.* Great Britain at the time was engaged in war with France. In 1797 large sums of gold were required abroad, and the price of gold began to rise. In September, 1799, the standard price of gold was £3, 17s., 6d. per ounce, and in June, 1800, it was £4, 5s. per ounce. The war with France ended in 1815. During this period and for several years after the war the people of Great Britain were obliged to use an irredeemable paper currency for their medium of exchange. Prior to the suspension of specie payments the condition of affairs in Great Britain was gloomy indeed. Sir Archibald Alison, the historian, in speaking of the period immediately preceding suspension says: "Nor was the internal suffering of this ill-omened period inferior to its external disaster. It began with the severe commercial distress of 1793, unprecedented at that period in intensity and duration, and which was only

*See Bank of England, page 92.

relieved by an extensive loan to the trading classes by government; and it terminated in the dreadful monetary crisis and run upon the bank and mutiny in the fleet, in the spring of 1797, which brought the nation to the brink of ruin, and forced upon the government the necessity of suspending cash payments." The British Government and people had been vainly trying to carry on great operations with an inadequate medium of exchange. The suspension of the Bank of England led to the use of irredeemable paper money to an enormous amount, or, to use an expression now greatly ridiculed by the bullionists, "to an amount equal to the wants of trade." The result was magical. We will again quote from Sir Archibald Alison. He says: "The next eighteen years of the war, from 1797 to 1815, were, as all the world knows, the most glorious, and, taken as a whole, the most prosperous, which Great Britain had ever known. Ushered in by a combination of circumstances the most calamitous, both with reference to external security and internal industry, it terminated in a blaze of glory and a flood of prosperity which have never, since the beginning of the world, descended upon any nation. Hardly had the run upon the bank shaken to its center the whole fabric of our commercial prosperity, and the mutinies of the Nore, Plymouth and off Cadiz paralyzed the arm of our naval defenders, when the victories of St. Vincent and Camperdown again restored to us the dominion of the sea; and ere long the thunderbolts of the Nile and Trafalgar prostrated the naval strength of the enemy, and the victories of Wellington first arrested, and at length broke his military power. Prosperity, universal and unheard of, pervaded every department of the empire. Our colonial possessions encircled the earth—the whole West India Islands had fallen into our hands; an empire of sixty millions of men in

Hindostan acknowledged our rule; Java was added to our eastern possessions; and the flag of France had disappeared from every station beyond the sea. Agriculture, commerce and manufactures at home had increased in an unparalleled ratio; the landed proprietors were in affluence; wealth to an unheard of extent had been created among the farmers; the soil daily increasing in fertility and breadth of cultivated land, had become almost adequate to the maintenance of a rapidly increasing population; our exports, imports and tonnage had more than doubled since the war began; and though distress, especially during 1810 and 1811, had at times been severely experienced among the manufacturing operatives (occasioned by Bonaparte's decrees against British goods), yet, upon the whole, and in average years, their condition was one of extraordinary prosperity. The revenue raised by taxation within the year had risen to £72,000,000 in 1815 from £21,000,000 in 1796; the total expenditure from taxes and loans had reached in 1814 and 1815, the enormous amount of £117,000,000 each year. In the years 1813 and 1814, being the twentieth and twenty-first of the war, Great Britain had above a million of men in arms in Europe and Asia, and remitted £11,000,000 yearly in subsidies to the continental powers. Yet was this prodigious and unheard of expenditure so far from exhausting either the capital or resources of the country, that the loan in 1814 was obtained at the rate of £4, 11s., 1d. per cent., being a lower rate than that paid at the commencement of the war; although the annual loan at its close was above £35,000,000, and the population of the empire at that period was only eighteen millions."

All this was accomplished in Great Britain during the early part of the present century by irredeemable paper money. The bullionists try to blunt the force of this argument by attributing the prosperity of England during this period to the vast outlays of the government, but if this was the cause, why did it not produce the same effect during the period prior to the suspension, when the government was making similar outlays? The simple truth is that the people of Great Britain possessed patriotism and faith in the stability of their government and institutions, and when furnished with industry's most essential tool, an abundant and cheap medium of exchange, they were enabled to develop the producing forces of the nation to their utmost extent, with the marvelous results above given. And the logic of the whole matter is, that if paper money will perform such marvels in time of war, danger and uncertainty, it can be made to perform the same or greater marvels in time of peace, when no uncertainty need attend its use.

When the several acts of Parliament were passed continuing Pitts' "bank restriction" (continuing the suspension of specie payments), one clause was always retained, and that was that the bank was "to resume cash payments" within a few months after peace should be established. Doubleday, in his Financial, Monetary and Statistical History of England, says that "it has been asserted that Pitt never meant this clause to be enforced, at least as far as regarded the fundholders (bondholders); and that he intimated as much in Parliament on one occasion." However, it was adhered to. The bullionists immediately began to clamor for a return to specie payments. The bank of England, which had "bales of paper money" in circulation, was obliged to contract to an extent that would enable it to redeem the remainder in coin. This began to occasion distress amongst the merchants and manufacturers. In speaking of this period Doubleday says: "During former revulsions, such as that of 1810, caused by the decrees of Bonaparte against the admission of British goods, the bank had come promptly forward with loans and discounts to relieve the pressure. Now, however, the directors scarcely dared to move an inch. They knew that the political economists were strong in the House, and that they were bent upon cash payments at all risks. They knew that the Jews of Change Alley would secretly abet the same doctrine. Against a combination of usurers and theorists, one set all selfishness, the other all crotchets, there was no defense to be made. The country gentlemen, who were the dupes of the economists, were led to believe that cash payments were necessary for both the interest and security of themselves. Those who had the power were resolved, and nothing was left to the bank but to narrow its issues, and look about for gold and silver wherewith to meet the storm. This was altogether a difficult business. In the year 1816 alone thirty-seven country banks had become bankrupt. The commercial world required additional propping. But the government (the bank) was in the same dilemma; and to it the merchants were sacrificed. Between February and April, 1816, the directors lessened their discounts from £23,000,000 to £11,000,000; and before February, 1817, to £8,000,000; and before August of the same year to £7,000,000; whilst up to nearly the same period they held of Exchequer bills, etc., £25,000,000. * * This reduction of the bank issues, and destruction and crippling of the country banks, had another and still more important effect, inasmuch as by causing the price of gold to fall to nearly the mint price, it encouraged the political economists to press forward, and at last, in 1819, to pass an act, the most important in its consequences, and extraordinary in its circumstances, that ever was decided upon by any legislature, in any age or country. * * The Currency bill of (May.) 1819 was passed at the instance of a committee, amongst the members of whom were included all the parliamentary dabblers in political economy of any name or talent, and of whom Peel was chairman. Horner, the chairman of the bullion committee of 1810, was dead; but in his stead, they had Ricardo, a rich Jew stock-jobber, who having made an immense fortune by this worst species of gambling, had also contrived to obtain a reputation by the publication of some books on political economy. * * Backed by the authority of this rich and arrogant man, the economists obtained on this occasion an almost entire command of the House of Commons. * * The House made the plunge with one accord. There was hardly the semblance of an opposition. Ricardo had the enormous folly to tell the House that the bill was 'not worthy of half an hour of even their consideration;' and assured them that the whole question was one of 'three per cent;' this being the extent of the fall of prices, which this man calculated would take place, after all the one and two pound notes in the kingdom were burned, and the remainder, of five pound notes and upwards, made 'payable on demand in gold sovereigns worth £3, 17s., 10½d. the ounce.' In short there was only one man in the Commons who really understood and opposed the measure, and this man was Mr. Matthias Attwood, * * and Mr. Attwood was prevailed upon to quit the House that the vote might be unanimous. In the House of Lords, Lord Grey alone ventured to dissent from the measure; * * The Houses, however, for once 'were all in one accord.' * * As a bit of legislation, this ever-memorable act is remarkably brief and to the point; consisting only of thirteen not very long nor wordy clauses. It repeals, in the first place, all the acts for restraining the bank from paying its creditors, which had been passed from 1797 up to that time, the repeal going into effect 'from and after the first day of May, 1823.' This was a repeal of all bank notes on demand for sums less than five pounds. It then provides for a gradual return, in the meantime, by the bank to cash payments; beginning with an issue of gold at four pounds one shilling the ounce, in 1820, and ending with the standard mint price of £3, 17s., 10½d."

The premium on gold during this period fluctuated as follows:

1814	30⅛ per cent.	1817	2½ per cent.
1815	18¾ "	1818	5 "
1826	2¼ "	1819	6⅓ "
1816, Oct. to Dec. 1	"	1820	par.

Although the Currency bill passed Parliament unanimously, it did not fail to excite great alarm and opposition among the industrial and business classes of the kingdom. The Directors of the Bank of England protested against its passage, declaring that "they could not venture to advise an unrelenting continuance of pecuniary pressure upon the commercial world, the consequences of which it was impossible for them to foresee or estimate," or countenance a measure in which "the whole community was so deeply involved, and which would possibly compromise the universal interests of the empire in all the relations of agriculture, manufactures, commerce and revenue." The bankers and merchants of London joined in a petition against it, in which they predicted the most disastrous results.

The contraction of the currency, which was augmented by the passage of the bill, soon produced the most alarming results. We again quote from Alison's History of Europe. He says: "The effects of this extraordinary piece of legislation were soon apparent. The industry of the nation was speedily congealed, as a flowing stream is by the severity of an Arctic winter. The alarm became as universal and widespread as confidence and activity had recently been. The country bankers, who had advanced largely on the stocks of goods imported, refused to continue their support to their customers, and they were forced to bring their stocks into the market. Prices in consequence fell rapidly; that of cotton, in particular, sank in three months to half its former level. The country bankers' association was contracted by no less than five millions sterling ($24,000,000); and the entire circulation of England fell from $235,545,000* in 1818 to $174,385,000 in 1820, and in the sneeeeding year it sank as low as $142,757,000. * * The effects of this sudden and prodigious contraction of the currency were soon apparent, and they rendered the next three years a period of ceaseless distress and suffering in the British Islands. The accommodation granted by bankers diminished so much in consequence of the obligation laid upon them to pay in specie, which was not to be got, that the paper under discount at the Bank of England, which in 1810 had been $115,000,000, and in 1815 not less than $103,000,000, sank in 1820 to $23,360,000, and in 1821 to $13,610,000. The effect upon prices was not less immediate or appalling. They declined in general, within six months, to half their former amount, and remained at that low level for the next three years. Distress was universal in the latter months of 1819, and that distrust and discouragement were felt in all branches of industry which are at once the forerunner and cause of disaster." From Mr. Doubleday's history we also quote as follows: "We have already seen the fall in prices produced by the immense narrowing of the paper circulation. The distress, ruin and bankruptcy which now took place were universal, affecting the great interests both of land and trade; but especially among land owners, whose estates were burthened by mortgages, settlements, legacies, etc.,

*Amounts are given in dollars instead of pounds.

the effects were most marked and out of the ordinary course. In hundreds of cases, from the tremendous reduction which now took place, the estates barely sold for as much as would pay off the mortgages; and hence the owners were stripped of all and made beggars." Before the close of the year 1819 the distress became insufferable. Great meetings were held throughout England and Scotland during the summer. In August 60,000 people, men, women and children, assembled near Manchester. A collision occurred between the people and the troops, in which a number were killed and many wounded. This created intense excitement, and the meetings of the people held in Liverpool, York, Leeds, and various other cities, were attended by vast multitudes of suffering people, demanding vengeance. Serious riots occurred, which were only quelled by military force. In 1820 a conspiracy was discovered, which had for its object the murder of all the King's Ministers, and which was only frustrated through the cowardice of one of the conspirators, who betrayed his associates. Military training went on amongst the people, and the government was obliged to provide a large military force to prevent an outbreak. "On Sunday morning, the 2d of April," says Alison, "a treasonable proclamation was found placarded all over the streets of Glasgow, Paisley, Stirling, and the neighboring towns and villages, *in the name of a provisional government*, calling on the people to desist from labor; on all manufacturers to close their workshops; and on all the friends of their country to come forward and effect a revolution by force, with a view to the establishment of an entire equality of civil rights. Strange to say, this proclamation, unsigned and proceeding from an unknown authority, was widely obeyed. Work immediately ceased; the manufactories were closed, from the desertion of workmen; the streets were filled with anxious crowds eagerly expecting news from the south; the sounds of industry were no longer heard, and two hundred thousand persons in the busiest districts of the country were thrown into a state of compulsory idleness by the mandates of an unseen and unknown power." Five thousand troops were immediately assembled at Glasgow, and the insurgents were overawed. Before the end of the year the government had increased its volunteer force to 35,000 men. "Without doubt," says Alison, "this powerful volunteer force, organized especially in the manufacturing districts at this period, and the decisive demonstration it afforded of moral and physical strength on the part of the government, was the chief cause through which Great Britain escaped an alarming convulsion."

Thus were the masses of Great Britain, whose valor and labor had carried the nation to the acme of glory and prosperity, ruthlessly and wantonly sacrificed on the altar of so called "honest money," only to further enrich the moneyed class of the kingdom. But after all forced specie resumption proved a failure. Parliament was obliged to retrace its steps. In 1822 an act was passed authorizing the issue of one and two pound notes for a period of ten years longer, and the one pound notes *were made a legal tender* everywhere except at the bank of England. "This act," says Alison, "coupled with the grant of £4,000,000 Exchequer bills, which the government was authorized to issue in aid of the agricultural interest, had a surprising effect in restoring confidence and raising prices; and by doing so, it repealed, so long as it continued, the most injurious parts of the act of 1819." But the ruin, suffering and misery which had attended the attempt to force specie payments could not be undone, nor could the broken fortunes be restored. By a return to specie payments finally, the specie basis banking and credit system, the whole tendency of which is to concentrate wealth in the hands of the few, was re-established; and the industrial classes, especially the agricultural class, have never since been able to recover from the blow then received.

> "Princes and lords may flourish, or may fade,—
> A breath can make them, as a breath has made:
> But a bold peasantry, their country's pride,
> When once destroyed, can never be supplied."

In 1822 the land owners of England numbered 165,000. According to the census of 1861 the number was about 30,000, and one-half of the whole kingdom is now owned by not more than twelve persons.

From this mere outline of the disastrous events which attended specie resumption in Great Britain, revolutionizing the whole structure of British society, and shaking to the center the foundations of the government itself, some idea may be formed of what the American people will be obliged to suffer during the next few years. Great Britain then possessed many advantages which are not possessed by the United States at the present time. Her industries were in full operation; the balance of trade was largely in her favor; she had a large supply of specie to begin with; the premium on gold was only about five per cent.; and, as the country was limited in extent and densely populated, money circulated with great rapidity. On the other hand, the industries of the United States are already prostrate; the balance of trade is against the country; the specie in the country is inconsiderable in amount; the premium on gold is over twice as high as it was in England; and the immense extent of the country precludes any possibility of money circulating with rapidity. In addition to this, British thought and habit had been educated under the specie basis and credit system of money; whilst, in the United States, experience has fully demonstrated that the system is inconsistent with the genius of American institutions and repugnant to American habits and ideas.

There is every reason, therefore, to believe that the disaster and distress which will attend an attempt to force specie payments in the United States will exceed in intensity that which marked the experience of Great Britain an hundred fold. The contraction which took place just after the war was carried on wholly by the government. The evil consequences of this contraction were partially averted by the emission of over $350,000,000 of bank currency. But now a different kind of contraction is going on. The National Banking system has already enabled the banks to acquire possession of over two-thirds of the greenback circulation, and it is a question of but a short time until they will hold almost the entire amount. Their own notes are encumbered with interest, and are not subject to the natural laws of trade, but to the will of the banks. It will take but a short time, therefore, to call them all in. The organs of the banks are constantly repeating the statement that there is plenty of money in the banks, and that any one can get it who has anything to get it with, and the statement is echoed and re-echoed by all the demagogues and weak minded tools of the money power in the country. Properly considered, we submit that this fact alone confirms all the objections which we have urged against the system of banks of issue. Why is money plenty in the banks, and why is it not occupying the channels of trade and honestly performing the functions for which money is designed? For the simple reason that a medium of exchange consisting, even in part, of bank currency will not obey the natural laws of trade, because it is burdened with interest which robs the industry of the nation of more than its average profit. In ordinary times, after industry had been driven to the wall and a commercial crash had brought about an adjustment, the banks began to expand their circulation, and the banks and the people would enter upon another era of inflation, only to end in the same manner. But now the specie resumption act not only prevents any such expansion, but compels both the banks and the people to contract in every way possible to prepare for the impending crash. True enough, money is plenty in the banks, and it will grow plentier there before the nation is a year older. In fact the contraction of the banks has scarcely more than begun. But as failures multiply, as they are now doing with startling rapidity, loans and discounts will grow less common, until finally the country is entirely deprived of a circulating medium. This can end only in the complete destruction of all values. It will be as difficult to pay a small debt as a large one, for money will be everything and property nothing. Taxes cannot be paid, for there will be no money to pay them with. Not only will individual bankruptcy be general, but the decline in the public revenues, which must follow, will render it impossible for the Federal or State Governments to meet their obligations. This is the only kind of repudiation that need ever be feared in America. The people are being rapidly deprived by the policy of the money power, not only of the ability to sustain the government, but of the ability to provide for themselves and families. That a nation possessing the wonderful advantages and the skill and energy possessed by the American people should be brought to even its present distressed condition in the pursuit of a phantom, is simply monstrous. And when the crisis is reached, what will have been attained? "Honest money?" No. Nothing but a circulating medium consisting of bank currency, only nominally redeemable in coin. Assuming that the government will be able to redeem the greenback circulation and that the amount is paid to the banks, it is not difficult to foretell the result. The banks will issue bank currency, redeemable in coin. Whenever a demand for specie arises abroad, American securities will be thrown upon the market, and the gold in the country will disappear in a day. The banks will be obliged to suspend specie payments, precisely as the old State banks of issue were obliged to do, time and again, under similar circumstances. Under the old State banking system the people were compelled to use bank currency, even when they knew it was a fraud and a lie, because they had nothing else to use. But under the National Banking arrangement the notes of the banks will be taken without hesitation, not because they are convertible into coin, but because they are guaranteed by the Federal Government—based upon the faith and wealth of the nation. In the end, therefore, so far as specie circulation is concerned it will prove, as in the days before the war, a fraud and a delusion. The National Banks, however, will have accomplished their end. They will have obtained absolute control over the monetary and political affairs of the nation. The whole affair is in fact but a grand scheme to accomplish that purpose, and it is marvelous that intelligent people can be decieved in believing otherwise. In 1791, when Hamilton sought to establish his funding and banking scheme, the great Pitt said: "Let the Americans adopt their funding system and go into their banking institutions, and their independence will be a mere phantom." What Hamilton, with all his genius and great ability and influence was unable to accomplish in the infancy of the republic, a pack of venal demagogues have well nigh accomplished nearly a century later. People are wont to say, and apparently seem to think that it is an evidence of their good sense, "that they don't know nor care anything about this financial question." It is high time that everybody should seek to understand this question, because until the National Banks are destroyed and a system of money is founded upon sound principles, there can be no enduring prosperity in the country, and the "independence of the people will be a mere phantom." The demoralization which is now going on throughout the country in consequence of the enforced idleness and poverty of millions of people, is a matter of serious import, and one which should awaken to a sense of duty and action every christian man and woman in the land, and especially ministers of the Gospel, who profess to follow Him whose tenderest care was ever manifested for the weak, the lowly and the oppressed.

There is another fact which may convey a warning to those who are lending themselves to the ignoble cause of enriching the money power at the expense of ruin, poverty and distress to the masses. When the American people are driven to the extremity that the English and Scotch people were, by an attempt to force resumption, and gather in vast multitudes, as the English did at Peterloo and the Scotch at Glasgow, to demand redress, matters will assume a very different shape in the United States from what they did in Great Britain. It is true that an organ of a notorious Wall street operator, the New York *Tribune*, has intimated that any such demonstrations would promptly be met with "shot and slaughter;" but in the United States that is more easily said than done. The day has not yet arrived when Americans can be intimidated by such threats. As yet they "their *duties* know, but know their RIGHTS, and knowing *dare* maintain them." While the American people undoubtedly possess too much patriotism and intelligence to jeopardize the stability of their institutions, they nevertheless may possibly forget, in the hour of their distress, that the Lord hath said, "vengeance is mine." In that day the Shermans and McCullochs had better never have been born.

CHAPTER IX.

A MONETARY SYSTEM FOUNDED UPON SOUND PRINCIPLES.

It is a common error, inculcated by the bullionists, to suppose that metallic coins alone are money, and that money is the same thing in all parts of the world. Nothing could be further from the truth. Population, commerce and trade have long since outgrown the world's supply of the precious metals. Every nation builds up a monetary system of its own, and no two systems are or can be alike. The monetary system of a nation is an outgrowth of its civilization, precisely as are its manners, its customs, its language and its government. For example, Great Britain and France both use metallic coins and paper money, and yet the monetary systems of the two nations differ in almost every particular. Several centuries ago the increase in population, trade and manufactures and the limited supply of gold and silver rendered it impossible for the people of Great Britain to secure a sufficient amount of coin to form an adequate medium of exchange. The true nature and functions of money were but imperfectly understood, and no effort was made, on the part of the government of that kingdom, to remedy the difficulty under which the people labored in effecting their exchanges. The people were obliged to do the best they could. Exchanges of property and commodities thus came to be effected to a great extent by means of promissory notes, book accounts, and other devices of the credit system. In the course of time the Bank of England was established. Soon after it was established its managers conceived the idea of issuing bank notes, to be exchanged for the notes of individuals. Merchants and others gladly availed themselves of an opportunity to substitute the notes of a responsible and widely known institution for the notes of individuals, which could only circulate in a limited sphere. Bank notes were found to be capable of greatly facilitating the operations of trade, and became the chief medium of exchange of the nation. Bank notes, it will be perceived, are purely an offshoot or development of the credit system, invented to remedy the want of an adequate medium of exchange. In this manner a monetary system of a peculiar character has been developed in Great Britain, which has exercised a powerful influence upon the destinies of the people of that kingdom and also upon the rest of the world. The monetary system thus developed in Great Britain, although based on specie, is made up almost wholly of credit. The statement of Sir John Lubbock, given on page 48, shows that of £19,000,000, paid into his bank in a few days, only one-half of one per cent. consisted of coin. Every dollar in coin in Great Britain thus becomes the basis of an immense superstructure of credit. Gold coins are the legal tender money of the country, silver being a tender only for small sums. As the exchanges of the country are carried on with a medium of exchange only a small percentage of which is coin, whenever a stringency occurs, or a want of confidence prevails, which inevitably happens as soon as the credit of the nation becomes fully inflated, everybody seeks to obtain possession of this small percentage of the circulating medium, which alone is a tender in payment of debts. Coin consequently rises in value and is no longer a proper measure of other values. In this respect at least its functions as money are totally perverted. Money thus instituted is given a tremendous power over property and labor, and the whole tendency of the system is to make the rich richer and the poor poorer. The system, however, is in accord with the views held by the aristocratic or governing class of Great Britain, and finds its champions in a school of political economists, who profess to believe, and strive to inculcate, the doctrine that it is natural and proper that poverty and want and disease and misery should be next door neighbors of wealth and unbounded prosperity. It is due chiefly to this system of money that such great extremes of wealth and poverty are to be found in Great Britain.

France, like Great Britain, uses both coin and paper money, but money in France is instituted upon entirely different principles. The policy of the French Government is to render money abundant and cheap, in order that the exchanges of the nation may be effected with the least cost possible, and that the productive ability of the people may be developed to the utmost extent. The men who moulded the French system were wise enough to know that labor is the true source of wealth, and that the surest way to render the government powerful was to enable the masses to become prosperous. This was not accomplished without a great struggle. Colwell, in his work on The Ways and Means of Payment, says: "The system of public finance in France, once so cumbrous and awkward, so expensive and otherwise disadvantageous to the nation, has, during the past half century,* under the able direction of Count Mollien, the Marquis D'Audriffet and other eminent men, undergone such radical changes as have completely modified both its principles and its mode of operation. These reforms were resisted, in every stage and with every weapon, by the parties (the money power) interested in maintaining old

*This was written prior to 1860.

abuses. The persevering efforts of honest and intelligent men for thirty or forty years overcame all opposition, and France now enjoys a financial system, in not a few respects, superior to any other nation." The people of France have the cash system and pay as they go. The circulation of the country consists of about $1,200,000,000 in specie and about $500,000,000 of irredeemable legal tender paper money, issued by the Bank of France. The London *Standard* of April 14, 1876, in commenting on the remarkable condition of the French finances, says:

"The Bank of France at the present time occupies in the financial world a position more remarkable than has ever been held by such an establishment. Its notes enjoy a forced currency and are a legal tender in all business transactions, yet those notes suffer no depreciation. They pass from hand to hand for precisely the same value as gold. A sufficient explanation of this fact may, perhaps, be found by some persons in the circumstance that the bank has accumulated in its coffers at this moment the greatest quantity of the precious metals that has ever yet been possessed by a single establishment. That, however, does not really account for the undiminished credit of the bank. For even in the agony of the last war, when the veteran armies of the empire were prisoners in Germany, when Paris was closely invested, and one-third of the departments were occupied by the invader, the bank's notes were at no greater discount than two or three per cent., and almost immediately rose to par. It is, then, the admirable management of the bank, not the satisfactory nature of its reserve, which gives to it the confidence it commands. It adds to the peculiarity of the position that, although the bank possesses a stock of gold and silver out of all proportion greater than is held by any other bank in the world, it does not propose immediately to resume specie payments. And what is more remarkable still, nobody demands that it shall do so."

A further examination of the monetary systems of other nations would disclose similar peculiarities and differences; in some gold is the only tender, in others silver, and in others gold, silver and paper. In Austria, for example, silver pieces of the denomination of one and one and a half florins are a legal tender to any amount. Gold is also coined into pieces of the denomination of four and eight florins (about $2 and $4), but as gold is not a tender, it is regarded as merchandise and fluctuates in value like other merchandise. The Austrian system is modeled after the British system, silver forming the basis instead of gold, and it has proved there as elsewhere a perpetual source of disaster.

From these facts it is manifest that a people should be far more concerned about the manner in which their monetary system is instituted than about the material of which their money is made. The chief function of money is to exchange property and commodities, and it should be instituted in such a manner as to enable this to be done economically and equitably, so that all classes may be duly rewarded in the distribution of the products of labor, according to their deserts.

People strive to accumulate wealth, and wealth, in its ordinary signification, consists of property and money. As money, by virtue of its legal properties, is an equivalent for all kinds of property, its possession is eagerly sought, and hence it seems that people are seeking solely for money, which is not the fact. Money is simply the means to attain the end, which is dominion over property. Real value belongs only to property or products, and money is the legal medium by which it is represented, measured and exchanged, and hence money, properly considered, is simply a tool of exchange.

As has already been explained, the population, commerce and trade of the world has long since outgrown the supply of the precious metals available for the purposes of a medium of exchange. Other forms of money are in use in all civilized nations. The larger operations of trade, both foreign and domestic, are carried on almost wholly by means of paper devices or substitutes for money, which represent and are based on the value of the commodities exchanged. Bills of exchange constitute the real "money of the world." The trade between different sections of the country, like the foreign trade, is carried on almost entirely by means of bills of exchange, checks, drafts, etc., and no one will say that it is not more economically and safely done than if it was carried on by means of gold and silver. The volume and amount of the bills of exchange, etc., used are limited only by the exchanges to be made. If any one were to suggest that bills of exchange, drafts, etc., whether foreign or domestic, should be limited in volume and amount by law, he would probably be denounced as a fool, and yet it is just as absurd and far more unjust to limit the volume and amount of the legal tender money to an amount manifestly inadequate to effect the exchanges of the nation.

Money, by reason of its legal properties, under any circumstances, has sufficient power over property to enable it to perform all the essential functions of money, namely, to exchange and accumulate value; but to limit it in amount, as by selecting a rare and expensive material like gold, or by arbitrarily declaring by law, as in the case of legal tender Treasury notes, that it shall not exceed a certain sum, without regard to population, extent of country, or exchanges to be effected, is to invest money with an extraordinary power over property, labor and trade, as unsound in principle as it has proved ruinous in practice.

THE REAL ISSUE.

The issue presented to the American people, then, in the present crisis, is not between specie and paper money, but between two systems of money, both involving the use of paper currency. No more important question could possibly arise, for upon its proper solution depends not only the present prosperity of the nation, but the welfare of the people for generations to come. "Monetary laws," says Kellogg, "are the most important that are enacted, for by these laws money is made the tender for debts and the medium of exchange for products. All individuals are compelled to found their contracts for the necessaries of life upon the standard fixed by law. However good the intention of the parties, their contracts will partake of the evil of the monetary laws upon which they are founded, and every law that goes to support the fulfillment of the contracts will partake of the same evil. * * The laws make money the foundation for all business contracts. The value of this foundation is unjust and continually varying, so that parties in fulfilling their contracts are compelled to give either more or less than a just equivalent for their purchases. The results of all contracts are as varying and unjust as their foundation. The continual fluctuations in the value of money makes a sort of gambling system of all trade."

The distinguishing features of the two systems of money, The Specie Basis or Bank Currency System and The Legal Tender Paper Money System, which are now presented to the American people for their adoption or rejection, have been duly explained in the foregoing pages. It only remains now to bring them together, in order that the advantages and disadvantages of each may be fully discerned.

THE SPECIE BASIS OR BANK CURRENCY SYSTEM.

The specie basis or bank currency system originated with the Bank of England;* it was introduced into the United States about the time of the Revolution, and has exercised a powerful influence upon the business and social relations of the people of the United States since that time.

The fact that banks of issue have existed in the United States for over three-quarters of a century has led many to suppose that issuing and lending bank notes constitute the chief business of banks. Issuing or lending bank notes, on the contrary, is a mere incident of the business of banking. The great function of banking is the adjustment of payments, growing out of the exchange of property and commodities, by means of devices of the credit system, such as bills of exchange, etc. Banking, as we have explained,† is an agency of trade, second in importance only to money itself. For many purposes of trade the means of payment afforded by banks are preferable to the use of cash, as where they obviate the necessity of transferring or retransferring money between individuals, localities and nations having mutual dealings. The great error of the specie basis and bank currency system of banking consists in this, that the banks, not satisfied with furnishing the means of payment best adapted for carrying on the larger operations of trade, seek to compel the public to use the same means of payment (devices of the credit system) in all the operations of trade, although for many purposes cash is preferable to credit. No dividing line can be established between the use of cash and credit, and it is manifestly but the part of wisdom to have money so instituted that commerce and trade can avail

*See page 89. †See page 76.

themselves of either cash or credit in such proportions as may be most advantageous. If the circulation consists of bank currency this cannot be done, because bank currency is credit and not cash. "The banks of the United States," says Colwell, one of the most conscientious as well as profound writers upon the subject of money, "are, properly speaking, dealers in credit. So far as their capital is paid up in gold or silver, it is reserved as a security for their circulation. It is a rare thing that a bank lends gold or silver. Their business consists mainly in purchasing commercial paper—that is, the evidences of debt taken by men of business in the ordinary course of their affairs; in paying for that paper with bank notes, or with credits granted upon their books; in receiving upon deposit their own notes and claims or transfers upon other banks; in allowing a constant transfer of deposits, in the way of payment, among their customers and those with whom they deal. The banks, then, are not lenders of money, though compelled to pay their obligations in money. They are founded on the idea that an association of men, with a paid up capital, and a corporate existence, is entitled to a higher credit than individuals, and that the latter might find it greatly for their advantage to avail themselves in their business transactions of this superior credit." It is undoubtedly highly advantageous to individuals to be enabled to avail themselves of this superior credit in many of the operations of trade, but it is equally important that they should be enabled also to avail themselves of the use of cash in other operations. Under the bank currency system cash does not circulate in the channels of trade, but bank notes, and these are continually being returned to the banks in payment of debts.

The following extracts from The Ways and Means of Payment, to which we are already so much indebted, will convey a clearer idea of the leading principles, which underlie the specie basis system, than we could otherwise hope to give. It should be remembered that Mr. Colwell's work was written prior to 1860:

"We have seen," says Colwell, "that the credit system rests upon the fact, that the business of purchasing and selling commodities is separated from the business of payments; and upon the further fact, that the commodities which men sell are made to pay for those they purchase. So far as credits and payments are concerned it is the main object of every man to apply his credits to pay his debts; to employ what is due to him by others in discharging that which he owes to others. The main agency in this is the banks. It is well known that all the large transactions of business are made upon the credit of the parties concerned in them; that the great staples of the country, as well as foreign goods in large quantities, are bought and sold upon individual credit. The market value involved in every transaction is expressed in money of account, and appears on the face of the bills of exchange and promissory notes which the purchaser gives, and the seller takes, as evidence of the debt incurred and credit given in each case. These evidences of debt and credit, which represent, in various shapes, the market value of the commodities, foreign and and domestic, as they move in the channels of trade are the very articles in which it is the object and proper business of the banks to deal. The parties to these evidences of debt, or this commercial paper, having delivered and received the commodities upon which the credits and indebtedness are alike founded, have the remaining duty of payment to fulfill." * *

"Men extensively engaged in commercial and industrial pursuits are, by the very nature of their business, both buyers and sellers—both debtors and creditors. It is important to pay their debts, and realize their credits, with the least trouble, expense and waste of time possible. When any two of them have mutual accounts against each other on their books, they compare and balance them: of course debts so paid, and credits so realized, are as satisfactorily paid and realized as if gold had passed on each transaction. So each man of business indebted upon promissory notes and bills of exchange, and holding such paper of others for debts due to him, is only desirous of applying his credits to his debts. He never thinks of looking for gold or silver to effect a discharge of his debts, and as little does he think of exacting such payment from those who are indebted to him." * *

"The banks of the United States are the chief agencies in this mode of payment. They offer the means and facilities of payment which the parties to this business paper require. They receive this paper, having some months to run to maturity, and deducting interest for the time, give the parties bank notes, or a credit on their books for the proceeds. This is not turning individual notes into money, it is simply turning them into promissory notes of the bank, or deposits; these being of higher credit, and fitted, from the manner in which they are issued, to be used as a currency or a medium of payment. The real basis of the individual notes discounted by the bank is the commodities which the person giving the notes received. These persons contracted debts to the several amounts of their notes, and against these debts they hold the purchased commodities. They offer the goods thus purchased to the public, and expect, from their sale, to realize the means of paying the debts. The discounted paper, therefore, exhibits on its face the true market value of the commodities purchased by it;

and the bank notes, or bank credits, given for this individual paper have the same basis, with the added guarantee of the bank. All bank notes and bank credits issued upon real business paper are virtually issued for commodities actually moving in the regular channels of trade. The purchasers of these commodities expect to realize enough, by their sale, not only to pay for them, but a profit beside.

"It is this process *which is continually absorbing bank notes and returning them to the banks.* The sellers of goods receive the paper of the purchasers, and dispose of it to the bank, taking therefor bank notes and bank credits, the latter of which they employ in paying their debts, and the former pass into circulation in the retail business, and in this way soon reach the hands of the debtors of the banks, to whom they are always as valuable as the equivalent, or same nominal amount of gold or silver, and even more desirable, because they pay debts to the bank equally well, and with less trouble, expense and hazard." * *

"If the banks in any community have discounted notes to the amount of a million, averaging sixty days to maturity, granting credits therefor to the amount of $990,000, they will promptly give up any or all the notes going to make up the million, for a return of their credits to the amount. The banks give nothing for the notes discounted but credits on their books: what they gave for the notes they are willing to receive in kind for them. The profits of the bank, being the interest, for which they issued no credits, must of course be paid when the notes are retired. The main business of the banks consists, then, in purchasing commercial securities and evidences of debt, paying for them with their own notes and bank credits, and deducting the interest for their profit. In doing this, they not only furnish a medium of payment in which these commercial securities can be discharged, *but a currency which may be employed in the interval*, before it is applied to the extinction of these debts. What chiefly makes this currency available and effective is, that there is an active and urgent demand for it, to the whole amount due to the banks; that is, for more than all the banks have issued. This demand is active, urgent, daily, unremitting: the notes in bank are maturing daily, and the demand, therefore, never flags; every day has its payments, which are to be effected with money, or the issues of the banks. The latter, in any community where there are banks of circulation, being the chief medium of payment, is the medium most in demand.

"We have shown that, in all cases where the notes discounted by the banks were given by the makers of them for commodities of daily use and consumption, these commodities are immediately offered to the public for bank notes, or checks on bank deposits, as the proper fund with which to pay the discounted notes. The commodities, by their sale, give origin to promissory notes; the promissory notes give rise to the bank notes and credits; these become, in their turn, a medium with which to purchase the commodities; and the bank notes and bank credits coming thus, by circulation, into the hands of the debtors to the banks, are returned to the banks in payment of the discounted notes." * *

"In cases where banks discount paper not given for property transferred at the time, it is, or should be, on well grounded confidence that the maker of the paper has the power or means of redeeming from the hands of the public an equal amount of the issues of the bank. The banks being large holders of individual paper, either discounted or deposited with them for collection, they are of course constantly looked to for the means of payment; and a credit on the books of a bank, granted by the bank, or derived from another quarter, being all that is required, it is earnestly sought for that purpose. Where there are many banks, and large transactions in business and upon credit, the movement of these payments in banks, and the consequent movement of bank-credits or deposits, become far too complicated to be followed up by any process of analysis. One great feature, however, must ever be prominent, and that the most effective of all in sustaining the present banking system; that is, that every debtor of a bank is an active agent in purchasing and returning to the bank its notes and credits; that the issues of the banks, whether notes or credits on their books, are more available, convenient and economical for these debtors, than the legal currency of coins. They are more abundant, more easily obtained, and equally effective. It is this which gives to bank notes and bank credits their efficiency and rapidity of movement. The amount of the circulation of the New York banks averaged over $8,000,000 in 1857, and the deposits averaged over $87,000,000. These constitute the medium in which the payments of the City of New York are chiefly made. With these, there is a daily payment to be made of from $30,000,000 to $50,000,000, and they are quite capable of making that amount of payments each day, for both notes and deposits may be paid many times during the day. It is very safe to assume that over $30,000,000 of city bank notes and deposits are paid each business day in New York. There is a demand, then, upon these notes and deposits in every week, for payments, to the amount of $200,000,000, and in every month for $800,000,000. This demand daily, weekly, monthly, constantly pressing upon a fund of bank notes and deposits, which may at no time exceed $100,000,000, is certainly active and pressing enough to keep up the value of a fund so much used, and so indispensable to the men who have $200,000,000 to pay every week.

"That these sums are far within the actual daily payments of New York is apparent from the operations of the Clearing-house. The amount cleared daily, in 1857, was over $20,000,000, and these clearings are but the balances on the transactions between the banks. A vast sum of payments is made every day in the business of such a city as New York, which is in no way embraced in the transactions of the Clearing-house. If we assume that the whole of the payments effected yearly through the agency of banks in the United States, is only ten times greater than the amount paid yearly in New York, we shall have an aggregate 400 times greater than the amount of the precious metals in the country; 500 times the amount of the bank note circulation of the United States; 400 times the amount of bank deposits; and 30 times the annual value of the whole productive industry of the country." * *

"In the great movements of industry and trade, goods and services pay for goods and services; the promissory notes, bank notes, bank credits, or other currency, which intervene, are devices of adjustment, and not the very payment ultimately aimed at. Men give what they have to spare, to obtain what they desire. If they do not, in the first instance, sell for money, and with that purchase what they want, they take a security or evidence of debt; they make their purchases upon their individual credit, and give evidences of debt. The debt and credit extinguish each other in the banks, and the parties have, in substance, exchanged goods; all the rest is merely keeping and balancing accounts between them. These securities are issued, in this country, to an amount not less than $1,000,000,000 every three months, in which period this amount continually runs off and is renewed, making $4,000,000,000 in the year. Of this $1,000,000,000 of securities, the banks become the owners and collectors; and for half this amount they are under a constant engagement to pay money on demand. To meet this engagement, the banks hold $60,000,000 against $500,000,000, or twelve per cent. of the amount. Of course, absolute convertibility of all this fund of securities into specie, on demand, is an impossibility. If all the gold and silver in the country, estimated at $250,000,000, were in the banks, it would be an impossibility. It must, therefore, continue to be impossible; and hence arises one of the gravest difficulties connected with banks of circulation.

"If bank notes, like checks upon banks, were confined in their use and circulation to those at whose special instance they are issued, and whose debts are to be adjusted by them, there would be less occasion for any public intervention or concern. For the public have little interest, whether men thus mutually indebted discharged their debts by balancing accounts, by bank notes, or by checks on banks. But the experience of a century and a half has shown that, where bank notes are offered as a currency, they are freely received, and soon become the chief medium of exchange. It is almost invariably true that, wherever bank notes are offered as a currency, with even the slightest pretensions to regularity and security, they are accepted, and pass rapidly into general circulation. This facility of converting bank paper into a currency is a strong temptation to resort to it, and accounts in part for the multiplication of banks of circulation in this country and elsewhere; but it has given rise, also, to that ceaseless jealousy with which this system of banking has been watched. There is, perhaps, more ground for this jealousy than many friends of the system have been willing to acknowledge. If the circulation of bank notes had been confined to the payment of the debts in which they originate, no more mischief could ensue than now arises from the employment of checks upon banks, which the parties using them are interested to keep within legitimate and safe bounds. But as bank notes, wherever offered, secure a wide circulation, it is not enough to say, let people take them at their risk, as they take them at their discretion." * *

"We have said, and the figures we have adduced show, that convertibility of the notes and deposits of our banks is impossible, even when the banks are in the best condition. And that this must continue to be the case, constituted as the banks of the United States are, is as certain. The main feature of the business of these banks is the discount of notes maturing at a future time: we have previously assumed that the average time to run, of the paper thus discounted, is ninety days, or one-fourth of a year. They issue to the parties at whose instance these discounts are made, their notes payable on demand, or give them credit on their books for the proceeds, payable in like manner on demand. The deposits of the banks are made up, almost altogether, from the notes thus issued, and the credits thus granted. The circulation and deposits of 1856 amounted to $443,000,000, for which the banks, by this mode of doing business, became liable on demand; that is, they received from their customers claims on the public maturing in three months, and they become liable to pay a certain amount on demand; in the year 1856, for instance, in every three months, $445,000,-000, and in 1857, in every like period, $500,000,000. The paper discounted by the banks not being payable on demand would only be paid, and could only be demanded as it matured from day to day; whether the sums thus paid into the banks were eight or ten millions daily, it was all the banks could exact, and if the notes had not been discounted, the amount required to pay them would have been the same. But the banks became liable to the payment of from $445,000,000 to $500,000,000 in any one day in 1856 and 1857—a position, stripped of the mists and prejudice which constantly surround it, which should be called, as it really is, stupendously absurd; and, in times of commercial revulsion, not less dangerous than absurd." * *

"Banks of circulation, however, here and elsewhere, are and continue to be placed under stringent legal obligations to pay their liabilities in coins. If any law could compel them to do this, and still leave them power sufficient to carry on the business of banking with the same advantage to their customers and the public as at present, the currency they would furnish would indeed be the best attainable for circulation. For a paper currency of sufficient amount, absolutely and at all times convertible, would combine almost every conceivable advantage. The obstacle is, that such a convertibility is impossible; no legislation can accomplish it; the omnipotence of the British Parliament could not achieve it. Even the unusual provision in the constitution of the State of New York, which denies the power to the Legislature of legalizing a suspension of specie payments, availed not in 1857, during the fearful panic of the hundred days. This precaution about the notes did not extend to the deposits. The banks suspended upon their deposits, which were ten times the amount of their notes. They have since resumed, and have now $31,000,000 of specie to $90,000,000 of notes and deposits. With this enormous and unusual accumulation of gold, payment on demand rests only on the forbearance of the people. The depositors could bring the banks to a state of suspension in two hours.

Upon this state of facts, the common phrase that our bank circulation is based on gold and silver is absolutely untrue. If our paper currency had no other basis than this very uncertain, insecure, and ultimately impossible convertibility, it could not be upheld for a week, nor even a day. The real basis of our paper currency, that which does sustain it through extraordinary emergencies, is the individual promissory notes, and other evidences of debt, in exchange for which it is issued. These must all be paid, or the debtors must fail or suspend. The business men of the United States owed the banks, in 1856, the sum of $684,000,000; and the banks were indebted, for their circulation and deposits, $445,000,000. If we suppose that these debtors to the banks were 100,000 in number, owing an average of $6,840 each, all this mass of business men would be active agents in redeeming the issues of the banks, of which the average burden of each would be $4,450. The products of the industry of a country being sold, individual paper being given therefor, and the issues of the bank being given for that individual paper, it is evident not only that the issues are based upon that paper, but it is equally evident that the commodities for which the individuals issued their paper have come into their hands, that they have these commodities to offer to the public for the notes in circulation, and for checks on the banks, with which to pay their debts. The real strength of the banks is in this, that their business is founded on the trade and industry of the country; and all the business men, with the commodities of daily consumption in their hands, are under the strongest inducements to offer these commodities for the notes and deposits of the bank.

"It must not, then, we repeat, be supposed that the basis of our paper currency is specie; the fact is, and must be, otherwise; that is no foundation to be relied upon, which must go with the first flood. No superstructure like our banking system should be reared upon a quicksand. We do not urge this as an argument against convertibility on demand, in the aspect of a check upon the banks. It may be necessary or expedient, but cannot be so on the ground of its being the basis, or adequate security, of bank issues. We should not make the concession even by implication, that $50,000,000 or $60,000,000 of gold and silver can be any proper basis for issues or liabilities of the banks to the amount of $445,000,000 to $500,000,000: it is a mere delusion, to regard the former amounts as sufficient to sustain a demand for the latter." * *

"We object, then, to a phrase so likely to mislead, as that of calling gold or silver the basis of paper currency, under the present constitution of our banks. The obligation to pay on demand can be nothing more than a check on the abuse of banking, or a security to the public, and as such only should it be regarded and discussed. If it be indispensable, it is upon the ground that no other adequate security is attainable. We do not believe this, and regard this attempt to place the credit system on the back of our coinage system, as partaking of that caution and wisdom which would place a locomotive, for its best service, upon a one-horse cart."

THE COST OF THE SPECIE BASIS SYSTEM.

Under the specie basis system the money of the country is locked up in bank vaults as the basis of bank currency, and the business of the country is necessarily carried on with credit and currency. The amount of credit and currency is limited, not by the amount of specie held by the banks, but by the amount of property and commodities moving in the channels of trade. The cost of such a medium of exchange is enormous. The amount of the loans and discounts of the banks during the year 1875 amounted, on an average, to nearly $1,000,000,000, the interest on which at 10 per cent. is $100,000,000.* The loans and discounts made outside of the banks doubtless exceed the loans and discounts of the banks, but assuming that they are the same ($1,000,000,000), and that the rate of interest averages 15 per cent. for the year, it would amount to $150,000,000, or in all $250,000,000 paid yearly in the way of interest.

But there is another method of arriving at an approximate cost of the system, which makes the amount much larger. The clearings of the banks of New York city average about $20,000,000 daily. Estimating the payments of the city of New York at $40,000,000 daily, and the payments of the whole country at five times that amount, or $200,000,000 daily, will give $60,000,000,000 for the year. If this vast sum of payments costs the payers on an average 60 days' interest, or say one per cent. on the whole amount, it will make the sum paid yearly under the credit system $600,000,000. This vast sum is paid by the industries of the country. With a medium of exchange occupying the channels of trade, unencumbered by interest, such as specie or legal tender Treasury notes, the greater portion of this enormous sum would be saved to the producing classes of the nation. The interest paid for a medium of exchange furnished by the banks and for the use of credit rendered necessary by the bank currency system, is a burden upon production and trade, that can only be removed by the extinction of banks of issue and the substitution of legal tender Treasury notes for bank currency.

*See Page 263.

COMMERCIAL CRASHES AND MONEY PANICS.

When the business affairs of the country are in active operation, the whole amount of credit and currency available for the purposes of trade is in constant demand. As trade increases the demand for credit and currency increases, until it becomes inflated to a dangerous extent, or a demand for specie may arise abroad. In either event the banks are obliged to provide for their own safety, and the withdrawal from business men of the required amount of currency and credit produces a stringency, which inevitably leads to disaster. The manner in which this happens is thus explained by Colwell:

"It is not difficult to see what abundant food for panic there is in such a condition of things. Persons in the United States have claims to the amount of $400,000,000 on the banks, payable on demand; these claimants know that the banks cannot pay in specie the fifth part of them, and often not the tenth part. And although the specie is not what they need, or would ever have asked, yet they know that the banks may stop payment in an hour; that they will then be branded as bankrupt; and that they may thereupon be subjected to injurious and damaging legal proceedings: panic becomes, therefore, inevitable. Men in such circumstances feel themselves to be involved in a widespread, complicated calamity. They fear the result, not only for the amount of their present deposits, and the bank notes they hold, but they tremble for other debts due to them, and are in equal dread about what they owe. They know that if this machinery of the credit system is stopped, or seriously disturbed, debts cannot be paid. The banks, under the influence of a panic, knowing that they can neither trust one another, nor the unreasoning public, for an hour, adopt what seems to them the only safe course; they receive in payment all their issues as fast as current payments return them, without, however, as usual, keeping up the currency by fresh discounts. If the payments at the banks amount in the United States, for each day, to $300,000,000, the withdrawal of the usual facilities at the banks by contraction, to the extent of even one-half, would rapidly absorb the stock of bank notes and deposits applicable to current payments, and of course make these payments daily more difficult, and finally, to a large extent, impossible. High interest, such as eighteen, twenty-four or thirty-six per cent. per annum, supervenes in this hour of trial to check still further the circulation of that portion of the bank notes and deposits not absorbed by the banks." * *

"The contraction in New York, in the panic of 1857, is a specimen of what the banks are constrained to do, to save themselves. They can only protect their coffers by refusing to issue the usual supply of currency. The diminution of loans and deposits in the banks of New York stood thus in August and October, 1857:

	Loans.	Deposits.
15th of August	$121,241,472	$92,356,328
19th of September	108,777,421	75,772,774
17th of October	97,245,826	52,894,623

"This exhibits a reduction of discounts, in one month, of $13,000,000, and the succeeding month of $11,000,000; that is, $24,000,000 in sixty days: in one month deposits ran down, under this operation, $17,000,000; in the succeeding month, $23,000,000; making, in the two months, a reduction in the chief medium of payment of $40,000,000. The deposits were thus reduced nearly one-half. It cannot be surprising that, under such a process of contraction, interest went up to between fifteen and thirty-six per cent., and exchange down to nine or ten per cent. below par. What the banks did in New York was done, in a greater or less degree, in other cities; bankruptcy, ruin and destruction followed. It is estimated that from five to six thousand failures occurred, involving an indebtedness of from $280,000,000 to $300,000,000, with a loss to creditors of more than $150,000,000. But this loss bears no comparison with that arising from the depreciation of securities, and from the fall in price of real and personal property, which, judging from the results of estimates carefully made, cannot be less than $500,000,000, and may not improbably be twice that sum. The loss sustained by the men who labor for their living is even more severe in its consequences, if not equal in pecuniary amount. A million of men idle for six months involves a loss to the country of $150,000,000, besides the loss upon the machinery, shops, tools and factories, which stand idle when the workmen are unemployed.

"The late panic has inflicted, in all its bearings and ramifications, a loss upon the country which may be variously estimated from $500,000,000 to $1,000,000,000. No doubt the ill effects of the panic were much enhanced by the previous abuse of credit, and that a considerable portion of this devastation should be set down to that account. With every allowance in that respect, we shall have a vast sum of loss to charge to the panic; and whether this sum be $400,000,000, or $800,000,000, matters not to our view. The loss was, to great extent, unnecessary, cruel, terrible—a loss which has carried privation, distress and ruin to a million of homes. For a time, at least, not yet passed, it reduced hundreds of thousands of the best people to a state of entire dependence, if not beggary.

"What was the occasion of these dire calamities? The banks of the United States had a reserve of specie for several years previous to 1857, and during the first half of that year, amounting to somewhat over $50,000,000; and of this, the banks in the city of New York held a little more than one-fifth. To save this amount of specie, the banks contracted the currency one-half, denied the usual facilities upon their books, put up the rate of interest from twelve to thirty-six per cent., put down exchange upon England to nine or ten per cent. below par, reduced the revenue from customs to less than half the usual amount, drew a surplus of $20,000,000 of gold out of the public treasury, and drove the government to an issue of paper promises to pay its current expenses, deprived hundreds of thousands, perhaps millions, of their customary employment, caused some five or six thousand failures among men of business, and finally inflicted a loss on the country, in the depreciation of securities, in the reduction of prices and by insolvency, of several hundred millions.—Not to save this sum of fifty millions from being lost, sunk in the ocean, or thrown away, were all these evils encountered, but merely to prevent it from passing into circulation among the people, or at the worst, to prevent it from being exported in payment of debts due in foreign countries. Nine-tenths of the debts of the country are paid, as we have seen, by the agency of discounts and deposits, with some aid from the circulation of the banks; but the banks have been placed under such heavy penalties to pay all their liabilities in specie on demand, that when they are threatened with a panic, a commercial revulsion, or a heavy export of specie to foreign countries, they are compelled, like Sampson in the temple of the Philistines, to pull down the whole fabric of credit, public and private, about the ears of the people, to disturb and check the progress of industry in all its departments, to make bankrupts of their customers, and to sow pauperism broadcast in the field of labor.

"This compelled policy of the banks, under the stringency

of the laws which govern them, has been called paying specie. But with how little propriety. Instead of paying their liabilities with commercial promptness and the faithfulness of those who are discharging a legal and moral obligation, they resist it with all the power and weapons they can command. In the struggles incident to this resistance, they strike down friends as well as enemies, and deprive the public of an amount of currency necessary to business, ten times greater than the specie they are unwilling to pay out. And this is the convertibility so long aimed at, and to secure which so much legislation and so much thought has been expended! This is the triumph of banks which pass through a season of panic and revulsion without suspending!—a triumph like the victory which leaves 100,000 dead bodies on the field of battle, which makes 10,000 widows, 50,000 orphans, and 200,000 paupers."

THE LEGAL TENDER PAPER MONEY SYSTEM.

With the clear and comprehensive analysis of the principles of the bank currency system, contained in the foregoing extracts from The Ways and Means of Payment, before us, it is not difficult to understand how public notes issued by the government can perform the fnuctions of a medium of exchange.

The great object of trade is the exchange of commodities and services, and it is immaterial to the parties interested whether this exchange is effected by means of a medium possessing intrinsic value, or representative value, as long as it is done with equal safety, convenience and cost.

Public notes, like bank notes, are virtually based on commodities moving in the channels of trade. There is a constant interchange of commodities and services on a vast scale going on between individuals, growing out of the necessities of government, Federal, State and local. To effect this exchange a medium is required. On the one side are the people, who are obliged to contribute out of their substance in proportion to their means towards the expenses of government. On the other, there is a vast multitude of people to whom the government, Federal, State and local, is indebted for commodities and services. The people possess abundant property and products desired by the creditors of the government, and the only problem to be solved is as to the manner in which the exchange can be equitably, speedily and economically accomplished. This can be done, and as it is a matter in which the entire nation is directly interested, it is eminently proper that it should be done, through the instrumentality of public notes issued by the government. Individuals engaged in trade employ the superior credit of banks to enable them to exchange commodities and services; and this superior credit of the banks, for reasons which have been fully explained, serves the purposes of money, in the interval between the time it is issued, in the form of bank notes, to creditors of the banks, until it is returned by the debtors of the banks. In the same manner the superior credit of the government, issued in the form of public notes to the creditors of the government, performs the functions of money, until it is returned to the Federal Treasury by the debtors (tax payers) of the government. The bank notes rest upon the credit of the institutions which issue them, and are a lien upon the assets of the banks, which consist of the property of the banks and of their debtors. The public notes rest upon the credit of the government, and are a lien upon the whole property of the nation. Thus far the analogy between public notes and bank notes is complete, with the advantage largely in favor of public notes, for two reasons: in the first place, public notes constitute a more economical medium of exchange, because they do not bear interest, and in the second place their security is more ample. There is not an objection to the use of public notes, as a medium of exchange, that does not apply with ten fold more force to the use of bank currency; while there are a great many objections to the use of bank currency, which cannot be urged against the use of public notes. It is said by the bullionists and bankers that the "security, though ample, is too general and intangible for the purpose; and that the 'whole property' can only be reached and applied through the slow process of taxation." This is begging the question. The process of taxation is going on constantly, and in point of fact the "whole property" of the people can be reached by a tax warrant much more speedily and certainly than the property of the banks and their debtors can be reached by process of law.

Again it is contended by the bullionists and bankers that a paper currency, in order to perform the functions of money, should be convertible into gold on demand. It has already been sufficiently explained that this is impossible under the bank currency system, unless the amount of notes issued does not exceed the amount of gold held for their redemption; and in that event there is no need to issue any notes, for the public might as well use the gold. Nothing can be clearer than that paper currency is used chiefly for the purpose of supplying the deficiency of money occasioned by the scarcity of the precious metals; and to issue paper notes to the amount of three, five or ten times the amount of gold held for their redemption, and say that they are convertible into gold on demand, is nothing more nor less than a fraud and a delusion, which inevitably leads to disaster.

There is but one way to make paper money equal to

specie, and that is to clothe it with the ability to perform the same functions that specie will perform. That this can be done is fully demonstrated by the instances referred to by Jefferson* and Calhoun,† and by the experience of the French people at the present time. The partial legal tender paper money of the United States now in use fails to circulate at a par with gold, because it is not clothed with the same powers as gold. That Treasury notes of the government, when made a full legal tender, will circulate at par with specie was clearly established by the "old demand notes" issued in 1861, which, after they were made a full legal tender, went up with gold to $2.85, as compared with greenbacks; and at the present time we find the currency bonds of the United States government quoted at a premium of three or four per cent. over gold bonds.

WHAT IS A DOLLAR?

Much confusion arises in regard to the nature and functions of money, from the fact that people have been led to believe that gold, in some way or other, has been made a standard of value. Such is not the fact, either theoretically or practically, as will be fully shown.

The idea of value is something that exists in the minds of the people independent of coins. The unit of value, which is established by custom and education, whatever may have been its origin, is used abstractly. When once a unit of value becomes fixed in the minds of the people, or in other words has passed into the "money of account," it measures all values and is capable of measuring the value of gold and silver, the same as any other commodities. "The value of the unit, or beginning point, being once firmly fixed in men's minds by constant use," says Colwell, "remains there wholly independent of subsequent changes of price which

*See page 56.   †See page 59.

may affect the specific article from which it took its rise. Thus if it sprung from a coin, or a certain quantity of gold or silver, it becomes afterwards so independent of these as to be quite capable of expressing the changing prices of that or any other coin. It is, then, a matter of fact that all commercial people keep their accounts, compute money, and express prices by the use of a money of account. The naming a price with them is not naming a coin, or any specific quantity of gold or silver; but it is the employment of the denominations of the money of account, which all understand to express a price. There is scarcely any mental operation more generally and constantly in exercise than that which is used to express prices." It was thus that the people of Great Britain came to keep their accounts in pounds, shillings and pence. The unit of value with them had its origin in comparing values with the value of a pound of silver, which was divided into twenty parts denominated shillings. This unit of value was changed by successive changes in the silver coinage, until about a century ago, since which time the unit of value in England has remained unchanged. From about 1660 until 1816, the pound sterling had no corresponding piece of coin. The English guinea had been intended to represent a pound, but it had not been properly adjusted, and, owing also to the fluctuations in the price of gold, it varied in value until 1717, when its value was fixed at twenty-one shillings. In 1816, after much deliberation, it was decided to fix the weight of the sovereign at 5 pennyweights, 3 grains and 171-623 thousandths of a grain. It is manifest that the whole difficulty was in establishing a coin whose value should correspond to the unit of value of the money of account, carried in the minds of the people. The English sovereign has since been changed several times.

The people of the United States have undergone a similar

experience. Prior to the Revolution the money of account of the colonies was expressed in pounds, shillings and pence. The unit of value, the pound, not only differed from the English pound sterling, but was different in different colonies. The pound in the following named colonies varied from the present money of account in the United States as follows:

£1—New England and Virginia, $3.33 or 6s. to the dollar.
" New York and North Carolina, 2.50 or 8s. "
" Pennsyl'nia and Middle States, 2.66 or 7s., 6d. "
" South Carolina, 4.28 or 4s., 8d. "

There were no coins in existence corresponding to these amounts. These different units of value had their origin in various causes, which we will not stop to discuss; but when industry and trade had become sufficiently advanced they became fixed. The trade of the colonies with the West Indies had introduced into the country a considerable amount of Spanish coins. The names and values of these coins did not correspond to the money of account of the people, and their value was estimated in the money of account of the several colonies precisely as that of wheat, or any other commodity, was estimated. In 1792 an act was passed by Congress with a view to establishing a uniform money of account throughout the country. People reckoned in pounds, shillings and pence, and paid in Spanish dollars. It will be remembered that continental money was payable in "Spanish milled dollars, or the value thereof in gold or silver." The Act of Congress of April, 1792, declared—"That the money of account of the United States shall be expressed in dollars or units, dimes or tenths, cents or hundreths, and mills or thousandths; a dime being the tenth part of a dollar, a cent the hundreth part of a dollar, etc.; and that all accounts in the public offices, and all proceedings in the courts of the United States, shall be kept and had in conformity to this regulation." This is believed to be the first time that a money of account was ever established by law—moneys of account having in all nations grown up in the minds of the people. The word dollar, however, expressed a value which was fully understood by the people, without any reference to a fixed amount of gold or silver. The great difficulty consisted in fixing the amount of gold and silver that would be equal to a dollar. By the same act a coinage of gold and silver was provided for; "Dollars, or units, each to be of the value of a Spanish milled dollar, as the same is now current, and to contain 371 4-16 grains of pure, or 416 grains of standard silver. * * Eagles, each to be of the value of ten dollars, and to contain 247½ grains of pure or 270 grains of standard gold." Other coins were to be in the same proportion. It was then declared and established, that 371 4-16 grains of pure and 416 grains of standard silver, shall be current as money at the price of one dollar, the value of the unit of the money of account; and gold eagles and half eagles were made current in like manner. The act further provides, "that the proportional value of gold to silver, in all coins which shall be current as money within the United States, shall be as fifteen to one, according to quantity in weight, of pure gold or pure silver."

This attempt to fix the price of gold and silver by law proved a failure. The price of gold as compared with silver was fixed lower, as it proved, than the market price, and the result was that gold ceased to circulate as money to any extent until 1834, when the amount of pure gold in the eagle was changed from 247½ grains to 232. After the discovery of gold in California and Australia, gold depreciated in value, and silver, becoming the more valuable metal of the two, according to the standard established by Congress, deserted the channels of trade. This was remedied, in a measure, by the act of 1853, which changed the coinage of silver about seven per cent. The weight of silver half dollars was fixed at 192 grains, and the smaller coins in the same proportion. The simple fact is, that gold and silver fluctuate in value like other merchandise, being governed entirely by the uncontrollable law of supply and demand, and it is about as absurd to attempt to fix, by law, an unchangeable price on gold or silver as upon a bushel of wheat or a day's labor.

Sir James Stewart, in his work on political economy, says: "Money which I call money of account, is no more than a scale of equal parts, invented for measuring the respective value of things vendible. * * Money of account performs the same office, with regard to the value of things, that degrees, minutes, seconds, etc., do with regard to angles, or as scales do to geographical maps, or to plans of any kind. In all these inventions there is some denominative taken for the unit. In angles, it is the degree; in geography, it is the mile; in plans, it is the foot or yard; in money, it is the pound, livre, florin, etc. The degree has no determinate length, so neither has that part of the scale upon plans or maps which marks the unit; the usefulness of all these being solely confined to the marking of proportions. Just so, the unit in money can have no invariable determinate proportion to any part of value; that is to say, it cannot be fixed in perpetuity to any particular quantity of gold or silver, or any other commodity. The value of commodities depends upon circumstances—their value ought to be considered as changing with respect to one another only; consequently anything which troubles or perplexes the ascertaining these changes of proportion by the means of a general determinate and invariable scale, must be hurtful to trade; and this is the infallible consequence of every vice in the policy of money or coin. * * It does not follow, from this adjusting of the metals to the scale of value, that they themselves should, therefore, become the scale."

It is of course denied by the bullionists that any such currency can be established, as will naturally conform to the money of account; but upon what other hypothesis can the success of the greenback, as a currency, be accounted for? During and since the rebellion the greenback has performed all the functions of money. Gold in the meantime has ranged from par to $2.85. If gold was the standard of value the price of all commodities would fluctuate with gold; but commodities rise and fall in price, as measured by the greenback, without reference to the price of gold (except articles on which duties are paid in gold.) It is said, however, that now that matters have become settled the price of gold shows the depreciation of the greenback; and only recently a distinguished ex-United States Senator,* in a letter to the Hon. S. S. Cox, proposed to change the unit of value (the dollar) from 100 cents to say 85, or the supposed present value of the greenback as compared with gold. If gold coins and greenbacks were on the same footing, such reasoning might carry some weight, for there would be reason to believe that the money of account of the country had undergone a change; but until greenbacks are made a full legal tender, it is entitled to no consideration whatever. If gold was only a partial legal tender and greenbacks were a full legal tender, greenbacks would probably bear a premium over gold, just as currency bonds bear a higher premium than gold bonds, because they possess a slight advantage over gold bonds in point of time. The inconvertible inscriptions of credit of the Bank of Venice were at a premium of 20 per cent. over gold for centuries, simply because they were endowed with superior

*Hon. Edgar Cowan, of Pennsylvania.

powers to coin; and for centuries these inscriptions of credit, conforming as they did by law to the money of account of the people, constituted an unvarying standard of value, by which all commodities, including gold, were measured. The standard of value of the Venetians thus instituted changed only with the money of account of the country.

Gold, if not made a legal tender in payment of debts, performs the functions of a medium of exchange simply as an equivalent; but when made a tender it is invested with additional powers. If the amount of gold put in a dollar is less in value than the money of account, injustice is done to the creditor; if more, injustice is done to the debtor; and when too much gold is put in a coin, it will cease, if there is any other tender, to circulate as money at all. The fact is that the precious metals, considered in their true light, have simply come to perform, in the commercial world, the functions of an universal equivalent, and pass by weight, except when made a tender in the shape of coins; and are subject, in regard to price, to the same laws which govern other commodities. At the present time silver is some two or three per cent. below par, while gold is about twelve per cent. above, as measured by the greenback. This is due almost entirely to the character of the legislation which regulates the circulation of gold, silver and paper.

Gold, then, performs the functions of a medium of exchange by reason of its intrinsic value; and public notes and bank notes perform the same offices by reason of their possessing representative value, not of gold, but of property and commodities, including gold. (It will be observed that in using the words "public notes," Treasury notes are referred to, not as a legal tender, but as a device of the credit system, the same as bank notes.) The bank note virtually represents the commodities moving in the channels of trade, which brought it into circulation, and rests upon the credit of the institution which issued it; in like manner the public note virtually represents the property or commodities levied by the government to defray its expenses and discharge its obligations, and is backed by the credit of the government and the entire property of the nation. It was in this sense that Calhoun asked, "Why not use its own credit (the credit of the government) to the amount of its own transactions? Why should it not be safe in its own hands, while it shall be considered safe in the hands of eight hundred private institutions, scattered all over the country, and which have no other object but their own private profit; to increase which they extend their business to the most dangerous extremes? And why should the community be compelled to give six per cent. discount for the government credit, blended with that of the banks, when the superior credit of the government could be furnished separate, without discount, to the mutual advantage of the government and the community?"

Public notes issued by the government for the purpose of effecting the exchange of property and products constantly taking place between the people on the one side and the creditors of the government on the other, should naturally conform to the money of account in which they are stated, and would undoubtedly do so if founded upon sound principles. The nation possesses abundant property and products of almost every description, subject to the demands of the government; and the government unquestionably possesses the ability to command every dollar's worth of property and products belonging to the nation. The credit of the government, therefore, should be beyond question, and its paper should represent and command property and products to the exact amount stated on its face. A note of the government is virtually an order given by the people collectively upon themselves, payable in property and products. To make this order payable in precious metals, when the people have no precious metals, or only a very limited amount, is to render it impossible for the people to comply with the order, and compel them to dishonor the public credit. A law making public notes payable in diamonds of a certain degree of purity and weight would be considered very oppressive, as well as absurd, and yet it is upon precisely the same principle that the public note is made redeemable in gold. The public note will command property and products, if properly instituted, to the precise amount inscribed on its face, and gold coins can do no more. The creditor of the government wants property and products, and the tax payer must have money (public notes) to pay his taxes. It is this that, in the first instance, gives circulation to public notes. The tax payers constitute a vast army of agents engaged in selling commodities for public notes, with which to discharge their obligations to the State, just as the debtors of the banks form a large body of agents engaged in collecting bank notes to pay their debts in bank.

LEGAL TENDER.

People cannot be compelled to part with their property for money, but public policy requires that some equivalent of property should be established as a tender in payment of debts, and this equivalent is styled money. To the creditor it should be immaterial whether this equivalent possessed intrinsic or representative value, provided it commanded property to the amount attached to it by law. A dollar's worth of gold, when coined and declared the only tender, is endowed with great advantages over all other kinds of property, as well as over the public note which represents property. Creditors can refuse to take property or public notes, at no matter what valuation, but gold coins they are obliged to take at the price fixed by law. Hence it is that a public note, which represents property to the amount inscribed on its face, and should command property of any kind, including gold, will not command gold. The gold has been transformed into money by being made a legal tender. Gold being clothed with special powers over property, as well as over the public note, comes to be in great demand, and, as it is limited in amount, is absorbed by capital, to be used as an instrument to control property and public notes; its functions as a medium of exchange are thus capable of being perverted, and the object of the legal tender law is consequently also perverted, greatly to the injury of society and of the public credit.

The public note is intended to perform the functions of a medium of exchange for the exchange of all kinds of property, including gold, and should, therefore, be made a legal tender. If any commodity is to be made a tender, it should be such a commodity as the people possess or can readily acquire at its market value. The great object of trade is the exchange of property, not property for money or money for property; and money which is designed to effect this exchange should be instituted in such a manner as to form an unvarying representative and measure of value, conforming to the money of account of the nation. But if money is made of a commodity, it will rise or fall in value according to circumstances, and will render trade uncertain, or, as Kellogg aptly expressed it, will make a gambling system of all trade.

The responsibility of furnishing a medium of exchange, or declaring what shall be a tender, rests with the Federal Government. It is a matter of vital importance to the nation, individually and collectively, to have money so instituted as to clog the production and exchanges of the nation as little as possible. In this advanced age credit is everywhere used in trade, when credit can be used to exchange products more advantageously than a medium of exchange possessing intrinsic value. It is not only eminently proper, but it is a matter of public advantage, therefore, for the government to use its own credit, at least to the extent of its own operations. To do this its notes should be made a full legal tender, otherwise the people can repudiate individually what they have done collectively, which inevitably works injustice to the creditor of the government, and impairs the credit of the nation.

The bullionists assert that a paper money, not redeemable in gold, issued by the government, can possess no value; and that it virtually consists of bits of paper with figures and words printed on them; and political economists are found so shallow, or worse, as to adopt this theory. If this is true, then are all the paper devices of civilization, by means of which property is held or exchanged, a fraud and a delusion. But public notes are not simply bits of paper, to be issued to an unlimited extent. Every dollar emitted by the Federal Government in payment for property, services, or in discharge of its obligations, costs the people precisely one dollar in property or products, to redeem it and return it to the public Treasury. When public notes, representing commodities moving in the channels of trade, are issued by the government to the extent of its own transactions and are made a legal tender, they conform to the money of account of the nation, and become the measure of all values, the standard of all payments and the basis of all money contracts; they, therefore, perform all the offices of money, and pass into general circulation. They are paid out by the government for property or services at their face value; being a tender they pay debts at their face value; and in the end are returned to the Federal Treasury in the shape of taxes, in lieu of property, to the amount inscribed on their face. No evidence of debt or device of the credit system ever devised possessed greater elements of strength and security than the public note of a rich and powerful nation, made a legal tender and issued to the extent of its own transactions. The notes of the Bank of France, as we have seen, although not redeemable in specie, circulate at par to the amount of hundreds of millions of dollars, when made a legal tender and backed by the credit of the people. Who will say that the revenues of the United States are not as certain as those of France, or that the ability of the American people to produce wealth does not equal that of the French people, or that the Federal Government is not as stable as the French Government? The French people are uncertain as to whether they will be living under a monarchical or a republican form of government in ten years from to-day, and yet we see, at the present time, $500,000,000 of inconvertible notes of the Bank of France, made a legal tender, circulating at par, on the credit of the government; while in the United States the notes of the government, not exceeding $400,000,000 in amount, circulate at a depreciation, as compared with gold, of over twelve per cent. This is clearly the fault of legislation—making the notes of the government only a partial tender, when in order to conform to the money of account of the nation, they ought to be made a full tender.

THE QUANTITY OF MONEY REQUIRED BY A NATION.

The question as to how much money a nation needs has led to a great deal of mystification. A nation evidently needs a sufficient amount of money to enable it to effect its exchanges in the most economical manner possible. As has been explained, many of the operations of trade, especially of a large character, can be conducted most speedily, economically and safely by means of the devices of the credit system, such as bills of exchange, notes, checks, etc.; while, on the other hand, in other operations cash is an almost indispensable agency. By cash is meant money, such as gold or silver coins, or public notes, made a legal tender in payment of debts. There should, therefore, be a sufficient amount of money in circulation to enable those engaged in exchanging property or services to avail themselves of either cash or credit, or both, in such proportions as may be most advantageous.

Under the bank currency system, money, as we have seen, scarcely circulates at all. The medium of exchange consists of bank currency, which is used as a substitute for cash. Bank currency bears interest, and it, therefore, constitutes a very expensive medium—far more expensive than gold or silver, or legal tender public notes, which bear interest only when used as capital in individual transactions. The volume of bank currency is regulated, not by the wants of trade or the exchanges to be effected, but by artificial circumstances; and it frequently happens that bank currency, as at the present time, will desert the channels of circulation almost entirely, because industry cannot afford to pay the tax which it entails upon the community.

The precious metals can be obtained only by digging them out of the ground in localities where they exist, or by exchanging products for them at their market value; and when obtained can be retained in the country only by importing commodities to a less amount than are exported.

Legal tender public notes, like bank notes, can be issued to an unlimited amount; and the only question to be considered is as to the amount which the government ought to issue. It is perfectly clear that the government ought to issue, at least, an amount sufficient to conduct its own transactions with the people. This amount is based on commodities moving in the channels of trade (between the tax payers and the creditors of the government), as certainly and as securely as any commercial paper or bank currency was ever based on commodities, to which they owed their origin. The revenues of the government, for example, amount to about $300,000,000 a year. This requires an exchange of property or products to that amount. How much money will it take to effect this exchange? Who can tell? The public note, when issued by the government to effect this exchange, passes into circulation and performs the offices of a medium of exchange, not only for the purposes of the government, but for the trade of the nation. Its offices are limited, therefore, not by the immediate transactions of the government, but by the exchanges or trade of the entire nation. It follows, then, that the amount of public notes put in circulation by the government should be limited only by the exchanges of the nation. This theory, as to the amount of money required by a nation, is fully recognized and endorsed by political economists, who stand high with the bullionists. Professor Bonamy Price, in the quotation given on page 236, says: "A cart transfers weight; money, ownership; and all the world knows that the cartage to be done determines the number of carts," etc.; and again, in speaking of the amount of bank notes that will circulate, he says: "The answer is the same as that which has already been given to the parallel question respecting coin. So many bank notes as the public has a distinct want for will circulate, and no more. It is the universal law of all commodities in use, the law of demand and supply"

Money should be instituted in such a manner that the

amount in circulation will conform to the wants of trade, otherwise it will not prove an unvarying standard of measure and payment. If money is scarce and interest is high, all exchanges become difficult and expensive; property and products depreciate in value; wages fall and production is diminished. On the other hand, if money is redundant, it will depreciate in value, and property, products and wages will appreciate in value in a corresponding ratio. In either event, money fails to conform to the money of account of the nation, greatly to the derangement of all values, and especially of exchanges of property founded on contract.

It is far better, however, for a nation that money should be too plenty than too scarce, for when money is scarce production languishes, wages are low, and idleness prevails; but when it is too plenty capital alone suffers; and it is better for the interests of the nation and of society that capital should be idle than labor. In the one instance (if capital is idle), people are deluded with the idea that they are much better off than they really are, because property rules at high figures; and in the other (if labor is idle), the masses are much worse off than they ought to be, because property and labor are at a great discount; individuals are brought to want; the public revenues are cut down; the expenses of government become oppressive; and demoralization is rife.

It is said, however, that, in any event, the amount of public notes issued by the government should not exceed the annual revenues of the government; otherwise they will become redundant. Why limit the amount by the revenues of a year, instead of a shorter or longer period? This is illusory. The public note performs the offices of a medium for the entire trade of the nation, and to limit its issue to an amount corresponding to the exact amount of the immediate transactions of the government would be similar to limiting the amount of bills of exchange used in trade to the exact amount of property to be exchanged. It is possible that a less amount of public notes would suffice to effect the exchanges of the nation; it is probable that a larger quantity would be required. Whether the public notes issued can be redeemed in the revenues of the government in one, two or three years, is a matter that will not effect their value in the slightest degree, as long as their security is undoubted and their use is required in the channels of trade. This has been abundantly demonstrated by the greenback, both during and since the war.

It is idle, therefore, for people to speculate as to how much money should be issued by the government with a view to fixing the amount by law. As already suggested, innumerable contingencies are constantly arising which will cause the amount required to vary. How much is needed can never be known until money is properly instituted, and then people will not care to know. Some idea may be formed of the vast character of the exchanges constantly taking place in the nation, when we reflect that the annual product of industry, agricultural and manufacturing, in the United States exceeds $6,000,000,000 a year, and that this mighty mass of products is exchanged many times and in many forms. All that can be safely said is that money, the principal tool by means of which these exchanges are effected, should be commensurate in amount with the work to be performed.

When money becomes too plenty, or, as it is termed, redundant, prices go up, property enhances in value, and wages become high. This is detrimental to trade, works injustice to creditors, and impairs the public credit, if public notes constitute the money of the nation. It is, therefore, a matter of almost as much importance to the public that money should not be redundant as that it should not be too scarce. How is this to be remedied? Public notes are issued by the government for property or services, and are returned to the Treasury in the shape of taxes. An increase in the rate of taxation would soon relieve the nation of any redundancy in the currency, just as bank currency is returned to the banks under similar circumstances. But in this connection another question arises, which has an important bearing upon the subject, and that is the question of interest.

INTEREST.

The price paid for the use of money or its substitutes is termed interest. When money possesses intrinsic value, as in the case of gold coins, the value of the metal of which the coin is made is one thing, while the rate of interest which the coin will bear is quite another. The fluctuation in the price of the precious metals bears no relation to the fluctuation in the rates of interest of money. The price of gold depends upon the laws of demand and supply, which govern the commerce of the world; but the rate of interest of money, as money is now instituted, is regulated by causes of a local character. Gold may not vary a fraction in the markets of the world, and yet money and its substitutes may, at the same time, be in such demand for the purposes of trade as to command exorbitant rates of interest. It then fails to constitute an unvarying measure of value or standard of payment. A dollar that will command 12 per cent. interest is a very different thing from one that will only command 6 per cent. To make money an unvarying measure of value and standard of payment, it is necessary that it should bear a uniform rate of interest.

That money should bear interest is not only legitimate, but essential to the performance of its functions as a medium of exchange. Money represents value and should be able to accumulate value; otherwise it would not be accepted in exchange for property. But, as has been suggested, its power in this respect should be uniform, in order that it may prove an unvarying measure of value and standard of payment. It has long since been discovered that usury laws are in vain, because they are not based upon sound principles. But money can, and ought to be so instituted as to command only a uniform rate of interest, proportionate to the profits of labor. Money, by reason of its legal tender property, naturally possesses a command over property and labor, and if it is instituted, as at present, so that it can be made to command any rate of interest that can be extorted by capital, its functions are not only perverted, but it is enabled to rob labor of its entire profits.

On the other hand, if legal tender public notes are issued by the government in excess of the wants of trade, they will lose the power of money to accumulate value, and their functions as money will be totally perverted, greatly to the disadvantage of the nation and to the injury of the public credit. It is, therefore, as necessary to provide against a redundancy, which will lead to such results, as it is to issue public notes to supply the want of a medium of exchange.

Inflation, in the sense in which the word is now used, is undoubtedly an evil, second perhaps only to contraction. The application of the term, however, is limited by the bullionists to an over issue of public notes, which leads to error and confusion. Public notes, if properly instituted, do not depreciate in value when over issued, because the people do not possess sufficient property to redeem them, but because the excess is not required for the purposes of trade, and they, therefore, fail to accumulate value. It is not on account of the weakness of the credit of the people that public notes under such circumstances fail to circulate on a par with the money of account, but because of their redundancy. This is evident from the fact that bonds bearing interest, which rest upon the same foundation (the public credit) can be issued to a much greater amount than public notes. An excess of public notes is not, therefore, strictly speaking, an inflation of public credit, but simply a superfluous amount of money, an evil which can easily be remedied. But it is otherwise with bank currency. Then it is not money that becomes inflated, but it is credit, in all its forms, that becomes expanded. This is real inflation, and is far more dangerous to the interests of society than a redundancy of money, because it inevitably leads to commercial crashes and money panics. The advocates of the specie basis or bank currency system are, therefore, the real inflationists of the nation. It is possible, as the law now stands, to issue bank currency to the full amount of the bonded indebtedness of the country, about $1,700,000,000, and all that is wanting to call that amount of bank currency into circulation is an opportunity. The loans and discounts of the banks in 1875 amounted to about $1,000,000,000, which indicated the amount of credit used for the purposes of trade at that time.

Bonds of the government bearing interest can be issued to a larger amount than public notes, because the ability of the public note to accumulate value is limited to its use as a medium of exchange, while the amount of bonds which can be issued depends upon entirely different considerations. Public notes will not seek investment in a bond as long as they are needed in the channels of trade. During the war $500,000,000 of 5-20 bonds, with which greenbacks were convertible, were in the market for over a year, and the Secretary of the Treasury was unable to dispose of more than

$25,000,000. The reason is obvious. The greenbacks were needed for the purposes of trade, and could accumulate value more rapidly in the production and distribution of wealth than a six per cent. gold interest bond; and it was not until the channels of circulation were amply supplied with a medium of exchange that the 5-20 bonds could be sold.

We have already suggested that a redundancy of money (legal tender public notes) could be remedied by increased taxation; but it may happen, as was the case during the war, that taxation cannot be resorted to, to the extent of the wants of the government, or the necessities of the occasion, without producing distress and defeating the ends of the government. It then becomes necessary to employ the credit of the government in another form—in the shape of an interest bearing bond. This bond or evidence of indebtedness represents property or products, payable in the form of money in the future; while the public note represents property in the process of exchange between the tax payer and the creditor of the government, and is virtually payable in the present.

When money (legal tender public notes) becomes redundant, it is manifest that there are more notes in circulation than there is property or products moving in the channels of trade to be exchanged through their instrumentality, and consequently more than the exchanges growing out of the transactions of the government will justify. Taxation must be increased to increase the transactions between tax payer and creditor; or, if that is inexpedient or unnecessary, the form in which the government credit is issued must be changed, that is, the public note, not bearing interest, issued in excess of the wants of trade, must be converted into a bond bearing interest; or in other words, as the government note is no longer payable in the present, it must be made payable in the future, and justice requires that it should bear interest (accumulate value), just as the public note, when not redundant, was capable of accumulating value, and this, as is obvious, can only be done in the form of a bond.

A bond, inter-convertible with the public note of the government, is capable of performing a two-fold service; it will prevent a redundancy of public notes, and it will regulate the rate of interest which money will command. When public notes become redundant and are unable to accumulate value, the excess would naturally seek investment in an interest bearing bond; and when money (public notes) is able to accumulate value more rapidly in production and trade, and interest rises, the interest bearing bonds of the government would again be converted into money, and thus the equilibrium would be restored.

Money thus instituted could not do otherwise than conform, in value, to the money of account of the nation, and, in amount, to the wants of trade. It would then always circulate on a par with money of account—a dollar note would mean a dollar, neither more nor less, and would always command a dollar's worth of property; interest would not vary a fraction for any length of time; and money would prove, what it is designed to be, an unvarying standard of measure and payment. Under such a system of money the exchanges of the nation could be effected economically and equitably, and capital and labor would each secure a due share of the products of industry; and commercial crashes and money panics could not possibly occur.

The amount of interest which an inter-convertible bond should bear is a matter of detail which can be settled fully only by experience. Interest on money, as has been suggested, should be in proportion to the profits of industry, otherwise capital will be enabled to reap more than its due share of the profits of labor. The average rate of increase of wealth in the nation is estimated at about $3\frac{1}{2}$ per cent. Capital is entitled to a proportionate share of this increase, and hence the rate of interest of money should not exceed greatly, if at all, the average increase of wealth. For the sake of convenience in computing interest it is suggested that a bond bearing interest at the rate of one per cent. a day on $100, or 3.65 per cent. per annum, should be issued. This, as well as other details, can only be settled by experience. The important point is the institution of a monetary system based on sound principles, and its details can be safely left to the government, if its affairs are placed in the hands of capable and trustworthy men, in sympathy with the wants and interests of the nation.

It is urged by many who are favorable to the use of the public credit, in the shape of public notes, that a bond is not an essential part of the legal tender paper money system; that it would be absorbed by capital, and in the end would constitute a burden upon the nation. This is borrowing trouble. The public notes of the government would not be funded in an interest bearing bond as long as they could accumulate more value in production and trade; and, when funded, they would return to the channels of trade as soon as their services were required.

The inter-convertible bond plan is greatly derided by the bullionists and their tools, who do not fail to misrepresent the principles upon which it is based in every way possible. The public note is treated by them as simply a promise to pay money, and upon this hypothesis it is not difficult to prove that it is a very worthless piece of paper. The public note, as has been sufficiently explained, is a representative, not of money but of property, and as the great object of trade is to exchange property and not money, it is far more important that the public note should represent property than money (gold coins). The amount of property in the country is estimated at $40,000,000,000; the amount of gold at $100,000,000. It is to exchange this $40,000,000,000 of property that money is required and not the $100,000,000; and to base the public credit on $100,000,000 of gold, when it should be based on $40,000,000,000 of property, is in utter violation of the plainest principles of the credit system, to which all paper devices for the exchange of property, whether public or private, belong.

Again it is asserted that the inter-convertible note and bond is simply paying one paper debt with another. If the public note was simply a promise to pay money this would be true, but the public note, properly understood, is not a promise to pay money, but is a representative of property to the amount inscribed on its face, which the government is entitled to demand and receive forthwith from the people, and in this sense was described by Calhoun as a "promise to receive," and not a "promise to pay."*

HOW THE PUBLIC NOTE IS TO BE PUT INTO CIRCULATION.

How the paper money of the government is to be put into circulation is a matter worthy of consideration, especially as friends of the system, with the best intentions in the world, have frequently allowed themselves to be led into error by failing to carry the principles of the system to their logical results. As the public note represents property and products which the government is entitled to demand and receive forthwith, in the way of taxation, to the amount inscribed on its face, and is virtually based on such property or products in the process of transfer from the tax payer to the creditor, just as other devices of the credit system

*See page 60.

are based on commodities moving in the channels of trade, it is clear that it (the public note) should only be issued by the government for property or services. If the government should issue public notes without reference to the ability of the nation to respond in property and products in the way of taxation, as for example, to pay off the public debt in paper money, when a corresponding amount of property and products could not be transferred at the same time to the creditors of the government, would, as is manifest, be a gross infraction of the principles upon which the legal tender paper money system is founded. The creditors of the government are paid in property or products, and the public note must not only represent such property, but must be able to command it, which can be done only to the extent to which the people are able to respond in the way of taxation. Hence it is idle to talk about liquidating the public debt with paper money, or any other kind of money, any more rapidly than the people are enabled to produce wealth (property and products), which can be applied to that purpose.

It has already been explained that the amount of money which the government can issue is limited, not by the amount of the transactions of the government for any specified time, but by the transactions of the entire nation, which are constantly varying in amount. But when the channels of circulation are supplied with a medium of exchange no more public notes can be used; it is essential, therefore, that their emission by the government should go hand in hand with taxation.

THE NATIONAL DEBT.

Debt, whether individual or national, is inconsistent with true independence, and the payment of the national debt at the earliest day practicable should never be lost sight of for a moment.

If the bonds of the United States are payable in lawful money, it is then possible to redeem them in property or products, in which they should be redeemable, as rapidly as the nation can produce a surplus of products, but if made payable in gold, which does not circulate in the channels of trade, their redemption is rendered well nigh impossible. If forced resumption takes place the public debt of the United States may be regarded as permanent, and its increase inevitable. The experience of England in this respect is worthy of note. At the close of the Napoleonic wars in 1815 the producing forces of England were in full exercise, and the revenues of the government were enormous. England immediately began to reduce her public debt; but the money power interfered and resumption was decreed; and the liquidation of the public debt ceased. When the Rebellion ended in the United States production ran on, owing to the abundance of money in circulation, to a marvelous extent, and the Federal Government was enabled to reduce the public debt some $500,000,000. But the policy of contraction soon curtailed production, the revenues of the government began to decline, and the payment of the public debt practically ceased. It remains now to return to specie payments to render it permanent, and to accomplish this end the money power is exerting its best efforts. It is to the advantage of the money power to have nations involved in debt, as well as to have money scarce; in this way governments and nations are rendered subservient to capital.

No event in modern times has spread such alarm among the money kings of the world as the adoption of legal tender paper money by the people of the United States.

None know better than the money kings that if the system is adopted in its entirety, it will ultimately release the masses from the bondage in which they have been held for ages by capital, and hence the bitter opposition with which the system meets. For several hundred years past commerce and trade have been engaged in a constant struggle to cheapen money, the tool of exchange; but it was not until the United States made the public note a legal tender that any progress was made, except in the use of substitutes for money, which were controlled entirely by bankers and money lenders. When the American government began to issue legal tender paper money, the money kings of the world perceived the necessity of taking measures to reverse the tendency of affairs, and they organized not only to destroy legal tender paper money, but also to demonetize silver, in order that they might be able to maintain their rule. That an organized conspiracy exists to demonetize silver for the purpose of increasing the power of money, is evident from what has occurred in Europe and in America within the past few years. Silver has been demonetized in England, Germany and Holland, and practically in France and in the United States.

No country in the world produces so much gold and silver as the United States, and yet the people of the United States are unable to retain it in the country. The same condition of affairs prevailed prior to the war, when we had the specie basis system of money, so that the inability of the people to retain gold and silver cannot be charged to the use of public notes.

The simple fact is that gold and silver cannot be retained in the country until the producing forces of the nation are sufficiently developed to enable the nation to export more than it imports; and in the second place gold and silver and paper money will not all occupy the channels of circulation at the same time, unless they are all clothed with equal powers as money.

If specie circulation is desired, therefore, it can only be attained by making gold, silver and the public note equal legal tenders; then, as soon as the nation is able to retain the precious metals, they will occupy the channels of trade as a matter of course. The bullionists and bankers themselves are compelled to acknowledge that forced resumption will not give specie circulation, but they say it will fix prices at a gold standard. This, as has been fully shown, is not only a delusion but a barefaced fraud. The notes of banks of issue, which the public will be obliged to use, cannot be maintained on a par with coin, if redeemable only in coin, unless the banks can retain the coin to redeem them, and to say that the banks can retain specie in the country, when the nation cannot retain it, is absurd, as well as contrary to experience.

The only way in which the people can hope to reduce and eventually liquidate the public debt, is by the adoption of a system of money, such as has been described, which will give industry free development, and enable the nation not only to largely increase its production of wealth, but to render it available when produced.

CONCLUSION.

Those who desire to fully understand the money question can only hope to do so by always keeping in view the fact that the great object of commerce and trade is the exchange of property and products, and that money is designed to be simply a tool to accomplish that end. Money is nothing more than "one of man's own inventions, a contrivance which he has himself devised for rendering an indispensable service to the practical life of every civilized people."* Its institution is a governmental duty, and as political sovereignty in the United States, theoretically at least, resides in the people, it is incumbent upon them to take hold of this question and compel their servants to dispose of it in such a manner as will best subserve the interests, not of a single class, but of the entire nation. Thus far almost the entire course of Federal legislation has been controlled and directed by the few, in utter disregard of the rights of the many and of the honor of the government, and especially was this the case during the late Rebellion. Eulogies, it is true, are frequently heard from servile or subsidized sources of the patriotism of capital during that trying period. They are utterly false. "Not a patriotic act can be found in its history. It neither volunteered its services nor submitted to a draft. Its support of the government was purchased at the highest price ever paid by a bleeding people. It was in truth a traitor to the existence of the Union—a baser traitor than he who fought to destroy it upon the field of battle. It hid itself from danger, and sold its assistance only for enormous pay, while the rebel soldier offered his life on the field of battle for nothing, except his devotion to an erroneous principle. While the soldiers of the North, too, were freely going to the front by the million, the capitalists, who now trample upon them and their children, were allured from their safe retreats in the midst of their hoarded treasures only by vast golden bribes. Neither in law or in equity, neither in the sight of human courts or courts divine, have they any claim upon the forbearance or gratitude of the American people." And then, not content with the vast gains wrung from the people in the hour of their extremity, they perfected a plan, to quote again from the

*Currency and Banking, by Bonamy Price.

CONCLUSION. 361

same eloquent champion of the people's cause,* "to hold the bonds of the government as a foundation for banking. The wealthy classes were unwilling that the government should deal directly with the people and furnish them with a cheap and safe currency. They insisted upon standing between the government and people. They insisted upon becoming the 'middle men' in the matter of furnishing a circulating medium; and the profits that have accrued to them as such 'middle men' and have been paid by the tax payers, are without a parallel in the history of any other financial system upon the face of the globe. * * A government policy which thus taxes its people in order to fulfill a plain duty to them, can only be properly characterized as legalized robbery."

Since the war every energy has been directed by the money power towards the destruction of the greenback and a return to the specie basis system of money. The machinery of the government is in its hands, and it is now aiming to control the two great political organizations of the country, in order that it may consummate its purposes. The issue has been forced upon the nation by the bullionists, the bondholders and the money lenders, whose tools are to be found in every party convention and caucus held in the country. The crisis has arrived, and the masses must arise in their majesty and assert their rights, or liberty in America will be a mere phantom. It is not from kings or emperors that the American people need fear the loss of liberty, but from a moneyed aristocracy, whose hand now rests heavily upon the nation. The question is one of paramount importance, involving as it does not only the present welfare of the people, but the well being of the nation for many generations to come. It is a question, too, in which the down-

*Hon. D. W. Vorhees.

trodden masses of other nations have a deep interest, for, if the money power is able to accomplish its designs in free, republican America, where else can the people hope to escape its bondage?

The contest will undoubtedly be bitter, surpassing in that respect the memorable contest between the money power and the people under the lead of General Jackson in 1832, but "the flower safety is only plucked from the nettle danger." The political organizations of the country are no longer faithful exponents of the popular will, nor can they be until the money changers are driven from their temples. The people must regain control of their party machinery, or be led like sheep to the slaughter. But it is to be hoped, in the language of Jackson's farewell address touching the same subject, "that, while the people remain * * uncorrupted and incorruptible, and jealous of their rights, the government is safe, and the cause of freedom will continue to triumph over all its enemies."

APPENDIX.

THE 3.65 INTER-CONVERTIBLE BOND SYSTEM.

BELOW we give an able article from the pen of Horace Greeley, on the subject of the inter-convertible bond, which appeared in the New York *Tribune* of November 9, 1871. It will be observed that Mr. Greeley suggested that the bonds should bear a moderate gold interest. This is unnecessary, and would be taken advantage of by the gold gamblers. The currency bonds of the United States Government to-day bear a large premium over the gold bonds, simply because they possess a slight advantage in point of the time they have to run. It may be, however, that, if the public note was properly instituted (made a full legal tender and sustained by a bond), it would practically make no difference whether the bonds of the government were payable both principal and interest in gold or legal tender notes. This view is held by many eminent persons. The Hon. Francis W. Hughes, of Pennsylvania, a distinguished leader in the democratic party, as well as one of the most profound lawyers in the country, in a speech at Scranton, Pa., in October, 1875, in discussing this point, said:

"What better system could be devised and what better guarantee could be afforded, that our paper legal tenders will always remain equal to par with gold, than that whenever there shall be an excess of currency it can and will go into government bonds *payable in gold*. I say gold, because I regard it as immaterial whether under such a system the bonds be payable in gold or not—either way they can be made, as now, *better than gold*. Our government bonds sell at 20 and 24 per cent. above par in our *partial* legal tender currency, and from three to eight per cent. above par in gold. Did our government not discredit our greenbacks by refusing to take them for duties on imports, and did it not thereby make a market for gold, the paper legal tenders would have always remained at par with gold. The $60,000,000 of full legal tenders first issued remained at par with gold, when the latter was as to partial legal tenders at a premium of 285. Let the bonds be payable in gold, and what then? Why, whenever the issue of legal tenders is in excess of the wants of business, by a law of its own nature as fixed as the law of gravity, such excess of currency will go back into such gold bonds. Can such legal tenders ever get below par in gold? Never, so long as government bonds shall be at a given rate of interest. Let experience determine this. I believe that under such a system the government credit would be so assured that 3.65 bonds, as have been proposed, would go above par in gold. In such case the interest should be less. Let results determine the proper rate of interest, or, if need be, perhaps some functionaries under careful guards, might be authorized to lessen or increase the rate of interest. This is a subject for legislation, and from the many suggestions that have been made a proper method can readily be adopted." * *

"It is not proposed to abolish gold as a legal tender. Whether as an article of merchandise or as a coin, let us have the benefit of it to the extent we may. But let us also have a NATIONAL CURRENCY. One that will not keep us involved in European money complications. but secure to us perfect independence therefrom."

The following is Mr. Greeley's editorial:

HOW TO REDUCE THE INTEREST OF THE NATIONAL DEBT.

"Mr. Boutwell's plan of funding the national debt has had a pretty fair trial. True, the times have been adverse, but we have generally found them, so when we needed to borrow money.

The sum and substance of the Secretary's success is the funding of $200,000,000 at 5 per cent. on the payment of the bonus of 1½ per cent. to the syndicate of foreign bankers who have agreed to take the loan. We would not disparage this achievement, for we regard it as decidedly better than nothing. Add to the interest ($3,000,000) $1,000,000 more for the aggregate cost of printing the new bonds, advertising, explaining and commending the loan, and the entire cost of funding the $200,000,000 at 5 per cent. for ten years is $4,000,000. It seems to me that this does not justify a hope that our $1,500,000,000 of instantly or presently redeemable sixes can be promptly funded even at 5 per cent.

Having given to the Secretary's efforts a hearty support throughout, we urge that a radically different plan may next have a fair trial. Before we send another bond abroad to be hawked from banking house to banking house throughout Europe, we ask the government to try—just earnestly to try—to fund the bulk of our debt at home. We could not have sold our bonds during the dark hours of our civil war to Europe at any price, no matter how ruinous, if we had not first shown our faith in them by taking hundreds of millions of them ourselves. So now, having seen how reluctantly they take our reissues at 5 per cent., with a discount, let us show them that we stand ready to take a larger amount at a lower rate of interest at par. Here is the gist of our proposition.

Let Congress make our greenbacks fundable, at the pleasure of the holder, in bonds of $100, $1,000 and $10,000, drawing interest at the rate of one cent per day on each $100 (or 3.65 per annum), and exchangeable in greenbacks at the pleasure of the holder. Now authorize the Treasury to purchase and extinguish our outstanding bonds so fast as it is supplied with the means of so doing by receipts of customs or otherwise, and to issue new greenbacks whenever larger amounts shall be required, every one being fundable in sums of $100, 1,000 or $10,000, as aforesaid, at the pleasure of the holder, in bonds drawing an annual interest of 3.65 in coin per annum, and these bonds exchangeable into greenbacks whenever a holder shall desire it.

The benefits of this system would be these:

1. Our greenbacks, which are now virtual falsehoods, would be truths. The government would pay them on demand in bonds as aforesaid, which is in substantial accordance with the plan on which the greenbacks were first authorized.

2. Every person having greenbacks for which he had no present need would present them at some Sub-Treasury and exchange them at par for these bonds. Suppose he had $10,000 which he expected to use a month hence, he can make them earn him $30 meantime, without incurring the

smallest danger of loss by bank failures or otherwise, and with a positive certainty that the money would be ready for him whenever he chose to take it.

3. A merchant leaves New York with a million of dollars which he proposes to invest in wheat at the West or in cotton at the South. He calls at our Sub-Treasury, exchanges his greenbacks for these bonds, and takes or sends these to Chicago, Saint Paul, New Orleans, or Galveston, to be exchanged for use when needed. After looking about for a month, he buys half the produce he originally intended, converts half his bonds into greenbacks, receives $50 per day or $1,500 in all, as interest, and makes his payments. After traveling and looking for another month, he invests the remainder of his capital, receives $3,000 as interest thereon for the two months he has held the last half million of bonds, and lays his course homeward. His bonds may have lain nearly all the time he owned them in the vaults of some bank; but they were earning money, not for that bank but for him.

4. Our greenbacks, no longer false, but convertible at pleasure into bonds bearing a moderate gold interest, and exchangeable as aforesaid, could not fail to appreciate steadily until they nearly reached the level of gold. Indeed, they would, unless issued too profusely, be really better than gold. Drawing a higher rate of interest than British consuls, and convertible at pleasure, as these are not, they would in time obtain currency even in the Old World.

5. The trouble so inveterately borrowed by thousands with respect to over-issues, redundant currency, etc., would (or at least should) be hereby dispelled. If there were at any time an excess of currency, it would tend to precipitate itself into the bonds aforesaid. If there should ever be a scarcity of currency, bonds would be exchanged at the Treasury for greenbacks till the want was fully supplied. Black Fridays and the locking up of greenbacks would soon be numbered with lost arts and hobgoblin terrors.

6. Though the demand for these bonds might for months be moderate, their convenience and manifest utility would soon diffuse their popularity and stimulate an ever widening demand for them. They would be a favorite investment with guardians and trustees who would expect to be required to pay over the funds held by them at an early day, whether fixed or uncertain. They would say, though I might invest

or deposit these funds where they would command a higher interest, I choose to place them where I know they will be safe and at hand when called for.

7. Ultimately, we believe they would become so popular that hundreds of millions of them would be absorbed at or very near the par of specie, and that with the proceeds an equal amount of our outstanding sixes might be redeemed and cancelled, without advertising for loans or paying bankers to shin for us throughout Europe. The interest thus saved to our country would be an important item.

Such are the rude outlines of a plan which we did not originate, but which we heartily endorse. Why not give it a trial? We should dearly like to inform Europe that, since she seems not to want any more of our bonds at 5 per cent., we have concluded to take the balance ourselves at $3\frac{2}{3}$."

THE LEGAL TENDER BILL AS IT PASSED THE HOUSE OF REPRESENTATIVES.

The following is a copy of the principal sections of the first legal tender bill as it passed the House of Representatives, February 6, 1862:

"*An Act to authorize the issue of United States notes, and for the redemption or funding thereof, and for funding the floating debt of the United States.*

SECTION 1. *Be it enacted by the Senate and House of Representatives of the United States, in Congress Assembled:* That to meet the necessities of the Treasury of the United States, and to provide a currency receivable for the public dues, the Secretary of the Treasury is hereby authorized to issue, on the credit of the United States, $150,000,000 of United States notes, not bearing interest, payable to bearer at the Treasury of the United States, at Washington or New York, and of such denominations as he may deem expedient, not less than five dollars each. Provided, however, that $50,000,000 of said notes shall be in lieu of the demand Treasury notes authorized to be issued by the Act of July 17, 1861; which said demand notes shall be taken up as rapidly as practicable, and the notes herein provided for substituted for them: And provided, further, that the amount of the two kinds of notes together, shall, at no time, exceed the sum of $150,000,000. And such notes, herein authorized, shall be receivable in payment of all taxes, duties, imports, excise, debts and demands of every kind due to the United States, and for all salaries, debts and demands owing by the United States to individuals, corporations and associations within the United States, and shall also be lawful money and a legal tender, in payment of all debts, public and private, within the United States. And any holders of said United States notes, depositing any sum not less than $50, or some multiple of $50, with the Treasurer of the United States, or either of the Assistant Treasurers, shall receive in exchange therefor duplicate certificates of deposit, one of which may be transmitted to the Secretary of the Treasury, who shall thereupon issue to the holder an equal amount of bonds of the United States, coupon or registered, as may by said holder be desired, bearing interest at the rate of six per centum per annum, payable semi-annually, at the Treasury or Sub-Treasury of the United States, and redeemable at the pleasure of the United States, after twenty years from the date thereof. Provided, that the Secretary of the Treasury shall, upon presentation of said certificates of deposit, issue to the holder thereof, at his option, and instead of the bonds already described, an equal amount of bonds of the United States, coupon or registered, as may by said holder be desired, bearing interest at the rate of seven per cent. per annum, payable semi-annually, and redeemable at the pleasure of the United States, after five years from the date thereof. And such United States notes shall be received the same as coin, at their par value, in payments for any loans that may be hereafter sold or negotiated by the Secretary of the Treasury, and may be reissued from time to time, as the exigencies of the public interests shall require. There shall be printed on the back of the United States notes, which may be issued under the provisions of this act, the following words: 'The within is a legal tender in payment of all debts, public and private, and is exchangeable for bonds of the United States, bearing six per centum interest at twenty years, or in seven per cent. bonds at five years.'

§ 2. *And be it further enacted*, That to enable the Secretary of the Treasury to fund the Treasury notes and floating debt of the United States, he is hereby authorized to issue, on the credit of the United States, coupon bonds, or registered bonds, to an amount not exceeding $500,000,000, and redeemable at the pleasure of the government, after twenty years from date, and bearing interest at the rate of six per centum per annum, payable semi-annually; and the bonds herein authorized shall be of such denominations, not less than fifty dollars, as may be determined upon by the Secretary of the Treasury; and the Secretary of the Treasury may dispose of such bonds at any time for lawful money of the United States, or for any of the Treasury notes that have been, or may hereafter be, issued under any former act of Congress, or for United States notes that may be issued under the provisions of this act; and all stocks, bonds, and other securities of the United States, held by individuals, corporations, or associations, within the United States, shall be exempt from taxation by any State or county.

§ 3. *And be it further enacted:* That the United States notes and the coupon or registered bonds, authorized by this act, shall be in such forms as the Secretary of the Treasury may direct, and shall bear the written or engraved signatures of the Treasurer of the United States, and the Registry of the Treasury, and also as evidence of lawful issue, the imprint of a copy of the seal of the Treasury Department, which imprint shall be made under the direction of the Secretary, after the said notes or bonds shall be received from the engravers, and before they are issued; or the said notes and bonds shall be signed by the Treasurer of the United States, or for the Treasurer by such persons as may be especially appointed by the Secretary of the Treasury for that purpose, and shall be countersigned by the Register of the Treasury, or for the Register by such persons as the Secretary of the Treasury may especially appoint for that purpose; and all the provisions of the act entitled 'An act to authorize the issue of Treasury notes,' approved the 23d day of December, 1857, so far as they can be applied to this act, and not inconsistent therewith, are hereby revived and re-enacted; and the sum of $300,000 is hereby appropriated, out of any money in the Treasury not otherwise appropriated, to enable the Secretary of the Treasury to carry this act into effect."

Two *penal* sections (§ 4 and § 5) were adopted as part of this bill, to guard against counterfeiting, but it is not important to insert them here, as they do not affect the principles of the bill.

THE LEGAL TENDER ACT AS IT FINALLY PASSED BOTH HOUSES AND BECAME A LAW.

"*An Act to authorize the issue of United States notes, and for the redemption or funding thereof, and for funding the floating debt of the United States.*

Be it enacted by the Senate and House of Representatives of the United States, in Congress assembled: That the Secretary of the Treasury is hereby authorized to issue on the credit of the United States one hundred and fifty millions of dollars of United States notes, not bearing interest, payable to bearer, at the Treasury of the United States, and of such denominations as he may deem expedient, not less than five dollars each.

Provided, however, that fifty millions of said notes shall be in lieu of the demand Treasury notes authorized to be issued by the act of July 17th, 1861, which said demand notes shall be taken up as rapidly as practicable, and the notes herein provided for substituted for them; and

Provided further, That the amount of the two kinds of notes together shall at no time exceed the sum of one hundred and fifty millions of dollars; and such notes herein authorized shall be receivable in payment of all taxes, internal duties, excises, debts and demands of every kind due to the United States, except duties on imports, and of all claims and demands against the United States of every kind whatsoever, except for interest upon bonds and notes, which shall be paid in coin; and shall also be lawful money and a legal tender in payment of all debts, public and private, within the United States, except duties on imports and interest as aforesaid; and any holder of said United States notes depositing any sum not less than fifty dollars, or some multiple of fifty dollars, with the Treasurer of the United States, or either of the Assistant Treasurers, shall receive in exchange therefor duplicate certificates of deposit, one of which may be transmitted to the Secretary of the Treasury, who shall thereupon issue to the holder an equal amount of the bonds of the United States, coupon or registered, as may by said holder be desired, bearing interest at the rate of six per centum per annum, payable semi-annually, and redeemable at the pleasure of the United States after five years, and payable twenty years from the date thereof; and such United States notes shall be received the same as coin, at their par value, in payment for any loans that may be hereafter sold or negotiated by the Secretary of the Treasury, and may be reissued from time to time as the exigencies of the public interests shall require.

§ 2. *And be it further enacted*, That to enable the Secretary of the Treasury to fund the Treasury notes and floating debt of the United States, he is hereby authorized to issue on the credit of the United States coupon bonds or registered bonds, to an amount not exceeding five hundred million dollars, and redeemable at the pleasure of the United States after five years, and payable twenty years from date, and bearing interest at the rate of six per centum per annum, payable semi-annually; and the bonds herein authorized shall be of such denomination, not less than fifty dollars, as may be determined upon by the Secretary of the Treasury; and the Secretary of the Treasury may dispose of such bonds at any time at the market value thereof, for lawful money, the coin of the United States, or for any of the Treasury notes that have been, or may hereafter be, issued under any former act of Congress, or for the United States notes that may be issued under the provisions of this act; and all stocks, bonds, and other securities of the United States held by individuals, corporations or associations within the United States, shall be exempt from taxation by or under State authority.

§ 3. *And be it further enacted*, That the United States notes and the coupon or registered bonds authorized by this act shall be in such form as the Secretary of the Treasury may direct, and shall bear the written or engraved signatures of the Treasurer of the United States and the Register of the Treasury, and also, as evidence of lawful issue, the imprint of a copy of the seal of the Treasury Department, which imprint shall be made under the direction of the Secretary, after the said notes or bonds shall be received from the engravers, and before they are issued; or the said notes and bonds shall be signed by the Treasurer of the United States, or for the Treasurer, by such persons as may be specially appointed by the Secretary of the Treasury for that purpose, and shall be countersigned by the Register of the Treasury, or for the Register, by such persons as the Secretary of the Treasury may appoint for that purpose; and all the provisions of the act entitled 'An act to authorize the issue of Treasury notes, approved the twenty-third day of December, eighteen hundred and fifty-seven, so far as they can be applied to this act, and not inconsistent therewith, are hereby revived and re-enacted; and the sum of three hundred thousand dollars is hereby appropriated, out of any money in the Treasury not otherwise appropriated, to enable the Secretary of the Treasury to carry this act into effect.

§ 4. *And be it further enacted*, That the Secretary of the Treasury may receive from any person or persons, or any corporation, United States notes on deposit for not less than thirty days, in sums of not less than one hundred dollars, with any of the assistant treasurers or designated depositories of the United States authorized by the Secretary of the Treasury to receive them, who shall issue therefor certificates of deposit, in such form as the Secretary of the Treasury shall prescribe, and said certificates of deposit shall bear interest at the rate of five per centum per annum; and any amount of United States notes so deposited may be withdrawn from deposit at any time after ten days' notice on the return of said certificates; *Provided*, that the interest on all such deposits shall cease and determine at the pleasure of the Secretary of the Treasury; and *Provided further*, that the aggregate of such deposits shall at no time exceed the amount of twenty-five million dollars.

§ 5. *And be it further enacted*, That all duties on imported goods which shall be paid in coin, or in notes payable on demand, heretofore authorized, to be received and by law receivable in payment of public dues, and the coin so paid shall be set apart as a special fund, and applied as follows:

First—To the payment in coin of the interest on the bonds and notes of the United States.

Second—To the purchase or payment of one per centum of the entire debt of the United States, to be made within each fiscal year after the first day of July, 1862; which is to be set apart as a sinking fund; and the interest of which shall in like manner be applied to the purchase or payment of the public debt, as the Secretary of the Treasury shall from time to time direct.

Third—The residue thereof to be paid into the Treasury of the United States."

The penal sections (§ 6 and § 7), in relation to counterfeiting, etc., of no importance here, are omitted.

SPEECH OF HON. THADDEUS STEVENS IN THE HOUSE OF REPRESENTATIVES, DECEMBER 19, 1862.

WHEN Congress convened in December, 1862, the Hon. Thaddeus Stevens, Chairman of the Committee of Ways and Means, offered a bill similar to the original legal tender bill, which passed the House of Representatives, February 6, 1862. This bill was intended to remedy the evils which had resulted from the partial legal tender act, but the money power raised a great hue and cry, and Mr. Stevens, finding that it was impossible to carry the measure, was forced to abandon it. His remarks upon the occasion were as follows:

Mr. STEVENS. I ask the gentleman from Maryland, (Mr. Crisfield,) who is entitled to the floor, to permit me to make a statement in reference to the national finances.

Mr. CRISFIELD. I yield to the gentleman for that purpose.

Mr. STEVENS. The bill which I introduced some days since, to provide means to defray the expenses of the government, produced a howl among the money-changers as hideous as that sent forth by their Jewish cousins when they were kicked out of the temple. It produced, what seemed to me, an unaccountable excitement in financial circles. This was caused, I suppose, by wrong information as to its origin, and a misunderstanding as to its object. This was partly the fault of letter writers, and partly the fault of stock-jobbing money editors. I perceive the money article of the Philadelphia Press, of Monday of this week, represents the bill as reported by the Committee of Ways and Means, notwithstanding the papers of last week stated its true origin. I suppose these money-article editors are some dishonest brokers who make gain by their misrepresentations. The bill, as all knew who wished to know, was introduced by me on my individual responsibility, on the call of the States, with the sole object, as I then stated, of referring it to the Committee of Ways and Means. Neither the Secretary of the Treasury nor the Committee of Ways and Means had ever been consulted with regard to it; nor, although referred to them on motion of the mover, has it ever been considered by the committee.

So much for the origin of the bill.

Its contents and objects seem to be equally misunderstood or misrepresented.

It is known to this House that I do not approve of the present financial system of the government. When this Congress assembled a year ago, all the banks of the Union, as well as the government, had suspended specie payments. The last $50,000,000 of loan, which had been taken by the banks at a discount of $5,500,000, payable in coin, was no longer paid in anything but the currency of suspended banks. The immense expenses of the government, (from $2,000,000 to $3,000,000 daily,) were to be provided for. It was impossible to negotiate loans, except at a ruinous discount. The Committee of Ways and Means were expected to provide the means, without any suggestions from any quarter to aid them. After careful deliberation, the committee, or rather as it turned out, the one-half of them, determined to inaugurate a system of national currency consisting of legal tender notes, receivable in all transactions between individuals, and between individuals and the government, and convertible into bonds of the United States, bearing six per cent. interest, payable semi-annually in lawful money, and redeemable in twenty years in gold or silver coin. The issue of $150,000,000 of such notes was authorized, and of $500,000,000 of twenty years bonds.

The system was simple in its machinery, and easily understood. It formed a uniform currency, sustained by the faith of the government, and furnishing but one currency for all classes of people. It was believed that as the legal tender notes accumulated in the hands of bankers and capitalists they would invest them in six per cent. bonds, so as to realize a profit from their capital. The instinct of avarice and gain would never allow them to remain long idle. This conversion and reconversion would have absorbed the $500,000,000 within the fiscal year, and supplied all the wants of government. So long as the legal tender notes remained unconverted the government would have had the benefit of the circulation without interest. This was the plan of the committee. The currency has proved the most acceptable ever offered to the people. This was the condition of the bills as presented originally, and as they passed the House.

But the simplicity and harmony of this system were doomed to be mangled and destroyed as it passed through the Senate. They began by making two kinds of currency for the same community—a fatal mistake wherever it occurs. They provided that bonds issued as above stated should receive the interest in gold, while the interest of all other bonds should be payable in legal tender notes, thus producing at the outset a depreciation of the United States notes, and creating a demand for gold to be taken advantage of semi-annually by bullion mongers. Without such provision there would have been no demand for a single dollar of gold to be used in this country. If merchants wished to import goods beyond our exports, and that required gold, I should feel but little sympathy for them, whatever premium they were obliged to pay. Being unable to defeat this provision, I procured to be inserted a provision making the duties on imports payable in gold. This was to enable the government to meet the payment of interest in coin. That had one good and one bad effect. It increased our tariff some thirty per cent., but it compelled our merchants to go among the Shylocks to purchase coin to pay their duties. These combined provisions form a mine of wealth for brokers and bankers. The duties and interest will require $60,000,000 of gold annually, and soon double that amount. Now, our banks and brokers have scarcely that amount on hand. They may put the price as high as they please, it must be paid. Suppose the banks in our three great commercial cities to have just that amount. If half-yearly they sell the half of it to the government and merchants at thirty per cent., using the other half to the end of the year and then selling it, they would clear by this single operation thirty per cent. on their capital, and have all the profits of loans, on deposits, and currency circulation besides. The gold would return to their vaults, possibly, by the payment of interest on the very bonds they held themselves, and so to be ready for the same operation at the next semi-annual payment, doubling their capital in three years. If a financial system which produces such results be wise, then I am laboring under a great mistake.

The next error was to change the twenty-year bonds into bonds redeemable at the option of the government in five years, and payable in twenty years. We all know these long loans sell much higher than short ones. But the most unsalable kind of bond is that payable in a short time if the obligor choose, or at any intermediate time up to a distant day at his option. Every man wishes to know when his investment will fall due, so as to know how to arrange for business for re-investment. The very uncertainty of the day of payment is a great fault; hence our bonds sell some five per cent. lower than an absolute twenty-year loan would; yet no one believes that we shall be able to redeem them short of that time. The only justification for this change would be the expectation of being able to pay in five years. He must be a very hopeful man who can indulge that idea.

Another change, which seems to me equally injudicious, was the allowing the holders of legal tender notes to deposit them with the government agent at interest not exceeding five per cent., and payable on call after ten days. This effectually destroyed the hope of any very speedy conversion of them into bonds. A holder of them would much prefer lending them on short call at a smaller interest, and wait for emergencies to speculate, than to fund them in government stock. The consequence is, that while $80,000,000 have been deposited on short loan, only about $20,000,000 have been invested in bonds. One singular feature of this provision is, that when $50,000,000 or more of these notes are thus borrowed by government, the Secretary of the Treasury shall keep on hand $50,000,000 of legal tender notes to meet the call, either by not issuing the amount authorized, or holding others. It is, in effect, the same as if the government agreed to take a loan of $50,000,000 at four per cent., and keep it in their vaults without use until the lender called for it; in other words, paying four per cent. interest for the privilege of holding unused a special deposit. How these short loans and the pressing demands for other claims are to be paid, at least after all the greenbacks are once issued, I do not well see. Had they twenty years to run, I should feel easy. These are the objections which I have to the present system.

I will now briefly state the provisions of the bill which I introduced. It was intended to restore the law just to the condition in which it left the House of Representatives, and nothing more.

The first section provides that the Secretary of the Treasury shall pay off and cancel all the five-twenty bonds and all others whose interest is payable in gold, and to exchange new bonds for them on such terms as shall be agreed on, or pay them in legal tenders.

Certain money editors have professed to see in this a violation of public faith, which promised the payment in gold. Nothing is more false. It proposed to lift these bonds, by negotiating with the holders, at such rates as could be agreed on. If the holder declined to sell, he would be entitled to receive his interest in gold, according to the original contract. I suppose no man could be found in this House base enough to propose repudiation. None but a very stupid man could so misread the bill. True, it proposed to issue no more bonds of that kind, and repealed the law authorizing it. And yet it has been thought of sufficient importance gravely to introduce the resolution here declaring in advance that we intended to make no change in the law. What business has anybody to inquire whether in our future issue of bonds we intend to pay the interest in coin or legal tender? It is enough for them to know that in contracts already executed the government will keep its faith.

It further proposed to pay off the legal tender interest-bearing deposits, and to repeal the law authorizing such loan. It has turned out just as the committee predicted, that such demand loan has prevented the conversion to any considerable amount. While $80,000,000 of legal tender are deposited on call, but about $20,000,000 have been invested in bonds. It is obvious that at that rate the sale of bonds will aid but little in carrying on the war.

It proposes to repeal the law requiring the payment of duties in coin, as well as the *interest on future issues* of bonds, except one-fifth of the amount of duties. This is retained so as to furnish the government with coin to defray the foreign diplomatic and consular expenses, and the charges of our courts in foreign ports, and the costs of destitute seamen. Thus the whole currency needed in this country would be legal tender United States notes. The bullion mongers would lose; the merchants and government would gain.

Having restored the law to its original shape, it proposes to raise money to pay the pressing debts due to depositors and gold-bearing bonds, the pay due soldiers, and other expenses, by issuing legal tender notes, not exceeding

$200,000,000 beyond those already authorized, and to issue $1,000,000,000 of bonds, bearing six per cent. interest, payable semi-annually in lawful money, and redeemable in twenty years in coin. With $500,000,000 of legal tender notes in circulation, they would accumulate so fast with capitalists and banks that the holders would be glad to turn them to profit by purchasing the loans; and I doubt not before the year would expire the whole $1,000,000,000 of bonds would be called for at par. In my opinion, with the present law this amount can never be sold except at ruinous discount. I believe that this disposes of the provisions of this bill, which were intended to restore the committee's project, and which was sanctioned by a large majority of the House.

The balance of the bill refers to State banks, and imposes a tax of fifty per cent. on all their circulation beyond one-half of their capital. This tax is obviously intended for prohibition, and not for revenue. I incline to think it should have taxed all above three-fourths, instead of one-half of the capital. The object of this provision was two-fold: first, to give a wider circulation to United States notes, and thus induce their conversion; secondly, to prevent the undue inflation of the currency. I suppose that such a law would drive at least $100,000,000 of bank notes out of circulation, leaving about the same amount afloat. These, together with the United States notes, would give a circulation of $600,000,000. I believe the business of this country requires that amount. Before the rebellion the paper issues were over $200,000,000, and the coin was at least $300,000,000. I suppose what may properly be called the present circulation amounts to more than that sum. The checks which pass as currency in our large cities are as much a paper circulation as bank notes. They amount to some $200,000,000, I imagine, and almost entirely supersede bank notes in New York and Boston. When it was said that the currency necessary to do the business of Great Britain was near two billion dollars, the bank note circulation was less than four hundred millions. The rest was supplied by bills of exchange.

But in times of suspension of specie payments, banks will expand to an unlimited amount unless restrained by some national law. I can account for the present high price of everything in no other way than by such expansion or the expectation of it. I fear the true amount of present circulation is not ascertained. Take, as an example, a very sound, well-managed bank in my own district; it has a capital of $320,000; it holds about $150,000 of United States six and seven-thirty per cent. bonds; it has on short loan $250,000 legal tender; it has $80,000 in coin; and its circulation is $800,000. In an adjoining district a bank with $400,000 capital has more than its whole capital invested in United States loans, and has a circulation of $1,000,000. Such issues must inflate the currency. The people will run mad with speculation, and in a few years a general crash will follow. My proposition would not reduce bank profits below a fair gain. While suspension continues they might hold, as they now have, their whole capital in government stocks, bearing at least six per cent. per annum. They could have the profits of a circulation equal to three-fourth of their capital, and bank on whatever deposits they have. This would give them at least ten per cent. interest to pay their expenses and dividends to stockholders. This is enough

But I ought perhaps to say, before I close, to my country banking friends that they need not be alarmed. There is no great prospect that we shall return to the system I have indicated, nor do much to protect the people from their own eager speculations. When, a few years hence, the people shall have been brought to general bankruptcy by their unregulated enterprise, I shall have the satisfaction to know that I attempted to prevent it.

Mr. Stevens' views in regard to the defects of the *partial* legal tender system have been fully confirmed by fourteen years' experience, and his predictions have been verified in a remarkable manner. Notwithstanding the defects of the system, however, and in spite of hostile legislation and the existence of the National Banks, it has proved immensely superior to the specie basis or bank currency system, which cursed the country for over half a century prior to the Rebellion, and which the bullionists and bankers are now seeking to re-establish. The people have been brought to the verge of bankruptcy by the machinations of the money power, and the interests of the nation demand that a *full* legal tender money system be now given a fair trial. This end can only be accomplished at the polls. The bullionists and bankers, and their tools, are already in the field, manipulating party conventions and caucuses all over the country, to carry out their designs. The masses must organize against them, throw party prejudice aside, and vote for no man for any official position, from the lowest to the highest, who is not known to be honestly in sympathy with the people's cause, and in favor of full legal tender money.

Monthly Range of the Gold Premium for Fourteen Years.

The following table shows the lowest and highest prices of gold at New York, for each month in the last fourteen years. The left-hand column of each year shows the lowest price, and the right-hand column the highest.*

*From the Tribune Almanac for 1876.

FRENCH ASSIGNATS.

FRENCH Assignats and Continental money are ghosts which have been conjured up to frighten the public by the bullionists and bankers, who wish to monopolize the right to furnish the circulating medium of the nation. The subject of Continental money was fully disposed of in the chapter on Banks of the United States;* and a word of explanation in regard to French Assignats seems to be necessary. Thiers, in his life of the celebrated John Law, tells what Assignats were as follows :

"Assignat was a name given to a peculiar species of paper money, issued during the first French revolution.   *   *
The first issue of assignats was made on the security of the forfeited [confiscated Ecclesiastical] property; and was adopted as a preferable alternative to throwing the forfeited lands on the market; which, * * so large an amount of property would glut. The holder of the assignats might use them as money or claim the land which they represented.

"The French revolutionary government wished to pay the debt of the monarchy and the expense of a universal war with the national property [confiscated church property], this property not being disposable, on account of the quantity and want of confidence, it anticipated the sale, and represented the results by papers called assignats.   *   *
But as the success of the revolution began to be distrusted, and doubts arose as to the maintenance of the national sale, they declined, and, as they declined, the government, to supply the deficiency, in value, was obliged to double the issue, and the repletion contributed, with distrust, to depreciate them."

Upon the overthrow of the revolutionary government and the formation of a responsible government, under Napoleon, the church property was restored to its lawful owners, and the assignats became worthless.

To compare the legal tender money of the United States to assignats, is simply an insult to the intelligence of the American people.

*See page 112.

EXTRACTS FROM KELLOGG.

"THE most fundamental and important truths in relation to the nature of money, have always been so covered up by the technicalities of law as completely to deceive the people respecting its true character, although they have always known and felt that there was something wrong in its power. Writers upon political economy, as well as the public in general, have taken it for granted that the laws of nations were right in founding the value of money in the innate value of the gold and silver metals out of which it was coined: hence the conclusions at which they must all arrive' are just as false as the premises upon which they start. And political economists may continue to write and the public may continue to argue upon these premises for centuries to come, and be just as far from the truth as when money was instituted upon this basis. Notwithstanding this mystification about money, its true character and power are very simple, and need only to be clearly and fairly stated to meet the approval of the common mind; and then the public must know that the present centralizing power of money is as gross an imposition upon the common sense of man, as it is upon the common rights of labor and property. For if the material of neither gold, silver nor paper money can in itself be used as food, clothing or shelter, then certainly the scarcity or abundance of money, or the scarcity or abundance of the materials of money, ought never in the least to interfere with a general and full supply of all the necessaries of life. For these necessaries of life are evidently the product of labor, and not the product of money. Yet the present power of money is such that the people are compelled first to work for money, and then to depend upon the power of money to supply the necessaries of life. Thus the power of money is first, and the power of labor is second. The money commands the labor instead of labor commanding the money. This is exactly reversing the true order of things, for it is making a dead centralizing power to rule and tyrannize over the living, productive power, whereas the productive ought always to command the unproductive power. If any writers upon political economy, or any financiers, have discovered the true nature, power and use of money, they have not made such discovery manifest to the understanding of the public. For the laws of nations, as well as the newspapers and other publications of the day, are still carrying forward and enforcing the idea that money is a productive, living power. Yet the power of money is entirely a dead power, and totally unproductive, notwithstanding its legal, accumulative powers."

"The avarice that pervades the civilized world has been ingrafted upon society by the too great power of money. In most countries it has made production by labor degrading to the child whose necessity compels him to perform it. The skill to gain by lending money, and by taking advantage of others in bargaining, has been, and is taken as evidence of superior talent, until, by example and precept, avarice has been instilled into the minds of childern. It has grown with their growth and strengthened with their strength until it has corrupted the very foundations of society. The per centage incomes on bank, railroad, State, and other stocks, and the rates at which money can be borrowed and lent, are the great leading topics of a business community. The topics are not, How shall we contrive to produce by our labor the greatest supply of all the necessaries of life for the general good? but, on the contrary, How shall we contrive to get the largest possible per centage income with the least possible production on our part? This state of society is directly at variance with such a one as a just monetary system would naturally induce. It is as much opposed to the natural rights of society as falsehood is to truth; and no continuance of competition in production or distribution, under the present monetary laws, will be any more likely to remedy the evils of this debasing system, than competition in falsehood would be likely to produce and sustain truth. We must begin improvement by doing away the great gain by unrighteous per centage interest on money; and then the wealth will naturally be widely distributed among those who do the most for the good of man, instead of being gathered in by a few, who thus become the great oppressors of the human family."

www.ingramcontent.com/pod-product-compliance
Lightning Source LLC
Chambersburg PA
CBHW022333230426
43664CB00040B/479